The SECOND GENERATION

The SECOND GENERATION

SYBIL WYNER

LIBERTY HILL PRESS

Liberty Hill Press
2301 Lucien Way #415
Maitland, FL 32751
407.339.4217
www.libertyhillpublishing.com

© 2020 by Sybil Wyner

All rights reserved solely by the author. The author guarantees all contents are original and do not infringe upon the legal rights of any other person or work. No part of this book may be reproduced in any form without the permission of the author. The views expressed in this book are not necessarily those of the publisher.

Paperback ISBN-13: 978-1-6312-9928-5
Ebook ISBN-13: 978-1-6312-9929-2

CONTENTS

Chapter 1..1
Chapter 2...13
Chapter 3...19
Chapter 4...23
Chapter 5...29
Chapter 6...37
Chapter 7...51
Chapter 8...61
Chapter 9...69
Chapter 10..83
Chapter 12...107
Chapter 13...123
Chapter 14...131
Chapter 15...145
Chapter 16...149
Chapter 17...157
Chapter 18...165
Chapter 19...171
Chapter 20...181
Chapter 21...183
Chapter 22...189
Chapter 23...203
Chapter 24...215

Chapter 25...227
Chapter 26...229
Chapter 27...233
Chapter 28...243
Chapter 29...259
Chapter 30...267
Chapter 31...273
Chapter 32...281
Chapter 33...291
Chapter 34...299
Chapter 35...313

CHAPTER 1

December 1979

AN ICY RAIN pelted the windowpanes as the howling wind hurled itself against the house, jealous of the quiet, warm stillness within. The branches of the ancient oak tree grabbed at the wooden shingles of the house, trying to secure themselves against the unmerciful gales of fury struggling to wrestle them to the ground.

CRACK! A large branch crashed in defeat to the earth, awakening Rabbi Eric Froman. His heart pounding, he listened to the desolate night that enveloped him. He felt a desperate need for the presence of another human being. The illuminated numbers on the clock showed 3:32 a.m. He threw back the covers, arose from the bed, and walked to the window. For a few minutes he watched the storm raging outside, fascinated by the patterns the trees created in front of the streetlight. A shiver flutter over his body making him aware of the cold seeping through the window. Trembling, he quickly returned to the security of the warm, soft bed. Normally, he loved to stretch out in his king-size bed and luxuriate in the warmth, but in his loneliness, he cuddled into a tight ball, snuggling his face into the soft pillow. The feeling of sadness began to dissipate in the grateful knowledge that he had three more hours to sleep before the alarm would sound.

He slowly drifted into a relaxed sleep, that scared time when peace descends up the soul and the spirit become released from its earthly prison.

Rin-n-ng. Rin-n-ng. The peace disintegrated. "Damn it!" Eric reached angrily for the telephone. "Hello!" He was surprised at the gruffness of his voice.

"Rabbi Froman?" a man's voice asked.

"Yes, speaking." Eric responded with a softer tone.

"This is Dr. Barry Glenn from memorial Hospital. Sorry to wake you, but we have a Jewish patient here who is dying. I'm not Jewish, but I think she should have a clergy to do the last rites, or whatever you people do when someone is dying."

Eric cringed at the words "you people."

"What is her name?"

"Jacqueline Sandrom."

"Jacqueline who?" Eric's heart quickened when he heard the name "Jacqueline" – he did not hear the last name.

"Sandrom."

"Is her family with her? I don't think she belongs to my congregation."

"Listen, Rabbi. We have had a pretty rough night here. Quite a few of our staff are out because of the storm and I really don't have time to chat." The doctor spoke quickly with irritated impatience. "I don't know what congregation she belongs to. I have called other rabbis but no one seems to want to come out on a night like this and…."

"I'll be right over," Eric responded before the doctor could finish his sentence.

"Thank you, Rabbi." Eric heard a sigh of relief with the click of the phone.

Eric threw off the warm blankets, wrapped his robe around him and sat on the side of the bed seeking the comfort of the dark room, hesitating to put on the light.

The name, Jacqueline, brought back memories of a girl he had loved in his teenage years. "Jacqueline Epstein. I wonder whatever happened to her," he mused as he walked to the window to see if the storm had calmed down a little, yawning and scratching the hair on his chest. The rain had turned to lightly falling snow that the wind was blowing in little circles around the bushes and cars. In his mind Eric heard music – music from the harp Jacky used to play. It seemed to Eric that the snow as performing q ballet, pirouetting around the scenery in the street and yards. The faster the snow danced, the faster Jacky played the harp, her petite body swaying as her hands gently stroked the strings.

CHAPTER 1

He brushed his hair back with his fingers as he leaned his head against the window, attracted by the graceful movement of the snowflakes and the music swirling in his mind.

Totally absorbed by the beauty of the scene before him, yet conscious of the urgency of the call, Eric pondered why more people seem to die in the early hours of the morning than at any other time. Perhaps it was true, as the doctors said, that it was the change of the barometric pressure on the earth but he believed what was written, that the presence of God hovers closest to the earth in the early morning. This is the time He comes for His souls.

A sudden gust of wind hugged the big oak tree in its grasp, and Eric though he heard the tree cry out with a moan as a large limb whipped across the window.

With a deep sigh, he turned on the light and began to pull gray woolen trousers over his lean muscular legs. As he slipped a heavy white turtleneck sweater over his head, he saw his reflection in the soft light of the dresser mirror. The olive-skinned imaged faced him with its thick black hair and dark eyes. He spoke to the image in the mirror as he put on his hat and heavy coat. "Better get moving, buddy, or the soul will leave this earth without you!"

Hurrying out into the cold darkness, Eric felt a heavy foreboding, a sense of tragedy descending upon him. "What is the matter with you, Eric?" he chided himself. "Get a hold of yourself! You're a rabbi and you have work to do!" He drove down the deserted street desperately trying to escape the feelings of depression.

▫ ▫ ▫

In the hospital, five doors down from Jacqueline Sandrom's room, a slightly built priest sat reciting prayers beside a bed on which lay an elderly lady. He had already given final rites to her and the withered hands no longer clutched the blanket. Her shallow breathing was peaceful. In the dim light, her thin white hair had the appearance of a halo and despite the brown age spots and bumps, there was a certain beauty in the wrinkled face framed by the pale blue pillow.

THE SECOND GENERATION

Father Paul Steiger tried to image Mrs. Serenato when she was a young girl. She was probably on the plump side but not fat, blood hair pulled back in an attractive bun with a pleasant smile on her full lips. "She must have walked proudly," thought Paul, "with shoulders back, accenting a full bosom. The mental scene caused the white collar to tighten around Paul Streiger's throat, and he began perspiring despite the coolness of the room.

"My God, not again!" he rebuked himself as he quickly arose and walked to the window to seek a cool flow of air to clear his head, running his fingers between his collar and his neck.

Sometimes when he saw or thought of a woman's breast, this strange emotion would envelop his body. The experience was not unpleasant, and he really did not know what was wrong with it, but within himself he felt feelings of sinfulness. He was unwilling to share these secret sensations with anyone because he considered them his own – personal and private. It would have been proper to speak of these feelings during confession, but he hesitated to speak with his superiors or even his colleagues. He was both ashamed and afraid they would think of him as being weak or even deranged. They all appeared so strong and sure of themselves. He wondered if they ever thought of women's breast. For the thousandth time, he tried to single out these feelings to better understand them.

They were like a wave of warm sweetness. He was sure they were not sexual because he did not have any feelings of arousal. They were more of a sensuous nature. He wanted a woman to hold him in her arms, to feel her hair sweep over his naked body. He longed to smell the tenderness of a woman remarkably close to him. He felt a desire to lay his head on her breasts and have her gently kiss him as she softly stroked his face and body with smooth, gentle hands. "Is this wrong for a Priest, a servant of God?" he asked the window. "Should I be dwelling in the thoughts of worldly flesh? Maybe I am being tested in some way?"

A soft whimper shattered his thoughts. He turned quickly and saw the old lady's wide eyes, staring straight in front of her with a look that seemed to see something unknown to human eyes.

"Heavenly Father! The Angel of Death came into this room and I was busy thinking about myself!" A surge of guilt and remorse tore

CHAPTER 1

at him as he rushed to the bed, surprised at the soft cry that came from his throat. He hesitated, then slowly reached down and closed Mrs. Serenato's eyes with a shaky hand. Death always seemed a foe to him, even when it could be considered a blessing. He clenched his fists. With all his might, he wanted to fight death; he

wanted to grasp life and push it back into the body lying on the bed. He wanted to see her eyes open, and the sweet toothless mouth smile again.

"You good priest," she always told him in her broken English. "But you hurt too much. No good. No good to be so sensitive. No good to hurt so much with your people. What you see all time is life. Birth, death, tears, laughter – good things, bad things. You in everybody life. You know everybody secrets. Learn to be strong. No let get to you. Always be strong!" Now the power of death had taken life and left only a piece of clay on the bed.

"I'll be strong," whispered Paul as he leaned over and gently placed a tender kiss on the old lady's forehead.

▫ ▫ ▫

Riding the elevator up to the tenth floor, Rabbi Froman wished he had more information about Jacqueline Sandrom. Did she have a family? Would they be there? Apparently not, or the doctor would not have called him; they would have called their own rabbi. She is probably an old lady who had outlived all her friends and family and was now left to die alone. Nevertheless, regardless of age, each time Eric had to give last rites to a dying person, he felt a fluttering in his stomach. He felt like crying when he saw the pathetic earthliness of the body once the soul had abandoned it.

The elevator stopped at the tenth floor, and Eric went to the nurses' station for information. "I'm Rabbi Froman. I was called for Jacqueline Sandrom."

"Room 1012," said the nurse as she picked up the ringing phone.

Not wanting to wait for more information, Eric went directly to room 1012. As he entered the room, he pulled out a Book of Psalms from his coat pocket, only to have it fall out of his hands. He reached down to pick up the book, and only then did he look at the bed. His knees weakened and a stab of pain shot through his stomach up into his chest. He grabbed at the chair next to the bed to steady himself.

A beautiful young woman lay on the bed. Her small face with its delicate features was framed by tendrils of black hair.

"Jacky, Jacky!" Eric whispered in a panicky voice. He expected her to open her eyes and acknowledge him, but there was not a flicker of motion anywhere in her face. He took her hand and studied the still countenance. Despite the deep blue circles under her eyes and the pale lips, she did not look as if she were dying. Jacqueline had always had silken, transparent skin. Even now, she looked deceptively healthy.

"Jacky," he called gently, "it's me, Eric." There was no response. "Jacqueline Epstein, for God's sake, open your eyes! It's me, Eric, Eric Froman!" Still no response. Eric could no longer control the hysterical fear consuming his body. He got up and ran to the nurses' station.

"Are you sure the woman whom you called me for…the one in room 1012, is the one to receive last rites?"

"Yes, Rabbi, pity, isn't it? So young and beautiful. These young people today are ruining their lives with drugs and alcohol."

"The doctor who called said her name was Jacqueline Sandrom. Where is her husband?"

"He's dead."

"How long were they married and how did her husband die?"

"Rabbi, we don't know any of her personal information. Her parents brought her in here two weeks ago and said her husband was dead. They had found her unconscious with a bottle of scotch and some "uppers" lying near her. If you want further information you can contact her parents."

"How do you know she is dying? She looks like she is only sleeping." Eric desperately tried to cling to the idea that there was some hope.

"She's comatose," the nurse replied. "She looks like she is just sleeping, but her vital signs are deteriorating. It's a shame, a real shame. I wish there were something we could do for her." From

CHAPTER 1

experience, Eric knew the nurse was stating the truth. Tears stung his eyes as he quietly turned and went back to room 1012.

He sat down on the side of the bed and took one of Jacky's hands into his, gently patting the long white fingers. "How beautifully these fingers played the harp," he said as he kissed each one individually. "Remember what everyone used to say, Jacky? That after 120 years, when you got to heaven, you would play for the angels to sing before God! Oh, Jacky, why did you do this? Why did you do this to yourself?" The hand felt cold. Death was already dancing up its fingers.

Eric held the hand against his cheek, covering it with his own, trying to bring warmth back into it.

"Please, Jacky, please don't die…try to live. Come on, you can do it. I'll help you. Together we'll pull you up from the shadow of death." He touched her eyelids and lips very lightly trying to force life to stay within them.

The teachings of his rabbi from the Yeshiva began to fill his head. "One is to be very careful not to disturb even the bed on which a comatose person is lying, for one is not to interfere while that person is communicating with God to receive his soul, as that is what the person is doing during the state of coma." The chanting voice of his rabbi resounded in his ears.

Eric quickly put down Jacky's hand and got up from the bed. He began to pray with every fiber of his soul. "Oh God, please, there is no end to Your compassion. Please, please let this woman live. Oh God, I believe in you so much. You know that. I love you with all my heart, with all my soul and with all my might. Please, God, let this woman live! Let it be a sign of Your power and might! The dead cannot praise Thy name! Please! Please!

Suddenly Jacqueline's breath became shallow. Her lips opened. Eric quickly pushed the nurse's call button. Within seconds the nurse was within the room.

"Give her oxygen! She is having trouble breathing! Eric ordered.

"I'm sorry but the family has requested that no means be used to keep her alive."

"But everything must be done to preserve life! Her family knows that. Call the doctor! Call her family! I'll speak with them."

"Rabbi, I'm sorry, but there is nothing more to be done. People die every day. I'm truly sorry." She lightly touched his arm, then briskly turned and walked out of the room.

Eric placed his hands on Jacqueline's head. He wanted to take her in his arms and like a child tell her everything was going to be all right. Shakily he began the prayer for the dying.

"*Adoshem melech, Adoshem Malach*"…… *The Lord is King, the Lord was King…*"

His last conversation with Jacqueline intermingled with his prayers.

"I don't want to be a rabbi's wife, Eric. I don't want people watching every move I make."

"*Yimlock l'olam vo'ed*……*the Lord shall be King for ever and ever.*

"You don't have to have anything to do with the people in the congregation. You will be MY wife!"

"*Blessed be His Name, whose glorious kingdom is forever and ever.*"

"It's not only that Eric. I want a husband who works from nine to five, not one who is always busy with other people day and night!"

"*The Lord, He is God.*"

"But, Jacqueline, I want to be a rabbi!"

"*The Lord, He is God.*"

"No, Eric, it won't work!"

"*Shma Yisroel, Adoshem, Elokeynu, Adoshem Echod – Hear, O Israel, the Lord is our God, the Lord is One!*"

"If you decide to go with your father in the silver business, Eric, let me know. Until then, I don't think we should see each other anymore."

"I never even knew you had gotten married!" Tears rolled down Eric's face and fell on Jacqueline's pillow. For one brief second, there seemed to be a smile on the pale lips and then stillness. Eric knew the soul was gone. He touched her face gently. "Good-bye, Jacky, good-bye, my precious love. Go, go play the harp for the angels to sing God's praise."

Rabbi Froman stood up, took a deep breath. "*Boruch Dayan HaEmet – blessed be God, the true Judge,*" he said automatically. For a few minutes he looked at Jacky, then turned and walked out of the room.

CHAPTER 1

"She's gone," he told the nurse. "Tell the family to contact me if they need me."

Eric rode the elevator in a daze. Everything around him had the intense irrational realness of a dream. What was Jacky doing in Albany? Could she have been looking for him?

He leaned against the wall of the elevator. Oh God, suppose she was looking for me! I could have saved her! Weakness overwhelmed his body and perspiration soaked his clothing. The elevator was spinning as the door opened. The sign "Chapel" caught his vision. He summoned all of his strength to walk out of the elevator. "I think I had better sit down for a while," he mumbled to himself.

With a trembling hand, Eric pushed open the panel doors. His dark eyes met a pair of questioning blue eyes.

"Good morning. I'm Father Paul Steiger," the owner of the light blue eyes spoke to him, almost in a whisper.

"Morning, Rabbi Eric Froman." Eric returned the greeting wearily, sitting down in a pew.

"Did you just lose one, Rabbi?" The priest sat down beside Eric.

"Yes," Eric answered with a deep sigh.

"So did I," replied the priest also with a tired sigh. "Old or young?"

"Young, only 32. How about yours?"

"Old…from cancer…she suffered terribly…but you know, I didn't want to let her die."

"I understand," sympathized Eric.

"What did your 32-year-old one die from, Rabbi?"

"Drugs and alcohol combination."

"Ach!"

"The Lord giveth and the Lord taketh away," muttered Eric. He was not in the mood for talking to anyone.

"True, but did you ever wonder why the Lord giveth if He has to almost immediately take it away? Like giving a piece of candy to a child, letting him taste it and then taking it back away from him!" Steiger spoke bitterly. Then when he realized what he had said, to a rabbi no less, he was ashamed of his words.

Eric saw the pained look in the priest's eyes. "I understand how you feel. I know we so-called 'men of God' are supposed to have complete faith. But I guess the 'man' part of us comes out in times like this. Furthermore, I think we are entitled to be human sometimes, don't you?"

Relief raced across Paul's face. Letting out a soft breath of air, he replied, "I sure do!"

Eric felt he had regained his composure. He rose, put out his hand. "Well, life goes on. Next time we meet, I hope it is under more pleasant circumstances."

The priest rose and grasped Eric's hand with a firm handshake. "Me too. And I do hope we will meet again."

Eric was near the door when he sensed the priest was watching him. He turned around.

"Shalom, Rabbi," said the priest with a smile and wave of the hand.

Eric returned the smile and with the tip of his hat, disappeared through the door.

When Eric stepped out into the fresh cold morning air, he took a deep breath and looked up towards the sky. The light of dawn was bringing the world out of darkness. "Oh Lord, please receive the soul of my beloved Jacky with favor." Tears flooded his eyes and his heart as he began to recite every Psalm he knew.

When Eric returned to his home, he hurried to wash his hands twice, one to wash away death and the second time for the morning washing before prayers. He put on his prayer shawl

and phylacteries and prayed as if his very soul were seeking God to beg on behalf of Jacky's soul "They will have to do without me at the synagogue this morning," Eric thought as he fell upon the bed into an exhausted sleep.

Father Steiger left the chapel soon after Eric. He never really felt the solace of peaceful prayer in the chapel since there was nothing in the room except a table, a couple of pews and different books of the Scripture. It was only a small room set aside for meditation. He preferred his church with its stained-glass windows, burning candles, and the altar covered with a beautifully embroidered cloth.

The first thing Paul did when he came into the church was to light a candle for the soul of Mrs. Serenato. He looked up at the anguished face of Jesus on the cross above the alter and echoed his words, "If it be thy will, take this cup from me," equating the bitterness he felt from losing Mrs. Serenato with the cup of vinegar

CHAPTER 1

given to the suffering Christ. "I'll miss you, Mrs. Serenato," he softly whispered as he crossed himself, glancing at the empty seat where she had faithfully sat for many years during Mass. Then he turned to the blue draped image of Mary, "Take her, take her soul in peace, Holy Mary." Again, he crossed himself and with a weary sigh, he slowly walked to his room to lie down. "Father Mahoney will have to say Mass without me this morning," he thought as he fell into a deep sleep.

CHAPTER 2

ERIC WAS THANKFUL that he was not called to officiate at Jacqueline's funeral. He was not even sure if the hospital had told hr family that he had been with Jacky when she died. He was even more puzzled that neither the Epstein family or his own family had notified him of Jacky's death.

The shock of seeing Jacky unnerved Eric. Deep within himself, he had always held the hope that after she had grown a little older and more mature, Jacky would come back to him. In fact, he had many times envisioned different scenarios. At times he imagined himself cool, unresponsive and indifferent, forcing her to beg him to take her back. Other times he had the mental image of taking her in his arms with great joy and happiness as she shed grateful tears that he was so forgiving and kind.

Now Jacky was dead. One of his enduring dreams died with her. "A man must hold on to something…a dream that may never come to fruition but nevertheless, it is there, with the hope of what might be!" Eric cried out loud as emptiness overwhelmed and consumed him. He sought the security of his large reclining chair by the window. His eyes focused on the telephone on the small table on his right. "Maybe I'll call mama. She is sometimes able to make everything all right; at least if not all right, then to make me feel better." Many times, in counseling, the people who came to see him sheepishly confessed their desires to talk with their mothers or fathers and he always reassured them this need was very natural. He knew of many people who were comforted by visiting the graves of their parents and speaking to the graves.

Eric put his hand on the 'phone but was unable to lift the receiver. "Come on, Eric," he chided himself, "You're a big boy now! You can handle this without your mother!" He withdrew his hand from the 'phone. "Why are you fooling yourself? You know your mother never cared for Jacky anyway!" He vividly remembered their conversation at the kitchen table the day he told her he was seriously thinking about marrying Jacky.

"She's not for you, son," his mother had told him as she poured tea. "She's too head-strong and hot-tempered. You will never get along together. You need a girl who is patient and willing to put up with your impatience."

"But Ma, she is full of life and exciting. We'll be able to work out these problems; we love each other!"

"Problems before a marriage are bigger problems after a marriage. And love? Love is not a cure-all. What good does love do? Look at me and your father. You know what kind of life I have had with him!"

Frustration began to well up in Eric. "Why in the hell does she have to turn every conversation to herself?" he thought but he held his temper and tried to turn the subject back to himself and Jacky.

"Precisely, Ma. You said you didn't love each other when you got married and look at the troubles you have had. Jacky and I love each other. We won't have the kind of troubles you've had precisely because we love each other!"

"There are other things in life besides love. There is respect. There is sharing with a partner. Do you respect each other? Tell me, Eric, is she willing to share with you? I mean share with you completely. She looks like a selfish girl to me. Does she worry only about herself, her own feelings before she worries about you…your feelings? Your father and me, we worry about each other!"

Eric felt cornered, and in defense he lashed out. "You and Papa… you, you're like…like oil and water. You are always complaining about him. You're a maid; you're a cook; he doesn't trust you; he's mean to you!" Eric knew he was angry with himself, not his mother for he, too, had a gnawing feeling that Jacky was self-centered and selfish. But he loved her and thought with time, it was something he could change in her.

His mother slapped her hand on the table. The cups and saucers jumped in the air, spilling the tea. "You don't talk about your father!" Her accent became heavy as it always did when she was

CHAPTER 2

angry. "I can talk. He is my husband. You cannot talk because he is your father. He gave you life. You show respect to your father!" She shook her head as she spoke to him. "I see now that I made a big mistake with you, Eric. You are my oldest. You always were sensitive, understanding. I made a mistake by treating you as my friend. I should have treated you only as a son. It is my fault!" Tears flooded her eyes. "It's my fault!"

"No, Mama, I'm sorry. You know I have a bad temper. I'm sorry, really I am!" Eric reached out and took his mother's hands in his. "Please, Mama, don't feel bad!" We are friends too! That is why we can be close and fight and still love each other very much! You're my best friend, Ma, why can't I be your best friend?"

Mrs. Froman looked lovingly at her son and spoke in a soft, gentle voice. "You are my life, my sweet Eric!" She brushed his cheek with her hand. "I don't want you making the same mistakes I have made in my life."

Eric moved away, sliding his chair a little and casually scratching his shoulder so that his withdrawal would not appear obvious. "Mama, you can't compare Jacky and me with you and Papa. It's altogether different. Compare Jacky and me with you and your first husband. You loved him and he loved you. Right?"

Mrs. Froman's eyes became misty. "He is who you are named after, you know." She arose and went to Eric. She peed his head and hugged him close. "My sweet, sweet Eric."

Eric always felt uncomfortable when she did that. He turned away, rising from the other side of the chair, and went to the refrigerator. "Do you have something cold to drink?"

"There's orange juice on the table."

"Oh, I didn't notice." Eric returned to the table, carefully bypassing his mother and poured a half glass of juice. "Well, I'd better get going, Ma." He gave her a light kiss on the check and left.

He always felt guilty with his impatience with his mother. He should not let her get on his nerves. "Oh, what the hell!" He reached for the 'phone.

After the fifth ring, he started to hang up when he heard his mother's voice. "Hello."

"Hi Mama, how are you doing?" he asked lightly.

"I'm all right, other than the normal aches and pains of an old woman."

"Ah, come on, Ma, you're not old. Everyone has aches and pains!" Eric hated when his mother said that.

"Wait until you get my age, you'll understand what I'm talking about."

Eric ignored her comment. "Ma, why didn't you tell me that Jacky Epstein was married?"

"She didn't marry a Jewish man. I didn't want to hurt you."

"When did she get married?" asked Eric.

"Last year, the end of April." His mother answered in a matter-of-fact voice.

"How did her husband die?" Eric tried to keep his voice without emotion.

"A drunk man was driving on the wrong side of the highway and crashed head-on into him. He was killed immediately."

"When did it happen?"

"Three months after they were married."

"Three months after they were married! Mama, you should have let me know!"

"She went crazy. I didn't want you to get mixed up with her again."

"But maybe I could have helped her!" Eric realized he was pleading.

"No! You could not have helped her. You know how she was. She would have pulled you down with her. You didn't need all that heartache and trouble!" His mother was adamant.

"What kind of work did her husband do?"

"He was a mind doctor."

"Do you mean a psychiatrist?"

"Yes, a psychiatrist."

"Mama, she may have been looking for me."

"No, she was NOT looking for you. Her husband had a friend who was a specialist with troubles of the mind and her parents were taking her to him. But she fought her parents. She did

Not want to go…she only agreed because her husband's friend convinced her to come. How did you find out she died?"

"I was with her, Mama, when she died."

CHAPTER 2

"WHAT?!"

"They called me from the hospital. There was a snowstorm and the hospital could not get a rabbi. They called me and I went." Eric's throat tightened and tears flooded his eyes. He swallowed a couple of times, gasped for a large breath of air as he tried to keep his voice normal.

"Are you all right, my child?" his mother asked softly.

"I'm okay, Ma. Tell me about the funeral."

"There were an awful lot of people there the same people that came to her funeral."

"Did the hospital tell her parents that I was there?"

"I don't know. They never said anything to me. I asked them not to call you."

"Ma, how could you do that? I'm not a little boy anymore. You don't have to protect me. I am a grown man and I am a rabbi. It is my job to go to funerals."

"But you don't understand......"

Eric's patience broke. "Yes, I do understand. You don't understand! You cannot run my life. I have my own life. I have to live the way I want to live it, not the way you want me to live. I must make my own decisions! I must work out my own problems! I want to do hat I want to do and not what you feel I should do!"

"Now you sound just like your father. I don't deserve to have you talk to me like this. I am your mother and you will give me respect. I never talked to my mother like that. What

Thing did I do? I tried to save you grief and heartache. Is that wrong for a mother to do? You are my child, my first-born. I don't have the right to try to spare you grief. Look at the grief I have had in my life because I had no mother to try to help me, to protect me," she declared as she began to cry.

"Okay, Mama, I'm sorry. I'm sorry. I didn't mean to make you cry. Sh-sh-sh-sh, it will be all right. I am just extremely nervous. I am sorry. Seeing Jacky die was hard for me."

"I know, son. It is okay. I always forgive your father when he is mean to me because I know he is a good man. Should I not forgive my precious son?" Eric could hear the tears in her voice.

"Okay, Ma. You take care of yourself. I'll talk to you later. Bye."

"Bye, son. You take care of yourself. A nice girl will come along, and you will get married and be very happy. Don't worry. Everything will be okay."

"Yeah, okay, bye Ma."

"Bye."

Eric leaned back exhausted into his recliner. The warm sunbeams shining through the window soothed his pain. Poor Mama. He felt sorry for her. She had a hard life. He had heard her tell the story many times – how after the Concentration Camp, she had met his father in the Displaced Persons Camp. He knew of the difficulties she had endured in the years they were married, and yet she took up for him. His father never talked. "I wonder what Papa's side of the story is?"

Eric would never know the complete story of his father and his mother, nor would he ever know the profound effect it had on his own life. Had Eric been fully cognizant of the violent fount from which the genes came that formed his mind and personality, he would have been a vessel unable to contain its powerful brew.

 # CHAPTER 3

August 1947 – Displaced Person's Camp – Germany

"YOU ARE A handsome woman, Miriam." Isaac Froman said to Miriam Gladstone as they sat together at the table drinking tea one afternoon.

"Thank you, Isaac, but four years in Auschwicz has not left me exactly a raving beauty."

With a shake of his head and a sigh, Isaac replied. "You have a special beauty from within, Miriam, you have a queenly countenance. I would be proud to have you as my wife." He took a bite from the sugar cube, immediately following it with a drink of tea.

"Isaac, you know I was married when the war started. I was deeply and completely in love with my husband, may he rest in peace. We were married only five months when the Nazis took him away." Miriam sat at the other side of the table, both of her hands around the glass of tea. Her large brown eyes in her strong olive-skinned face seemed to look hazily past Isaac into another world, another time.

Isaac let her have her moment of remembrance in silence as he took stock of her body. She was large boned, not delicately framed, but full of dignity and strength. She carried herself like a person of high breeding, like a queen.

Isaac felt a wave of jealously rising in his heart. His next words were a little stronger than he intended for them to be.

"That's the past, Miriam, he is gone. You can't have him anymore. You must now think about the future."

"I respect you, Isaac. I'm very fond of you, but I don't love you."

A sense of inferiority rose in Isaac. "Maybe she thinks I'm not good enough for her," he thought. Desperately, his anguished mind

THE SECOND GENERATION

sought words to convince her to marry him. "Love? Miriam, we can't afford the luxury of love. We are building on the graves of your husband, my wife and four children. The apple is eaten. All we have left is the core. Let's take the seeds from that core and plant new trees." Isaac reached across the table and laid his scarred, calloused hand on hers, his sunken black eyes pleaded to her from a pale, thin face.

"I don't know, Isaac. These past four years have taken more than life and love from me."

"Then live for revenge!" Isaac pulled back his hand and slammed it on the table. The tea glasses and sugar bowl rattled from the force of the blow.

"Revenge?" Miriam felt uneasy when she saw his sudden burst of temper.

Isaac saw her fear and quickly softened his voice. "It is the only way we can get back, get revenge on the Nazis!" His words had an urgent plea in them.

"Revenge on the Nazis? Miriam asked in a stunned voice.

"Miriam, Miriam," Isaac arose from his chair with a sigh and began to pace back and forth. Anger burned within him. "God didn't let me survive five years, five long torturous years, in the labor camp without reason." His large bony frame was giant-like, full of power. "Oh yes, they tried to kill me, but I lived!" He turned to Miriam and pounded his chest with clinched fists. "We can get revenge now, Miriam, by having children and more children until we replace those slaughtered by the Nazis. They tried to wipe us off of the face of the earth! We'll show them!" Again, he turned to Miriam and leaned over her, both hands on the table. "We'll have more and more children to show children to show them there is no destroying us!"

"Isaac, stop it!! Revenge is no reason to bring children into this world." Miriam spoke wearily as she got up from the table, pushing him back from her.

Isaac gently took Miriam by the arm and turned her towards him as he spoke with a low voice. "I'm not a bad person, Miriam. You, me – we're not so young anymore. The time is now. I promise I'll take care of you as long as I live." He pulled her slim body

CHAPTER 3

against him and tenderly patted her head. She looked up at his full face, accented with heavy grey hair and underlined with an equally darkish grey heavy beard. His piercing black eyes were crowned with thick, wild eyebrows. A large scar zipped across his left cheek along the side of his eye, disappearing into his hair line. She felt a fear of his strength and at the same time a deep sense of comfort and security. She placed her head against his broad chest and put her arms around him. Through the shirt her hands felt the welts and deep scars cut into his back from the whips of the slave labor camp.

"So, he is not educated or erudite. I could do a lot worse," she thought to herself. "I don't think I can ever love again. I am dead inside, but this man, he will take care of me and I'll work with him. And he is right, I am getting older, time is running out for me."

Tears streamed from her eyes. It was the first time she had cried in over two year Ten months later the night quietness of the camp was pierced with the cries of Eric Froman as he made his entrance into the world with clinched fists. "Hear that cry!" Isaac proclaimed to everyone waiting with him in the next room. "It is the cry of all those souls whose throats were silenced by the Nazis!"

 # CHAPTER 4

NEW LIFE IN the camp was always greeted with great joy and celebration. The phoenix had arisen from the ashes. With each new life, new hope was born.

The families who had babies were immediately put at the top of the waiting list to go to Israel. It was not long before the Froman family was on a ship sailing eastward.

"New life in a new land!" proudly announced Isaac as the little family stepped off the ship onto Israeli soil. The Froman family was lucky because a nephew of Isaac had arranged a small three-room apartment with a veranda. They were not forced to live in a Mabarah, the temporary housing constructed by the State for the overwhelming number of refugees who were coming to Israel after the war. Although the apartment was poor and of limited size, it became home for these two survivors who with torn, bruised hearts and souls, tried to bring some sort of normality to their battered lives. The tree-lined street teemed with the resurgence of humanity. The adults watched with great pleasure as the children freely ran and played in the warm sun of freedom during the day.

On the veranda at night, Miriam held the baby close and rocked him, crooning ancient lullabies. She felt a certain enjoyment and peace that had not been with her since her first husband had been pulled out of her arms.

Isaac lay in the bed in the darkness, closing his eyes and secretly pretending that it was his first wife, Ruthie, holding their little boy. For a few seconds, the horrors of the past five years vanished and he, too, felt a peace and contentment as he fell asleep.

Then the tide of memories in his dream, engulfed him and he heard ringing in his ears all over again, the cries of his children as they were ripped from his arms and dragged from the rail siding. He forced himself to open his eyes. "Miriam is a good woman," he said to himself over

and over. "She is a good woman. I will make a good life with her. The bad dreams will lessen," he tried to assure himself. "Time will dim them. Time will dim there." He fell asleep and began to dream again.

"Isaac, Isaac, we will meet again. It will be all right," he heard Ruthie's voice calling to him.

"You'll meet in hell, whore!" the Nazi's hand smacked across Ruthie's delicate fact. Blood poured out of her nose and mouth, but there was not a tear.

"It'll be all right, Isaac, my love. We will meet again! We will meet again!"

"Ruthie!" Isaac broke free from the soldier's grip on him and he ran to free her from the Nazi holding her. He saw from the side of his eye the Nazi raise his rifle butt; he tried to duck the blow. He felt himself falling into a dark abyss as he heard his voice calling. "Ru-th-ie-e-ee!"

It was bitterly cold in the slave labor camp. Isaac's whole body was numb. The striped pajamas all prisoners wore were paper-thin and offered extraordinarily little protection against the cold wind. He did not have gloves and whenever he touched the cold plates of steel they had to carry to the factory, pieces of skin from his hands tuck to the metal. In amazement he watched the skin tear off in big chunks. Why didn't he feel any pain? He held up his bloody hand to examine it. The Nazi's whip chewed into his back. Then there was no longer flesh on his back – only bone. The whip had eaten up all the flesh. Isaac turned around and faced Commandant Steigerhaus.

How could this be? The Nazi is an animal and I am a human being. Yet, he is dressed in his clean, crisply ironed uniform, well-fed, close-shaven. I, the human being, look like the animal – filthy, muddy, unshaven, eyes sunken into the head, full of lice.

"No! No!" shouted Isaac. I AM the human being! I have dignity! I am somebody!"

The Nazi's steel blue eyes became piercing balls of blue flame. "You are shit! You ARE an animal and animals were created for work to serve their masters! Now work, animal!"

CHAPTER 4

A myriad of colors exploded in Isaac's head as he lunged at the Nazi's throat. "You want an animal? You got an animal!" Isaac felt gushing hot blood spraying his cold body as his teeth sank into the Nazi's throbbing jugular vein. Isaac's dirty broken fingernails pulled out the Nazi's blue eyes as he shouted, "This if for my Ruthie!" Then Isaac's teeth found the soft part of the Nazi's belly. As he ripped it open and pulled out yards and yards of gut, he shouted, "This is for my children; this is for David, Rebecca and Ephraim!" In the height of his rage, his vision went blank.

"Am I dead?" wondered Isaac. "Am I in the ground, covered with earth?" There was no sound, only quiet blackness, with tremendous fear, his heart racing within his chest, echoing in his ears, he opened his eyes to reality.

Moonlight filled the room. "Oh, God, Oh my God," he moaned, as his cold clammy hands gripped his perspiring face. "When will you let me forget? When will you give me peace?" He was faintly aware that his pajamas were soaked with warm urine. He had an unbearable longing to be held, to be cuddled close in the arms of his Ruthie. His hand reached out for Miriam, but her side of the bed was empty. "Miriam," he mumbled, "I need you, Miriam." He was not sure any sound came from his lips as he got out of bed to find Miriam. He stumbled into Eric's room with half-closed eyes, afraid of opening them to face reality and afraid of closing them to escape reality.

The baby's crib was empty. Miriam was not in the apartment. The door to the veranda was slightly ajar. He silently peeped through the door. In the bright moonlight he could see Miriam's closed eyes and he heard her voice softly talking to Eric as she rocked back and forth, nursing him from her full breasts.

"Eric, Eric, my love, my dearest, my beloved. Eric, my sweetest joy in life, you live again. I hold you now in my arms as I once did when we shared each other. Oh, my love, my darling, my sweetheart, my beautiful love."

Resentment against the baby gnawed at Isaac as jealousy consumed him. His eyes burned with tears and his palpitating heart echoed in his ears. He put his body flat against the wall trying to find relief in its cool smoothness. He could not utter a sound, but he heard and felt his total being calling: "**I need to be in her arms!**" His wet

THE SECOND GENERATION

pajama bottoms were cold and clammy. Burning hot tears streamed down his face as he unsteadily made his way into the bathroom. All his desires turned to anger. "If she doesn't want me, I don't need her!" he declared in his thoughts as he closed the bathroom door tightly so the sound of running water would not penetrate outside. He washed himself hastily in the sink in fear that Miriam would hear the shower. Still shaken from his dream, he removed the wet sheets, flipped the mattress and put clean sheets on the bed. As he was tucking in the corners, eerie shadows on the bedroom wall became the faces of his dead children, mingling with the leather boots and electric chain fencing, dogs, whips, blood, death. With his last bit of strength, Isaac crawled exhausted into the empty bed. Gathering a pillow into his arms, he tightly closed his eyes trying to avoid seeing the grisly past. Ruthie's last words sounded in his ears, "We will meet again. It will be all right!" He fell into a dreamless sleep......the blessing of the cursed.

Three years later a girl was born into the Froman family. Her little round chubby face, highlighted by wisps of light brown hair, made her a favorite baby with the nurses. "She's a real cutie, Mrs. Froman," they told Miriam. "She'll break many hearts when she grows up!"

"Since you have your Eric, I think we'll call this one Ruthie, if that's all right with you, Miriam," said Isaac the first time he held the baby in his arms in the hospital. He shot a glance at Miriam.

"You're right. It is only fair." Miriam replied in a matter-of-fact voice.

Isaac gently rocked the baby in his arms. "Ruthie, my dear Ruthie," he uttered. "You live again. I have given you life again." Miriam lowered her eyes, bit her lips, but said nothing.

Eric was delighted with his new baby sister. Though he was only three years old, he was very proud of her, wondering at her tiny fingers and toes. "Mommy, look! The baby has tiny fingers and toenails!" he showed his mother in amazement.

Miriam sat down and took Eric in her lap. "You know, Eric, when you were first born, I looked at you the same way you are looking at Ruthie. I was also fascinated with your little fingers and toes. If fact, I thought you were so-o-o wonderful, that I was afraid to hold you too tight – maybe you would crack, or break, or something!" She touched her finger to his nose. "But just look at you now! What a

CHAPTER 4

big, handsome boy you have grown up to be!" She hugged him in her arms. "You will always be my favorite, Eric. Mommy loves you more than anyone else!" Miriam pressed his head against her chest and sighed deeply. Eric suddenly felt incredibly sad.

"What's wrong, Mommy? Aren't you happy with the new baby?"

"Of course, I'm happy with the new baby. Come, we'll take care of her together. You and I – we" be partners in taking care of Ruthie, okay?"

"Sure, Mommy!" Eric felt better as he jumped off Miriam's lap, but the feeling within him that something was wrong still lingered.

David and Rebecca, twins, followed Ruthie. The small three-room apartment was overcrowded, but there was no hope of finding a larger place. The economy of Israel in 1953 was nearly non-existent. Over two million refugees had poured into Israel from the war-torn countries of Europe. Even more refugees came from the Arab counties that expelled them during the Arab-Israeli War of 1948. Most came to Israel with little more than the clothes on their backs. In a small country, torn from war and constant attack from enemies on all sides, there was not enough food, clothing, housing, or employment to accommodate the great influx of so many people of different cultures at one time.

With the help of the nephew who had found the apartment for them, Isaac secured a job in a British hospital, cleaning the medical laboratories. It was menial and depressing to Isaac, and he felt degraded, cleaning after other people. Before the war, he had been a silversmith. His hands, though large, were refined in the art of silver, with a skill that had given Isaac the admiration of the community. This cleaning, on the other hand, was done by uneducated peasants and now he was cleaning the dirt left by other people. As Isaac sat on the Veranda with Miriam one hot evening, he looked at his gnarled, scarred hands with tears in his eyes.

"Look at these hands, Miriam. Would you believe they once created masterpieces? They were steady. They could weave lace out of strands of silver! Look at them now! Look how they shake! What can they do now? They can only mop floors! They can only clean sinks! They can only clean toilets! They no longer have dignity!" He began to beat his hands against the railing.

Miriam threw down her sewing and grabbed his hands in her own. "Isaac, stop it!"

Miriam saw the fist coming at her and ducked in time to have it graze the side of her mouth. Blood flowed freely where a tooth cut into her lip.

"I'll kill the son of a bitch Nazi who took the dignity from these hands!" Isaac shouted as the face of the Nazi tormentor, Commandant Steigerhaus, appeared before his eyes. He saw the bludgeon smash into his knuckles and a piece of white splintered bone rip through the skin. His bloody hands grabbed for Steigerhaus' throat when he heard a voice calling, "Isaac, it's Ruthie, your wife. You're hurting Ruthie!" Miriam shouted, hoping the name of his dead wife would break his craze. Slowly the haze lifted from his eyes and he looked at his hands around Miriam's throat. The strength drained out of his legs and he collapsed upon the floor. Miriam, trembling, sat down beside him, but she did not attempt to touch him.

"Isaac?"

"I'm so sorry, Miriam. I'm so sorry."

"Isaac, I understand. It's all right." She hesitated. "Dignity doesn't come from the hands, Isaac. Dignity comes from within the soul. These ands never lost their dignity, Isaac. They survived." As she spoke, she took his hands into her lap, holding them quietly. "These hands are putting bread in your children's mouths with honest work. That is dignity, Isaac. This job is not forever; it is only for now. Times will be better. You wait and see."

Isaac took her in his arms, and they lay together on the floor without speaking. Then he pulled back to unbutton the front of her dress and in the dim light, he saw the blue marks darkening on her throat. With a mixture of horror and remorse for what he had done, he became consumed with hatred for Steigerhaus and the ever-growing thirst for revenge. Strength rushed back into his body as he jumped up in anger. "I'll find you some day, Steigerhaus," he swore with raised fists and his eyes searing the air. "If you're still living, someday, somewhere, I'll find you!" Isaac Froman stalked out of the apartment, slamming the door behind him.

CHAPTER 5

THE BRITISH LABORATORY was quiet. Isaac sat down to rest as he viewed his work. "Good job!" he said out loud to himself. As he looked around the room, his eyes rested on the rack containing the white laboratory coats. On an impulse he got up, walked over to the rack, took a coat and put it on. He buttoned It and tried to view himself in the shiny aluminum cabinet. Suddenly, the door to the lab swung open and in walked the director. Dr. Shinegold. Isaac's heart umped and he quickly began to remove the coat. "I'm sorry, Sir." He almost whispered in embarrassment. As Isaac hung up the coat, the numbers engraved in his arm flashed before Shinegold's eyes.

"No, it is I who is sorry," Shinegold replied. "I didn't mean to startle you. I only came back for some reports I must finish tonight." He walked over to his desk and picked up some papers. Then he turned to Isaac who had not moved from where he had hung up the coat. "By the way, Isaac, it does get a little cool in here sometimes. If you feel cold, please feel free to wear any of those jackets any time you wish." Dr. Shinegold disappeared through the door as quietly as he had come in.

The white coat became a symbol of Isaac's restored dignity. He was now equal, in his mind, with the laboratory technicians who also wore white lab coats. When someone would ask what he did at the British hospital, he would proudly proclaim, "I work in the Laboratory!"

A couple of months later, Dr. Shinegold called Isaac into his office. "Isaac, I have something to discuss with you."

Isaac's heart quickened and his knees weakened. "Have I done something wrong?" he meekly asked.

THE SECOND GENERATION

"Oh no, to the contrary. We are very proud of your work. So much so, we would like to promote you to Assistant Administrator of Purchasing."

"An Assistant administrator?" Isaac did not believe what he had heard.

"Yes, an Assistant Administrator in the Purchasing Department. You will be in charge of helping secure all our supplies. How does that sound to you?"

"That's great!" said Isaac with a wide grin.

"You will also receive a raise in pay."

"That's great too!" Isaac grasped his hands in front of his chest and nervously shook them as he tightly squeezed them together.

"Okay, you can hang up your jacket tonight and start tomorrow in your new job!"

Isaac's face darkened. "I have to give up my white jacker?"

"Of course, you'll be working in Purchasing and in Purchasing they don't wear white jackets."

At home that evening, Isaac told Miriam, with great pride, that he had been offered an administrative job for more money, but he had refused because he would have to forgo his white lab coat. Miriam tried to convince him they needed the extra money for food, for the necessities of life. But Isaac weas adamant. "this is my dignity; no one is going to take away my dignity ever again!"

Though the apartment was too small for more people and food too little, Isaac insisted on trying to have more children. Miriam reluctantly agreed even though she was under constant strain caring for four small children in only three rooms, always worrying about not being able to feed her family with nourishing food. The tension in the house, which flared frequently, was hard on Miriam. She suffered two miscarriages, one in the fourth month and one in the sixth month. The lack of nourishment in the concentration camp, coupled with constant fear, had lowered Miriam's recuperative abilities. Her blood pressure was dangerously high and her resistance low. To Isaac's great disappointment, the doctor warned them to wait a couple of years before they thought of having children again. "Let her try to regain her strength both in body and spirit," Dr. Newman had advised.

CHAPTER 5

Miriam tried to make a happy surrounding for her children. Each task, each meal would be fun and games. Cleaning the house became a cooperative effort with everyone having a job to complete. Each meager plate of food was decorated to be appealing to the eye. Eric would always receive bigger portions, "because he is older," Miriam would explain. Many times, Isaac noticed that on Eric's plate were little morsels of goodies hidden underneath the lettuce or other vegetables, that the other plates did not contain, but he said nothing.

Most of Miriam's time was directed towards the children, a source of resentment to Isaac. "What about me?" he would demand. "You are my wife. I need you too! I need you more than the children. They have one another. There are four of them. I have only you!"

"Isaac, please," Miriam would plead. "They are only babies. They need both of us. Come, join in with us. Let's have fun together!"

"Fun? Fun? Isaac would shout and stomp angrily out of the room, to go to the bedroom, slamming the door or he would go out of the apartment completely. Eric learned quickly to stay out of Isaac's path when he was in one of those moods. He more he felt that his father hated him, the closer he clung to his mother. After Isaac left the room, Eric would come to his mother and pat her hand. "Don't worry, Mommy, I'll take care of you."

"Thank you, my sweet Eric," she would reply. "That makes me feel a whole lot better!"

The heavy burden of responsibility weighed heavily on Eric. In his child's mind, he thought that his father's anger and his mother's unhappiness were because of him. His father rarely touched him or give him attention even though he would hug and talk with the other children when he was in a good mood.

"Maybe if I take care of the children and leave Mommy more time to be with Papa, he'll loved me." Eric assured himself even though he did not relish the idea of his mother being alone with his father.

"Go Mommy," he would say when Isaac suggested the two of them go for a walk or to a movie. "I'll take care of the children. You don't have to worry about them!"

Eric hated taking care of the children by himself. Suppose there was a fire? Suppose the Arabs attacked? Suppose some sort of monsters came into the house with whips and guns like in Papa's nightmares? He made all kinds of plans in his mind. He even practiced tying a rope to the veranda to climb down for a fast escape. He would repeatedly look in all the closets and under the beds to see if something was there, all the time praying there wouldn't be anything. The least noise would start his heart pounding and when the noise became identifiable, he would feel both relieved and ashamed. He would go from bed to bed dozens of times to make sure each sleeping child was all right, each time terrified he would find something wrong.

The minute his parents walked out of the apartment, the fear rose in him and it did not subside until he heard their key in the lock. Then he would run to his bed and pretend to be asleep. He was afraid to talk to his mother for fear of adding to her unhappiness. Furthermore, she was beginning to suffer from headaches and would say to him, "Eric, darling, I have a terrible headache, would you please take care of the children for me?"

"Sure, Mommy," Eric would say as he began to change diapers and cuddle the little ones with all the ability his six-year-old mind could muster.

On Eric's seventh birthday, a letter arrived from America. Miriam's first cousin asked them to come to America. The cousin was going into the silver business and needed an experienced partner. It would not be charity, he assured them. They were really needed.

"Come to America," the letter read, "help me to get started. You'll have an equal share in the business. If, after the business is established, you want to return to Israel, you will be free to do so. By that time, you could be well situated financially and be able to make a good life for the whole family."

The idea of a trip to America and a business for Isaac appealed to the Froman family and for the first time in many, many months, there was merriment and true happiness in the small apartment as they made plans for a new life.

"But we will return to Israel." Miriam and Isaac assured each other and the children. "With money we will not be a liability to

CHAPTER 5

anyone or to our new State, but an asset. Tomorrow morning, I will go before work to apply for the quota," Isaac told his family.

That night for the first time in a long while, Isaac and Miriam lay in each other's arms with great enjoyment.

"Just think, Isaac, I'll not have to worry any more about rationed food or about making whole meal out of one eggplant and some tomato sauce. I never want to see another eggplant again!"

"As half-owner of a silver business, I'll have dignity, Miriam. When I go to the synagogue, they will always give an honor to me during services. Everyone will respect me!"

Miriam snuggled close to Isaac, closed her eyes and smiled to herself as her fingers stroked the hair on his chest. She had always snuggled to her husband, Eric, that way, but never with Isaac. Isaac pulled away from Miriam abruptly. Ruthie had always snuggled that way with him as she would whisper her love to him.

"What are you doing? Are you pretending I'm your Eric?" Isaac cried out in painful self-defense. His voice, bitter and harsh, startled Miriam.

"What's the matter with you?" She retorted. She was grateful it was dark for she felt her face burning. She had been pretending it was Eric. Yet, it was no secret that Isaac often murmured Ruthie's name as they were embraced in lovemaking. "How can we live a decent life together when you refuse to accept me as your wife?" Miriam asked in self-defense.

"That's what I want you to be. I want you to be MY wife. No one else's!"

"That goes two ways, Isaac. You can't have me and Ruthie too! Sometimes I think you only married me to have children for you, to get back the children you lost."

"I could have married anyone just to have children. I never lied to you. From the beginning I told you I wanted children!"

"Why do you act like you hate them, especially Eric?" Miriam's temples pulsated and her throat began to close.

"I don't hate them. I love them. They are my flesh and blood. But you spend all your time with them. You have no time left for me!"

"Isaac, why can't you understand? Children take a lot of time. And when you are mean to them, I try to make it up to them with more attention." The throbbing in her head became stronger.

Isaac ignored her statement completely. "Furthermore, you do not treat Eric as a normal child. Furthermore, you do not treat Eric as a normal child. You always sy, 'Eric and the children.' What does that mean, Miriam?"

The pounding in Miriam's head intensified. In desperation shed shouted, "Leave me alone! Leave me alone!" She clutched her head in her hands and crawled to the corner of the
bed, curling herself into as small a knot as she could muster.

Eric heard "leave me alone" and in terror he threw back his covers and ran to his parent's room, only to stand before the closed door in consternation. He had been warned never to open the door. "Mommy, Mommy, are you all right? Please come to my bed! Leave him by himself! I'll take care of you, Mommy!"

Isaac jumped out of the bed in fury. "See!" he pointed to the door. "Is that normal for a seven-year old child. What lies have you been telling him?"

"I have said nothing to him, Isaac. I swear to you! He is a very sensitive boy!"

Isaac went to the door and yanked it open. He hovered above his son, a naked giant in the dark. When he saw his father's angry face in the pale night light, Eric felt a strangling fear of facing not his father, but someone unknown to him, someone who would harm both his mother and him. He staggered backward, great waves of terror sweeping over him.

Miriam quickly got out of bed and pushed past Isaac. She hugged Eric, took his hand to lead him back to bed.

"I'm all right, sweetheart. Your father and I were just talking."

"Mommy, please don't go back to him. Stay here with me. I don't take up much room." His hand swept across the bed as he pushed himself tightly against the wall. "See, there is plenty of room for you."

Miriam held Eric close to her heart. "I would much rather stay with you, my sweetest, but I must go back to your father. After all, he is my husband. Now go to sleep. Everything will be all right."

CHAPTER 5

She gave him a kiss on both cheeks and then on the tip of his nose. She pulled the covers up to his chin and gave him an extra kiss on the forehead. Before closing the door, she looked back at the outline of the child in his bed, illuminated by the faint light from the window.

With all her heart, she wanted to go back and crawl in his bed to feel his warmth next to her.

Eric pulled down the covers from his nose and looked towards her. She blew another kiss to him and quietly closed the door.

Loneliness tugged at Eric's little being. "Why are they always fighting? What does he want from Mommy?" The bright light of the moon painted the walls of his room an eerie grey. He stretched his head sideways to look at the window which he thought he had closed before he got into bed. His heartbeat was fast. It was open! Someone or something could come in! He thought of getting up and closing it. No!!! There could be something under the bed waiting to grab him. Eric wanted to cry out for his mother. He thought of running and cuddling in his mother's arms, but he was afraid of his father. He slowly pulled the covers over his head and fell into a fitful sleep dreaming of his father's angry face and monstrous figure towering before him.

 # CHAPTER 6

July 1, 1951 – Albany, New York

CURT STEIGER SAT ramrod straight in the plastic-orange chair at St. Mary's Hospital.

During the four hours of waiting for his wife to deliver their fourth child, he had retained his staunch composure even though perspiration covered his body. A nurse apologized for the unusually warm room, explaining the air conditioning was not working at full capacity because of the tremendous heat wave engulfing the city. Other men in the maternity area had removed their jackets and opened their shirts at the neck; however, Curt remained fully clothed. His icy blue eye, alert and without emotion, chiseled cheekbones and deeply cleft chin together with his strong athletic body lent an appearance of authority and power.

His erect back and serene calmness belied the turmoil in his heart. He picked up a copy of "*Field and Stream*" magazine and flipped through its pages. A picture of an open meadow, its grasses waving gently in the wind caught his attention. Curt visualized a strong, muscular young man with fair skin, beautiful blond hair and striking blue eyes running in the field like a young animal, bronzed muscles flexing in perfect harmony with each movement.

"Please let my baby be a boy! I want a boy!" he said in his mind as he again visualized the youth running in the field, his proud head held high, his back straight as his body cut the wind with legs rhythmically moving as if they were attuned to music.

From a distance Curt heard a voice, "You have a fine baby boy, Mr. Steiger." Almost afraid to come back to the reality of the waiting room, Curt slowly looked up to see the doctor standing in front of him. Curt immediately stood up. "A boy?!" He ignored all the men in the waiting room congratulating him.

"Yes, Mr. Steiger, a boy this time. Congratulations!" Curt did not notice that the doctor's soft blue eyes were grave.

Though Curt's heart was pounding, he retained his reserved manner. He extended his hand to the doctor. "That you, doctor. Is he all right? May I see him?"

"Oh yes, he is perfectly healthy, weights four pounds, five ounces. Quite a nice little boy!"

"I want to see him!" demanded Curt.

Doctor Schultz saw the satisfaction on Curt Steiger's face, and he dreaded telling him the rest of his report. Thirty-five years of delivering babies and he still ached when he could not save both the mother and the child at a delivery.

"I think you had better see your wife first, Mr. Steiger."

"My wife? Of course. After three girls, she must be happy with our son as well. She really came through this time, didn't she?"

"I'm sorry, Mr. Steiger…"

"What do you mean, you're sorry. Sorry about what?!" Curt interrupted before the doctor could complete his sentence.

"It was a difficult birth, a breech. I'm afraid your wife's heart was not strong enough…."

"I want to see Bertha. I want to see my wife! Right now!"

"We're having difficulty regulating her heart. She went into cardiac arrest during the delivery. I'm afraid it was all too much for her."

"She's a strong woman. She will get over this. She will be fine! Let me talk to her!"

"Don't you say anything to her!" Doctor Schultz's voice was stern. "Her will is strong, but her heart is weak. I warned you it would be dangerous for her to have another child. You already have three beautiful daughters."

"But I wanted a boy! We both wanted a boy! And see, we now have one!"

Curt's pugnacious attitude irritated Dr. Schultz. He shook his head with a deep sigh and turned to lead Curt to Bertha.

Curt came with quick, strong steps into the curtained area of intensive care where his wife was but stopped abruptly when he

CHAPTER 6

saw her face. He had seen that kind of face hundreds of times. The pale, waxy looking skin and bluish lips told him that the last vestige of life was clinging between the shades of two worlds. Softly he walked to her bed, pulled up a chair and sat next to her. Reverently he touched her forehead. "Bertha, my love, thank you for my wonderful son." He swallowed hard to dissipate the knot in his throat.

Bertha spoke but did not open her eyes. "We did it, Curt, we have a son!"

"Yes, yes, he will grow up to be a fine man. We will have many years of enjoyment from him. I'm so tired, Curt, so tired." She turned her cheek into the pillow and slept.

For a swift moment, Curt hated his son. How could a puny baby kill his Bertha? But then a sense of pride swept over Curt. "He must be a very strong young man," he murmured to himself.

Curt sat for a long time by Bertha's bed, watching her sleep, watching the liquid slowly drip into the tube connected to her arm. He thought of the good life they had shared together. Everyone said they were a perfect couple and they always happily agreed. Several times Bertha opened her eyes. Each time, Curt would lovingly touch her face and pat her hand and she would weakly smile back at him. He fought to hold back his tears. Not once in the many years they were married had she seen him cry. He was always a tower of strength to her and everyone around them. How proud she was of him, of his strength! Now he must be stronger than ever – for his son!

Bertha Steiger clung to life for six days before her tired heart finally claimed its rest.

On the seventh day, Curt Steiger had his son christened with the name of Paul Wolfgang Steiger.

His oldest daughter, Christina, though only eleven, devoted herself to Paul with the natural instincts of a mother. The housekeeper repeated to all who came in contact with her, "That child is a born mother. Look how she holds him. She already changes his diaper like a professional!"

Although his other two sisters played with him, loving, hugging, and kissing him, Paul reserved the special squeals of delight for Christina. He would place his head against her budding chest with great contentment as she rocked, sang lullabies and nursery rhymes to him. If he were sick or restless in the night, he would find peace only if Christina come into his room to hold him or just sit on the chair beside his bed.

Curt was pleased with the relationship between Paul and Christina. Christina was strong-willed. She had no qualms about killing a bird or an animal or even squashing any kind of bug. She rode a horse like a man, ran like a deer and was capable of figuring out the most difficult problems that would arise in everyday living. She ruled her two sisters, who happily completed all chores assigned to the three girls. In school she was a top student and a leading athlete. She created an atmosphere about her of security and self-confidence that enabled her to control everyone with whom she came in contact. Curt often thought that she would have made a wonderful boy. He wanted Paul to be influenced by her.

When Paul was ready to start school, although Curt would have preferred a military academy for his only son, he settled instead for the discipline of the local Catholic parochial school. Maybe the strict nuns and priests could hammer some discipline into him! Curt thought Paul cried too easily; he was too frightened of the world around him and above all, he was "too soft." His body, to Curt's disgust, was small and chubby.

People never commented that he 'looked like a little football player,' but always said, "What a sweet little boy!" One Sunday, a woman in church stroked Paul's head and said, "With those long eyelashes and beautiful blood ringlets, he would have made a gorgeous girl!" The next day Curt took Paul to the barber for a crew-cut and began to plan how he would help his son grow into manhood – like a man!

Curt decided that three older sisters and a female housekeeper had too much of a 'feminine' influence on Paul. He called a family meeting. "From now on," he announced to everyone, "Paul is going to be taught to grow up like a man!" No more constant attention from his sisters. "When you fall, Paul, and scrape a knee or have any kind of minor injury or even a disappointment, you are not to cry. Men do not cry. Part of being a man is to bear pain without emotion. Do you understand, Paul?"

CHAPTER 6

Paul enjoyed the attention he was getting. It sounded like a fun game. "Yes, father, I understand," he agreed.

Curt continued. "You are also to learn discipline. Do you know what that is, Paul?"

Paul shook his head negatively. "Is it fun?

"Stand up, Paul!"

The sharp command in his father's voice frightened Paul. He quickly stood up without saying anything.

"It means making yourself do things you don't like to do. Listen to me now very closely. These are rules and laws that you will follow from now on. Are you listening to me, Paul?"

"Yes, I'm listening," Paul nodded. He began to fear his father. He wanted to run to Christina, but he was afraid.

"From now on, when you speak to me, you are to say 'Sir. Yes Sir, No Sir. Do you understand?"

"Yes, Father."

"What!!? What did I just tell you?!!"

"Yes, Sir.

Curt smiled. "You are to get up an hour earlier each morning. You are to make your bed, and make sure your room is in orders – which means your drawers and closets as well. You are to shine your shoes every morning before school and if you have any time left, you are to begin studying German. I shall teach you the lesson the night before. Do you understand, Paul?"

Christina tried to interrupt. "Father, he is only six years old. He is still a little boy!"

Paul gave her a look of thankfulness that quickly vanished when he saw the look his father gave to Christina. She backed down without further words.

Curt, without a word to Christina, turned his attention back to Paul. "Your training in physical fitness is also to begin. Every Friday evening you and I will go hiking and spend the night in the woods, rain or shine. I will teach you how to survive on your own. And maybe we can start getting rid of that baby fat!" Curt squeezed Paul's upper arm. We'll get some hardness in those muscles! What do you say to that, Paul?"

When Paul heard the word 'baby,' he was insulted. He was determined to show his father that he was no baby! "Yes, Sir," he responded with all his might, swallowing hard.

The following Friday when Paul got home from school, his father was waiting for him with a backpack filled with cans of food and a blanket. "Change your clothes. Put on your heavy shoes, your jeans, your flannel shirt and jacket," he ordered Paul. It had rained all day. Paul thought his father would surely have cancelled the hike. "Maybe we don't spend the night in the woods," he tried to comfort himself in silence. "It is much too wet!" Not wanting to irritate his father, he quickly changed his clothes and came downstairs.

Without speaking, Curt strapped the heavy pack on Paul's back, buckling the straps across his chest. "Okay, son, let's go!" Curt poked him in the midriff. "Let's see if we can get rid of this pudginess!"

Paul resented his father making fun of his body, but he gritted his teeth and said nothing.

They had been walking about twenty minutes when the chest straps of Paul's heavy pack began to cut into his flesh. His body was delicate rather than muscular and strong, and the soft flesh seemed to give away without a fight under the weight of the unyielding straps. His backpack became heavier with each footstep. "Dad," quickly adding, "Sir."

"Yes?" Curt answered without breaking his stride.

"The straps are cutting into my chest and the pack is hurting my back. Can we please stop?"

Curt stopped abruptly and turned to his son, facing him with hands on his hips, legs apart. "I will not stand for any cry-baby complaining. You will toughen up. Do you understand?"

Anger flooded Paul when he heard the words, "cry-baby." His father had no right to call him that. "Yes, Sir!" he yelled with a sneer.

"Good!" his father answered and turned to continue his same steady pace.

As soon as his father's back was turned, Paul reached into his pack over his shoulder, lifted the top from the side and began to throw the heavy cans, one by one, until only a couple were left. In anger at being forced to carry the heavy pack, he threw the last can away as well as the raw Irish potato he found in the pack.

CHAPTER 6

That night, Paul learned a lesson he would never forget.

His father had said nothing the whole evening. Curt built a fire, roasted his potato in the fire, opened the cans he had brought and ate in front of Paul without giving him one bite of food.

All he said was "one must be self-sufficient and carry his own weight." After eating, Curt rolled up in his blanket to sleep.

Shivering, Paul lay on the cold, wet ground. His empty stomach growled ceaselessly, and he longed for his bed where his teddy bear stood guard on the pillow. He wanted to feel Christina's arm s around him, making everything all right. Tears flowed down Paul's face. He realized he had made a mistake by facing the fire when his father saw his tears.

"If I see one more tear from you, Paul, I shall put out the fire, and you will sleep here in the dark." The calm, stern voice indicated the threat was real.

Terror swept over Paul, but he knew better than to answer his father. "Yes Sir," he replied firmly, quickly wiping his face. "No more tears!" He shut his eyes tightly and pretended to sleep, trying his utmost to keep even the smallest tear from squeezing out from under his lids. He dared not turn his back for fear his father would think he was crying.

Sometimes when Paul had an unusually difficult day, Christina would slip quietly into his room in the middle of the night, hug and kiss him and rock him gently as she held him in her arms. He would hold his breath in fear that his father would hear and forbid her to come to him anymore. When she tried to whisper to him, he would place his finger over her mouth and shake his head, eyes wide and anxious.

When Christina and he were alone, rare though it was, she would try to explain to him that their father was not mean; that he loved them all very much but he just wanted Paul to grow into a strong man. When their father wasn't looking, the other sisters would also give Paul fast hugs and quick kisses. Their clandestine affection became a fun game followed by giggles of delight y the girls, but tension and fear of discovery haunted Paul who knew that punishment would surely follow.

For his seventh birthday, his father gave Paul a beautifully wrapped package. Paul eagerly opened it only to find a small black gun with a brown wooden handle. The sight of the gun frightened Paul, but he knew better than to look disappointed.

"Oh boy, a gun!" he shouted with pretended delight, trying extremely hard to look excited.

"Come, let's go and try it out," his father said, obviously pleased that his son liked the gun.

"But it's my birthday, Dad, I want to be here with everyone. Let's go another time," Paul tried to compromise.

"Oh, we will only be gone a short while," replied Curt.

While quietly walking through the woods, Paul prayed with all his might. "Please don't let any animal show up. Please, please……" Suddenly his father stopped and stood very still. From the side of his mouth, he whispered to Paul, "Look, there is a squirrel sitting on the limb in front of us on the first branch of the tree. Shoot it!"

Paul's heart fell. "I don't want to kill that little squirrel, father. He didn't do anything."

Curt quickly and quietly slipped behind Paul, took Paul's hand in his and aimed the gun towards the squirrel. "Don't look at it as not having done anything, son." His father's voice had a hypnotic effect on Paul. "He is the enemy. His innocent look is his disguise. Don't let your heart rule you. Let your mind be your master!"

He relaxed somewhat in the circle of his father's arms. "Perhaps we'll miss the shot," he thought to himself.

He heard his father say, "It's there for us to kill, it is only a rodent, part of the rat family!" as he felt the pressure of his father's finger on his on the trigger. The shot resounded throughout the woods. Paul watched in horror as the head of the squirrel flew to pieces and blood gushed out onto the limb. The little paws momentarily held onto the nut as the body fell to the earth with a thump.

Paul could no longer contain himself. His bowels released themselves as he began to throw up. He heard his voice screaming, yelling, and felt his feet running through the woods. He just wanted to get away from the gun, the dead squirrel and his father. He ran, hot tears scalding his cheeks, blinding him. Bushes ripped at his arms and legs, scratching his tender skin, but he felt nothing. All

CHAPTER 6

he could see was the sight of the squirrel's head flying to peaces. He faintly heard his father's voice calling from behind him, but he ran faster, faster. He had to get away!

With relief he saw his house; with distress and frustration he realized he couldn't go into the house with his pants soiled, full of excrement. There was a creek not far from the house; he quickly changed his course before anyone in the house could see him and headed for the stream. He hurried behind a thicket of brush which mad a natural screen, cutting off all view of him.

Stepping out of his trousers, he dropped his underwear to his feet. Disgustedly he kicked them away. With the toe of his shoe he dug a shallow depression in the loose soil and leaves, stomped in his underwear and then raked the soil and leaves over them with his hands. He took off his shoes, walked closer to the stream and sat down, letting the sound of the water soothe him.

He watched a leaf float down the middle of the creek. How he wished he could ride that leaf away, away from his father, away from the responsibility of "being a man" at seven years old. He closed his eyes and began to cry, "Mommy, mommy, I want you. Please hold me, mommy." He put his arms around himself and tried to feel what it would be like in his mother's arms, as he rocked back and forth. He closed his eyes to concentrate, but all he saw was the squirrel's head flying to pieces. With a scream, he jumped up and stumbled backwards. Losing his balance, he fell on his buttocks. The stones at the creek's edge cut into his bare flesh and soft testicles. The pain was too much for him to bear. He began grabbing hands full of rocks and throwing them with all his might until he fell, exhausted on his back. He lay on the ground, breathing heavily, looking at the umbrella of trees over him. High on a limb was a squirrel eating a nut just like the one he had killed. Paul immediately felt comforted. "Maybe he's not dead. Maybe it was all a bad dream."

Paul watched until the squirrel finished his nut and scurried away. Feeling better, Paul got up and waded into the water. He automatically began to wash himself with soft, bottom sand he scooped up from under the water. As he gently washed between his legs, he smiled with bitterness. His father had taught him to do that. He rinsed his soiled trousers and laid them over a bush to dry. He then lay down on a soft patch of grass to rest, but when he closed his eyes the horror of the squirrel's head flying apart and the blood pouring out on the limb flashed before him again. His stomach churned in revulsion, twisting like hot knives sticking him; his body furiously shook as sobs tore from his soul. "Why do living things have to die, God?" he cried bitterly. "Why?!"

He wanted with all his might to run back and put the squirrel's little head back together again, to put the little nut back into the little paws. He knew it was impossible and worst of all, he knew he had caused the squirrel to die horribly. For the first time, the death of his mother became a reality. "Did I also kill my mother?" His father had told him she had died giving birth to him. Panic rose up in him. "Maybe I killed my mother too!" He looked up at the trees. The wind was blowing the branches with a strange sound. He listened intently. His heart was beating in his ears like a drum...." Boom, boom, you killed your mother, you killed the squirrel, you killed your mother, you killed the squirrel!"

"No-o-o! No-o-o!" Paul screamed with all his strength, gasping for air. "No-o-o!" he screamed again as all went black.

When Paul awoke it was beginning to get dark. He put on his trousers and headed back to the house, dreading the sight of his father. Paul quietly slipped through the back door and listened. He heard his sisters and father in the living room. Apparently, no one had looked for him. The only way to get to the stairs was to go past the living room. His father, reading the paper, did not look up at him even though Paul was sure he saw him. His sisters were sewing and reading. Soft music played on the radio. Christina winked at him and the other two sisters smiled but made no motion for him to come into the room. He went directly to his room and lay down on the bed in the dark, pulling his teddy bear close to his chest. He could not sleep except in short, restless spurts as he listened and waited for Christina to come to him. He wanted her to hold him, to cuddle and soothe the anguished feelings he could not control. The teddy bear, for the first time, brought no comfort and with fury he flung it across the room at the picture sitting on the desk of his father and mother.

CHAPTER 6

Anger built in Paul as the hours ticked by and Christina did not come to him. When daybreak brought light to his room, he knew she would not come and he mumbled to himself as he fell into an exhausted sleep, "Witch, I hope you die too!"

Christina at eighteen had blossomed into a beautiful woman. He body had filled out with a full bosom and she was not comfortable with Paul's head snuggled against her breast. She knew if she went to his room, he would certainly seek comfort by laying his head on her chest as he always did when he was upset. "Perhaps I have babied him too much," she thought. "He shouldn't be so upset over a squirrel being shot. Father's right. It is time he began to grow up!"

The first rays of sunshine beamed into Paul's room when he heard voices outside of his door. "I'm going horseback riding with Jergen this morning. We'll be back by eight for breakfast."

"All right have a nice time!" he heard his father answer.

Paul imagined Jergen, Christina's boyfriend, sitting on the limb eating a nut, and the bullet shot his head off instead of the squirrel's head. With that satisfying thought, Paul fell back asleep.

Later he awakened to loud shouts of screaming and crying. He quickly jumped out of bed, threw on his pants and shirt and ran down the stairs. The living room was filled with people crying – his two sisters, neighbors, a policeman, Jergen, as well as several other people. He immediately knew Christina was not there. "Where's Christina?" he demanded, surprising himself with his bold voice. The room became awkwardly silent.

With a white face and tight lips, his father answered him. "She's dead! killed by one of your precious little animals!" There was a cold fury in his father's voice.

"What?" Paul was stunned.

Jergen broke in. "We were riding amazingly fast when a rabbit jumped up and spooked Christina's horse. He bolted and Christina was thrown to the ground. She landed on a rock and her neck was broken. She must have died instantly."

Paul saw lips moving and he knew they were speaking but he could not hear the words they said. He heard unintelligible sounds. Worse yet, he felt nothing. "It is wrong to feel nothing," he thought

THE SECOND GENERATION

to himself. "Why don't I feel something?" He did not know whether he was talking out loud or to himself. Reality, fantasy, yesterday, today, all became one for Paul. The words he had thought last night came back to him. "Witch, I hope you die too!" Terror swept his body. "I killed her. I killed Christina. I killed my mother. I killed the squirrel!"

The shrill words hung in the air, filling the room. For that moment, no one spoke, a silence descended upon him.

"What did you say?" his father was coming towards him.

"If I had shot the rabbit's head off instead of the squirrel, then maybe Christina would be alive now!" He glared at his father as his mind shouted. "You, you made me do it. You made me kill Christina. You made me kill the squirrel and you made me kill my m other. I don't know how, but you made me do it! I hate you! I hate your guts!" He felt the pain of his nails digging into the palms of his hands from his clenched fists. He banged them against the banister, enjoying the pain.

"Go back to bed, son." His father said softly with the flicker of a smile. "There will be time to kill many rabbis. We'll do it together!"

Paul turned and went up the stairs to his room. "Am I going up the stairs or am I dreaming? Is Christina really dead? I didn't mean what I said. Maybe this is a bad dream and I'll wake up any minute and Christina will be there, holding me in her arms. Yes, that is it! Let me go back to bed so I can wake up from this nightmare." Paul climbed back into his bed, put his arms around his pillow and stared vacantly at the dust in the sunbeam streaming in through the window.

At eh wake and then at the cemetery, not one tear came from Paul's eyes. He stood straight and proud, his fists tightened with determination. "No, I will not cry. I will be strong for Christina!" As the priest spoke, Paul looked up towards the sky, half-expecting to see the soul of Christina soar up to heaven. The light blue sky was filled with white puffy clouds, floating through the air. Perhaps the clouds were thousands of wings of angels who gather together to welcome dead people to heaven. "That's why we see shapes in clouds," he thought. "It's the angels' way of letting people know they are there." Oh, if only he, too, could soar upward, upward to

CHAPTER 6

those clouds. He imagined himself up in the clouds and looking down on all the people.

"The Lord giveth and the Lord taketh away," he heard the priest chant.

Paul looked down at the coffin and imagined the top opening, flowers flying everywhere. Cristina would jump up and shout, "The Lord decided not to taketh away!" He waited and watched but the flowers did not move. He wanted to open the coffin and help Christina out of there. He wanted her alive. "What is life? How can God take it away? Why?" He ached with longing to bring Christina back to life. "I need you, Christina. Please don't leave me!" Paul did not know whether he was speaking to himself or out loud. Reality was blending into fantasy as pain ripped down his chest into his stomach. He could not grasp enough air into his lungs. Black spots filled his vision and he felt his legs weakening.

His sister was nudging him and whispering, are you all right?" As Paul looked up at her, rays of sun suddenly swept across the cemetery, releasing the prison of the clouds. Their warmth comforted Paul. He nodded "yes" and formed the words, "I'm okay" with his lips. These sun rays are a kiss and a hug from my mother, the one I have never known. She is trying to tell me that she needs Christina with her." He took his sister's hand and squeezed it with a faint smile.

The priest's words became a soft drone in his mind as his eyes began to examine all the tombstones on the cemetery. He saw white robed figures rise from each of them, led by a beautiful slim lady with long golden hair that sparkled in the sunlight. Her eyes were soft and bright blue, her skin was soft and creamy…her lovely mouth was smiling as she extended her arms to Christina who was also wearing a silken white robe. Christina went into her arms with a happy laugh and all the people crowded around the tow as they rocked and laughed with great happiness and joy in each other's arms. He watched in amazement as little wings began to sprout on Christina's shoulders.

"Come on, son, it's time to go." His father put his hand on his shoulder and there was nothing left except the cold stones and the wind blowing the grass and flowers around them.

The sun was again hidden by the clouds. Paul was furious at his father for taking away his dream. He reached up and knocked off his father's hand from his shoulder. "Thank you, sir, I can go by myself!" He turned and briskly walked to the car.

 # CHAPTER 7

May 1955

WHEN THE FROMANS arrived in Brooklyn, they were surprised to find that the cousin had prepared a beautiful home for them in a tree-lined neighborhood. The houses were close to each other with only driveways between them. Each house had a small back yard with trees, grass and flowers.

As they walked into the house, Miriam clasped her hands in joy. "Oh Isaac," she exclaimed. "look at the size of these rooms and all the windows!"

"Bad conscience. He did it because we were in the Concentration Camps and he wasn't. Don't worry, I'll pay him back every cent for this house." Isaac remarked cynically.

"Nonsense!" reprimanded Miriam. "We're the only family he has left. Mark needs us as much as we need him. Look at all the trouble he went through to find us!"

"That's right, Isaac," Mark Handelman remarked as he came into the door. I haven't been able to hold my life and my business together. I lost everything. You and Miriam are all the family I have left." He hesitated. The veins in his prematurely grey temples were visibly quivering.

"With your help, I'm willing to give life one more shot. I know you would have preferred to get your own house and make your own way. I would have preferred to have been with my family now. But that is the way it is, Isaac. If we are going to work successfully together, we had just better get it straight right now. There is no give and take in this relationship. There is only a complete sharing – fifty/fifty. I don't have the nerves, energy or time for any self-pity or nonsense!" Mark's tormented brown eyes looked straight into

Isaac's surprised face, waiting for an answer. Light pellets of perspiration covered his forehead. Miriam held her breath in anticipation of what Isaac might say.

Isaac put forth is big hand. "Welcome to our house, Mark. Please consider it your home as well, which of course it is!" he added with a half laugh. Miriam released her breath with relief.

"Come," insisted Miriam, "let's celebrate our new home, our new life, our new family, with a cup of tea." She took Mark's arm and gently tugged. "Come, come, I know right where I put my tea kettle."

As they drank tea, the Fromans learned that Mark's wife had lingered painfully battling cancer before her death, and his son was shot down in a bombing mission over Germany. The telegram from the government had classified him "missing in action."

"A Jew shot down over Germany? Even if he had survived the crash, he didn't have a chance with the Germans!"

"Maybe the German didn't know he was Jewish. He had fair skin and blond hair like your wife, didn't he?" Miriam ventured some sort of comfort.

"The war is over. Why haven't I heard from him?" Mark bit his lips. "I'm only glad Jill died before she heard that her son was dead. She gave him a little golden mezuzah to wear around his neck for luck. You know, I think she believed that nothing would happen to him as long as he was wearing that mezuzah. It would be ironic if he were unconscious when the Germans found him, and that mezuzah told the Nazis he was Jewish."

"Joseph was smart." Miriam reasoned, "The moment he realized he was in trouble, I'm sure he would have pulled off the mezuzah."

"What happened to your daughter?" Isaac asked, thinking he was changing the subject. Miriam shot him a look with "stupid" written all over it.

Mark did not raise his eyes but stared at the cup of tea he was holding with both hands. "Two weeks after Jill died, we got the news about Joseph. Beth had a hard time coping. On her way home from school, I guess she didn't notice the light had changed when she stepped off the curb in front of the delivery truck. The driver tried to miss her, but it happened too quickly. I was too involved with my own pain. I didn't think of her. I should have comforted her, given her more attention. She was too sensitive. She wasn't strong. I didn't notice my little girl had pain too."

Miriam reached over and placed both of her hands-on Mark's hands. "Mark, terrible things happen to us in life. We don't know why, but they happen. Always there are the 'I should haves, and maybe ifs…' but we try to accept what has happened and go on with our lives. To torment ourselves with the past only embitters our lives. We just must pick ourselves up and keep going by looking to the future with faith that something good will come into our existence. To live in the past is to live in despair. Find peace in the fact that none of us really had any control over what happened to us; then perhaps we will find a bit of contentment. Mark, look at me." Miriam gently put her fingers under Mark's chin and lifted his head. "Your will-power to survive is amazing. You still want to start over again to build a new life. That is good. We may be three broken pieces of plate, but together we will glue the broken pieces back together, creating a dish so strong that it will hold whatever life offers us. We still have many years in front of us. Let's not waste them. Let's live for what the future holds. Okay?" Miriam's compassionate face glowed with optimism. Little wisps of grey hair escaped the kerchief on her head, accenting her sincerity.

Mark took both her hands in his. "You are truly a beautiful woman and a magnificent soul, Miriam. It is my luck that I have you."

Isaac, who had quietly witnessed the exchange of feelings between Miriam and Mark, felt both proud of Miriam and uncomfortable with his own inadequacy of expression, that seemed to be second nature with Miriam. "Come," he said as he got up from his chair, "let's look at the house together."

Miriam joyfully redecorated the whole house. With the four bedrooms upstairs, she arranged for the girls to share a room and each boy to have his own room. She painted to boys' rooms light blue. In David's room she put dark blue curtains and bedspread, but Eric's room she decorated with white. She papered the girls' room with a tiny pink primrose pattern, choosing to match, a pink spread for the bed and white bed ruffles.

The master bedroom was painted Grecian white with accompanying white lace curtains on the windows. She covered the bed with a patchwork quilt of many colors that she had sewn herself. Thick white furry throw rugs were on each side and at the foot of the bed.

On her knees, she through scrubbed the light brown rug on the stairway and living and dining room floors. She cleaned the large bay widow in the dining room until it sparkled in the sunlight. The living room was smaller but comfortable with small stained-glass windows on the sides. The kitchen was not large but had enough space to comfortable prepare meals. Most of all, Miriam loved the large porch in front of the house which she filled with chairs, a rocker and abundant plants on stands.

Miriam manicured the tiny back yard lawn, planted flowers along both the side fences and a grapevine on the back fence. She hung baskets of flowers of different lengths on all the fences. From the limbs of a tree extending into their yard, she hung bird feeders.

"Four years I sat in the dark rooms of the ghetto," she exclaimed, "without seeing anything green – no flowers, no trees, no butterflies and no birds. Even the sun was my enemy, ready to expose my hiding places. Now I want to see sun, flowers, birds, anytime I want, without fear."

Miriam had expressed the feelings of many Jewish families living on her street. Having survived ghettos, concentration camps, hellholes of hiding, they cherished every tree, every blade of grass, every flower. The tree-lined streets were spotlessly clean. Each family cleaned not only in front of their houses, but the street as well, picking up any paper or debris that blew onto the street or was thrown out of a passing car.

The Fromans were immediately welcomed into the neighborhood. "We have our own little Israel here," they were laughingly told. They had no trouble adjusting. On the holidays, the neighbors celebrated together, visiting each other's homes in joy and happiness. When the Sabbath arrived, a peace would fall upon the neighborhood. Sabbath candles shone through the clean windows as the sound of Sabbath songs permeated the evening stillness.

Every morning and evening, the men and boys would go together to pray in the little synagogue three streets over. The women would gather on each other's porches on summer evenings

CHAPTER 7

after dinner to talk and to share experiences of life. The children would play together in the tiny yards or in each other's rooms.

The Froman family, for the first time, experienced a nearly normal atmosphere. Next door to the Froman house lived the Epsteins. Eric's sister, Ruthie, became fast friends with their daughter, Jacqueline, who was the same age. In fact, from the first day they met, they became inseparable. Jacqueline spent half of her time in Ruthie's house, eating, sleeping, and studying. Eric envied their giggling together behind the closed door of Ruthie's bedroom. He knew they were only comparing crushes and teachers, trying on clothes and makeup, but still, he longed to be part of such a close friendship.

Eric loved to look at Jacqueline. She was small and delicate with jet-black hair encircling her face, wisps of curls enhanced the blue of her eyes. The palest of roses bloomed on her creamy cheeks. She reminded him of the ceramic dolls he had once see displayed in a department store window. Eric wanted to touch her, but he was afraid that if he did, she would surely break and fall apart. Jacqueline knew that Eric was fascinated with her, and she would swish her long hair in front of him and tempt him with glances, only to rebuke him when he came close to her.

Lola Epstein, Jacky's mother, was also very beautiful and sometimes when all his mother's lady friends would sit on the front porch, Eric would hear them discussing her. To his immense irritation, they would always drop their voices and speak in lowered tones to each other. Had they not changed the tone of their voices, he probably would not have paid any attention to what they were saying, but the whispers indicated something forbidden. Like most children, Eric was fascinated with the forbidden and he became determined to find out what they were talking about. The idea occurred to him one day to feign illness so would not have to go with his father for evening prayers. He planned to take a book to the living room and sit next to the window facing the porch. The ladies would not see him through the curtains and perhaps he would hear what they were whispering about. And if they did see him, well, he would just be reading a book!

THE SECOND GENERATION

The conversation about babies, children, shopping for bargains, and other such things bored Eric. He was about to give up and leave when he heard the voices drop. Eric leaned closer to the curtains to hear. In his intense concentration, he did not notice his mother get up from her chair and come into the house. He had only heard the words, "Nazi brothels" when he became aware that his mother was standing behind him, hands on her hips, her stern face glaring at him. "I thought you were sick. What are you doing here?" she demanded.

"I was reading when I felt I was going to faint, so I went to the window to try to get some fresh air!" Eric stuttered with panic in his voice.

"What? There are no windows in your room?" asked his mother in a seemingly surprised voice.

Before Eric could answer, his mother continued. "You are never again to try to listen to anyone's private conversation." She warned, "God sees all, and when you do what you are not supposed to do, He doesn't like it!" That statement, which his mother used whenever she caught him doing something wrong, always scared the living daylights out of Eric. "I think you had better go to your room and think about the bad thing you have done, Eric! Better yet, I think you should do some studying of the Torah to make up for it!"

Eric knew better than to claim he was innocent. His mother was too smart for that. The best thing was for him to look deeply ashamed and regretful. He rose, sunk his head downward and walked towards his room as if he were carrying the weight of the world on his back. His mother smiled to herself and returned to her friends on the porch.

Jacqueline's family was different from the Fromans. They believed that God had turned away from the Jewish people. They would go to the beach on Saturday instead of to the synagogue, and Mrs. Epstein laughed when Eric's mother discussed her elaborate preparations for the holidays. However, everyone in the neighborhood appeared to overlook the Epstein's attitude toward religion because of the word, "Nazi-brothel." Eric was determined to find out somehow what it meant.

CHAPTER 7

Though quite tall for his eight years, Eric was slim and rather frail. He lugged the heavy large dictionary his mother kept on the pedestal downstairs up the stairs to his room. He looked up the word, "brothel." Its definition, "house of prostitution," did not satisfy him so he looked up "prostitute" – one who sells sexual favors." He had studied prostitution and sexual laws at the Yeshiva. There was the story of Tamar and Judah in the Bible as well as all the laws; however, the full impact of their meaning was beyond his youthful and inexperienced comprehension. His inquisitive mind wanted to discuss and understand the whole subject. He knew girls were different; he had diapered his little sisters enough times to know that, but he was younger than, and had not considered the difference.

The words, "sexual favors" fascinated him. What exactly were "sexual favors." The dictionary said, "One who sells…." Was that "one" a man or a woman? He lowered his pants and examined himself and tried to remember the details of his sisters. He would like to examine a girl closely now. But whom? His sisters were too bug. Maybe Jacqueline? He blushed at the thought of it. Guilt welled up in him. He had been taught at the Yeshiva that boys do not touch girls, much less have anything sexual to do with them until marriage.

He heard the door slam downstairs. "God watches everything you do and when you do something bad, He doesn't like it!" rang in his ears. He quickly pulled up his pants and carried the large dictionary back down the stairs, hoping no one would see him. Then he returned to his room and fell upon his bed. His mind mulled over and over the unknown words.

As the years passed, Eric's attraction to Jacqueline did not lessen. The "religious girls" with their high knee socks, long sleeves and high-necked dresses reaching below the calf of their legs seemed dull next to Jacqueline, who always dressed in the latest styles, with her dresses only to her knees, not caring if her legs or arms showed. Sometimes she would leave an extra button open on her blouse exposing the creamy white of her throat and chest down to her breasts. His excitement when seeing her tormented Eric. Whenever she slept over with his sister, Eric could not sleep most

THE SECOND GENERATION

of the night as he fantasied Jacqueline in his bed, giggling and laughing with him.

On his 17th birthday, Eric's parents gave a surprise birthday party for him. His mother prepared a table of food in the living room. In the center of the table was a large chocolate cake with 18 candles, which included one for good luck. It was a buffet meal, and people were sitting in groups on the porch and in the living room, eating, talking and laughing. Eric kept watching the door for Jacqueline. "Where is she?" he kept thinking to himself. "Her parents are here."

As Eric blew out the candles, he felt someone helping him from the other side of the table. He looked up into the laughing eye of Jacqueline. "Hey, I didn't think you were going to make it!" The joy in his voice was difficult to disguise.

"No way would I miss your 17th birthday party! Furthermore, I demand the first piece of cake!"

"Yes, Madam!" Eric sliced the first piece of cake and gave it to Jacqueline. As he cut slices of cake, he handed them to Jacqueline who passed them out to the guests. When they had finished, Jacqueline took Eric's arm, "Come, let's talk."

"I can't leave, Jacqueline, it is my party."

"I know. Let's just sit over here on the stairs and talk. Okay?"

"Okay, good idea." They seated themselves on the steps to the upstairs.

"I guess it took a birthday party for me to notice how you have grown up, Eric. You look so nice and so distinguished all dressed up."

"You look pretty nice yourself. But then you always look nice."

"And today, Eric?"

"Especially nice. Purple is a good color for you, Jacky. It compliments your skin."

Jacquelin was wearing a dark purple suit dress with a white strip around the collar and down the front. She had on hanging silver earrings and white shoes. Her hair was pulled back into a bun at the neck.

"Well, Eric, what do we have her, the mutual admiration society?"

Eric leaned his elbows on the step behind him and stretched out his legs. His six-foot frame covered half the staircase. "I guess

CHAPTER 7

it is better than picking on each other, or teasing each other like we always seem to do, Jacky."

"I think we are a little too old for that now, don't you, Eric?"

Eric nodded, "Yep, I guess do. So, tell me, Jacky, what's doing in your life?"

From that time on, Eric and Jacquelin developed a close friendship. For hours they would share discussions of their philosophy of life, their studies, their feelings, and the world around them. The fires of youth blazed under their gentle touching and caressing, which were very reserved because of Eric's teachings.

Eric's parents did not outwardly show disapproval of the relationship, but they subtly made remarks. "Her fast temper and sharp tongue do not match her beauty. She doesn't care for the feelings of other people."

"Ah, Ma," Eric would come to her defense. "Her mother always taught her not to take anything from anyone, but to fight back at the slightest insult. Don't you teach me same thing?"

"But there are ways of fighting back, Eric. At your enemies, not at your friends. She wouldn't make a good wife. She is too selfish. She thinks too much about herself."

"Who's talking about marriage?" Eric would answer much too quickly. "We're not even finished with school!"

 # CHAPTER 8

September 1965

A NEW HOUSE, a new job and a new life in America did not solve the old problems between Eric's parents. When Eric was 18 years old, their last child, Ephraim, was born, and for a while he claimed the attention of the entire family, bring peace to the household. It was not long, however, before Eric heard his mother should at his father during a late-night argument. "Now you have ALL your children back again. Why aren't you satisfied?!"

"ÁLL my children do not equal YOUR one Eric in your heart!" his father retorted.

Eric felt his guts twist within his body. "Why does my father hate me? What have I done to him?" He turned the question over and over in his mind, trying to find the answer. "If I ever have children, I'll never do this to them," he swore to himself. His hatred for his father became companion to the compassion he felt for his mother.

At the B'nai Yakov Yeshiva, which Eric attended, many of the students were children of survivors of the Holocaust. To help them cope and understand family problems a Second-Generation Group led by a psychologist was established by the Jewish Federation in cooperation with the college. To fathom his father's actions, Eric joined the group of children of survivors who met to discuss the difficulties they had experienced with parents who had lived through the Holocaust. He was surprised to learn many members of the group had the same problems he had. Many of their parents had concentrated all their bitterness into hatred for one Nazi tormentor.

THE SECOND GENERATION

"If my father ever came face-to-face with Commandant Steigerhaus, I am sure he would rip him apart piece by piece," Eric remarked at one meeting.

Commandant Steigerhaus was notoriously known for breaking the spirit and will of his victims. It was a game to him. He placed bets with his fellow Nazis on how long it would take to break a person!" he was told.

"What do you mean, 'break a person'?" Eric questioned.

"How much slow, deliberate torture a person could endure before he would beg for mercy or death. The torture would be emotional as well as physical. Not too many of Steigerhaus' victims survived. He was a master of torture!"

Eric also learned that Steigerhaus was on the "Wanted List" of Nazi war criminals issued by the State of Israel. He had only known about Steigerhaus from the nightmares and outbursts of violence his father suffered from. "He never broke my father," Eric said with pride. "In fact, my father is still fighting him!" When Eric realized what he had said, tears began to well up in his eyes. The hatred in his heart for his father began to turn to profound pity.

"What a reason to be proud of a father!" he thought. He did not know whether he was feeling sorry for his father or for himself.

Eric tried to get Jacqueline to attend the meetings, but she refused. "I live with the Holocaust every day of my life," she commented, "I don't want to socialize with it as well."

One Second Generation Group meeting Eric attended profoundly affect him and provided a new insight which determined his life's direction. The speaker was a renowned psychiatrist who spoke of the results of "marriages of convenience" performed immediately after the war; how survivors tried to recapture the memories of their lost loved ones in the children they bore in those marriages. Eric sat dumbfounded as the psychiatrist's words 'Holocaust Syndrome' shed light on the behavior of his father and mother. He felt a new awareness and understanding of his past with a deep, deep sense of deliverance. Relief washed through him as he realized that he was a victim, not a catalyst, in the difficulties of his parents' marriage. As he left the meeting, he also left his childhood behind him.

CHAPTER 8

On the way home, Eric thought, "I would never have been able to eliminate the confusion about myself had I not attended that meeting." He felt sincere sorrow for those people who suffered their entire life because the truth was not available to them. "I want to work with these people. I want to help bring peace or at least some understanding to their lives." The more he thought about it, the happier he became. "There is no right or wrong side with my parents, nor with me. These survivors of the Holocaust are victims, pathetic victims of emotions, of situations they did not create. Their children are victims. We are all victims. I want to help these people. I want to make them see it is not their fault. Once they understand, they can grab hold of their lives and turn them around." All of Eric's loneliness and longing left him, and for the first time in his life, he went to bed at peace with himself and the world around him. He had found a direction for his life.

Eric graduated first in his class. His deep sensitivity had given him extraordinary insight into his studies, and he had become known as an "expert" on Jewish law. His innate understanding of human emotions and feelings, coupled with the voracious desire for knowledge, attracted other students to him for help with their problems. Whenever he was able to successfully aid, direct or counsel someone, the haunting void he felt was replaced by a deep satisfaction. By graduation time, Eric had made up his mind. He was going to choose the rabbinate as his profession. With the desire to help people and to make the world a better place in which his people could live, Eric registered to study for his ordination. He also registered in the City College to study for his B.A. at night and acquired a teaching job in the Yeshiva to pay for his studies.

One early summer night after all Eric's plans had been formulated, he sat on the front steps of his house talking with Jacqueline. They were both in a good mood and very happy in each other's company. She was proud that Eric had graduated with high honors. He told her that he had registered in college and about his teaching position. To his surprise, she threw her arms around him and gave him a big kiss on the lips. "That's wonderful, Eric. What are you going to study?" "Psychology."

THE SECOND GENERATION

"Wow! You'll make a great psychologist!" she remarked with enthusiasm. "And there is a lot of money in it too!"

"I don't want to be a psychologist, Jacky."

"What? Then why are you studying psychology?"

"To help me in my work as a rabbi." Eric like the sound of the words.

Jacqueline was stunned. She did not reply, so Eric continued. "You're the first one I have told. I haven't even discussed it with my parents. I also registered to start my studies for my ordination in September. There is something more, Jacky." He took her hands in his and his soft brown eyes searched her face. "When I'm ordained and you've completed school, I want you to be my wife, my Rebbitizen. Together we will guide our people and help them!"

Jacqueline pulled her hands away from him in shock, turning to anger. Her temper flared. "I shudder at the mention of the word,' Rebbitizen.' It is antiquated! It puts chains on your life, a life that is not your own! I will have to cover my head, wear long sleeves! Absolutely not!! I will not marry any rabbi!"

"But Jacky, don't you understand? I want to be a rabbi. Please, please understand!" Eric pleaded.

"And what about what I want?" Jacky stood up. "Call me when you cancel your plans for rabbinical college, Eric. If you don't change your mind, then forget my number!" She threw her black hair over her shoulders and stomped down the porch steps to go home.

Instead of feeling dejected Eric was furious. He detested being forced to choose between two options by anyone. "No one will ever dominate my life," he promised himself whenever his father would force him to do something simply to prove his mastery over his son.

When Eric told his parents of his plans to be a rabbi, they were not overly enthusiastic. "Are you going to sit, study and pray all day," asked his father, "and leave it to your wife to make a living?"

"No, Papa. I am going to be a rabbi of the people. I am going to guide, lead and help my people. I'll get paid like any other job."

"Do you think you know enough to be a rabbi, Eric?" his mother asked. "Maybe there's another profession you would rather be in." Eric was disappointed in both of his parents, especially his mother. "My mind is made up. I am going to be a rabbi. I have a job and

CHAPTER 8

will pay my own way. Subject closed!" Eric turned and walked outside into the cool summer air. He looked up at the stars. "Well, I passed Your first test, didn't I, God?" The thought of a test by God, however, did not lessen the ache in his heart.

Jacky and Eric continued to be with each other throughout the summer. The subject of rabbi was not mentioned. Eric knew that Jacky though he would be so enraptured with her by the time she went away to school, that he would give up the idea of the rabbinate. Eric was just as determined to stand his ground.

The first year of study was difficult for Eric; allowing him little time with Jacky. He would arrive at the Yeshiva at seven o'clock in the morning, study for his ordination, teach in the afternoon, and finally go to City University at night. Sometimes he began his homework at eleven or twelve o'clock at night. On the Sabbath, he spent the afternoon sleeping after he came home from the synagogue. Yet, he felt a special kind of exhilaration in his accomplishments. His studies intrigued him as he strove to acquire all the knowledge he could master. Yet, despite his feelings, Jacqueline was adamant. He would have to choose between her and the rabbinate.

O August 26th, the day before Jacqueline was to leave for Berkeley University in California, she and Eric took a walk to the park. They had very few words for each other, and when they spoke, it was with shaky voices. Both were filled with emotion and tension. Eric saw tears dropping off Jacqueline's chin. He reached out and caught a tear as it fell, brought it to his mouth and gave it a gentle kiss, then pretended to blow it away.

"Jacky?" he looked into her sad blue eyes and his heart tore. She didn't speak but looked at him, waiting for his words. "Let's not fight before you go away." She nodded her head in agreement. Eric sighed. "I'll tell you what." Her eyes met his. He sensed that she was waiting for him to say that he would give up his plans to be a rabbi. He felt cornered and awkward. He looked at her again. "I don't believe in making decisions out of emotion. Let's stay friends. Let's write to each other. You have your studies and I have my studies. We don't know what the future will being. Let's just leave everything at that right now. Okay?"

He saw the wave of disappointment sweep over her face and her eyes flash with anger. Her tears had stopped. Her mouth became firmly set. Her delicately shaped nostrils flared. "You will not receive one word from me until you change your decision to be a rabbi," she said through clenched teeth. "Until then, goodbye!" She turned and began walking away.

The way she threw back her head in defiance infuriated Eric. "I think you are a stubborn bitch!"

Jacqueline's face flushed red as she hurried away with long and purposeful steps.

Eric immediately regretted his words. "I'm sorry, Jacky," he called after her. "I didn't mean it. Please come back and let's talk!"

Never breaking her stride, Jacqueline looked back and raised her hand with only the middle finger extended.

Eric was up early the next day, waiting on the front steps to see her before she left. When she came out of the house, she came over to him. "Goodbye, Eric. Good luck in your studies to be a rabbi."

"Good luck to you too!" he replied.

She turned and got into the car already packed with her luggage. As the car pulled away, she threw him a kiss which he returned.

Despite his hectic schedule, Eric wrote a letter to Jacqueline every week for three months. He poured his heart out to her, explaining his desires, hopes and dreams in the minutest detail, but his mailbox was empty every day in return. He counted the days until she would be home during the Christmas holidays. At last, the long-awaited day came. He rushed straight to her house after school with his heart beating in his ears. He just knew that she missed him as much as he missed her and would be anxious to see him. "Our relationship, our friendship, our love – they're too strong, too set. She won't give me up. I just know it," he told himself with confidence.

She opened the door with cool politeness and invited him in. They exchanged information on their lives with great courtesy, as acquaintances, not good friends. The space between them grew tense. Finally, Jacqueline spike, "You're wasting your time with your letters. The answer is still no. In fact, Eric, you can make up your mind right now – this moment. You can have me without the

CHAPTER 8

rabbinate, or you can have the rabbinate without me. You cannot have both!"

"From the determination in her face and her voice, Eric knew it was no longer the subject of his being a rabbi, it was a test of wills – hers against his. It was a test to decide who was the strongest! Eric heard his mouth speaking. "Then it will be the rabbinate." He arose. "Goodbye, Jacky. Good luck." His words were soft, without anger. He walked home in a daze. Jacqueline returned to school a week later without saying goodbye. At home Eric was quiet and sullen. When his family saw how he and Jacky avoided each other, they knew there was trouble between them, but no one said a word.

Late one-night Eric heard a soft knock on his bedroom door. "Come in," he growled, expecting to see his mother. Ruthie came into the room in her pajamas and housecoat. She sat down on the bed where he was reading a book.

"Mind if I come in and talk a little with my older brother?"

"No."

"Things are pretty lousy with Jacky, aren't they?"

"She doesn't want me to be a rabbi!" he blurted out.

"Eric, you know I love you both." It was more of a statement than a question.

"Yes, I know, and I don't expect you to take sides or to get involved."

"I don't intend to," she replied. Eric, I know you're my older brother who always took care of me and gave me advice, and….."

"What do you want to say, Ruthie." Eric was losing his patience. "Please, out with it. I'm not in the mood for playing games."

"What I want to say is that….well, some things are just not *b'shert* – ordained. We sometimes get very angry and hurt when we can't have what we want, but maybe, just maybe, we're better off without having all our desires granted."

Eric looked at his sister without speaking. She continued when she saw he was listening to her.

"A little heartache now may be better than a lot of heartache later. Feeling sorry for yourself is not healthy either, for you or for the rest of our family."

THE SECOND GENERATION

Eric opened his mouth to speak, but Ruthie put her finger on it. "I have something more to say, as long as I am talking." She hesitated and looked deep into his eyes. "Eric, I am SO proud that you are going to be a rabbi. I think you will make the best rabbi there is in the whole world!" She threw her arms around him and gave him a sound kiss on the cheek. He hugged her with deep affection.

"You are the best sister a brother could have!" He kissed her on the forehead. "Thanks, Ruthie." Ruthie smiled, gave him another kiss on the nose and went back to her room.

Eric felt better. He turned out the light and easily went to sleep.

 # CHAPTER 9

October 1971

ONE SUNDAY AFTERNOON, Eric was studying in the New York Library when he became aware of a tall, willowy girl walking towards his table. Long brown hair fell past her shoulders. Even though her arms were full of books, she moved with proud gracefulness. Eric stood up and met her, "You have some load there, could I help you?"

"Oh, thank you. I just hate running back and forth to the stacks. I guess I overdid it!" Her voice had an ever-so-slight intriguing British accent.

"Could I offer you a table?" Eric nodded towards where he was sitting.

"Why, I would be delighted! Thank you again."

Eric put the books on the table. He looked at their titles. Chemistry books!" He looked up at the girl. "What are you studying?

She shrugged her shoulders. "Chemistry?" Her soft brown eyes seemed to be laughing at him.

Eric clicked his tongue. "No, I meant what is your major?"

She gently laughed as she replied, "Chemistry."

"Sh-h-h's" began to resound from the crowded tables around them.

"Let's get out of this anti-social place for a while. How about a cup of coffee?" Eric asked.

"Sounds good to me, but what about all these books?"

"Just leave them. We'll be back in a little while."

"Okay. But if someone takes them away, you'll have to help me find and lug them all back again!"

"Agreed! Come on!"

They did not return to the library but spent the rest of the day in a little café talking. Her name was Sandra Bergenson and she was studying at Columbia University to be a research scientist. She came from a long line of Scientists and she was "carrying on the tradition," she said with a slight laugh. Eric studied her as she spoke. Her face, though not beautiful, was striking, with its high cheekbones, long eyelashes, Grecian profile and perfectly shaped lips. She had a quiet, confident nature which gave Eric a calm feeling. There was a mystique about her that Eric could not quite identify but found extremely attractive.

When Eric spoke to her of his studies to be a rabbi, she was truly touched. "What a wonderful, worthwhile life, to be a rabbi!" she said. "Dedicating one's life to humanity. To me this type of unselfishness is the highest sphere of living." Eric glowed warmly from within.

Eric and Sandra became constant companions in the weeks after their first meeting. Sandra's mature calmness was like an oasis in the desert, following the fiery, tempestuous nature of Jacky. However, sometimes Eric felt inadequate in her presence precisely because he was unable to believe that anyone could maintain such a constantly composed personality. He was accustomed to fluctuating emotions with animated highs and lows. Even when they disagreed, she never raised her voice or try to forcefully put forth her point of view but spoke softly and calmly. When he showed anger, she waited until he became aware of it, at which time he would feel stupid for his behavior. Then she quietly spoke to him, as if to a child who had just thrown a temper tantrum.

"Don't you have feelings inside of you? Don't you ever feel like shouting and screaming? How can you just sit there without any emotion at all?!" Eric shouted at Sandra in agitated frustration when she began to speak to him like a child.

"Oh yes," she replied. "I have a great deal of emotion; however, I learned a long time ago to control this animalistic instinct in myself."

Eric opened his mouth to contradict the word "animalistic" when Sandra motioned with her hand to be quiet. "Please, Eric, I am speaking. Let me finish what I started to say."

CHAPTER 9

With a shrug of his shoulders and a sigh, Eric waited for her to continue.

"When we are angry, we humans tend to insult each other. We say things we don't mean just to 'hurt' the other person. The words cut and they hurt. They are not easily forgiven or forgotten."

"My God, thought Eric, "she sounds like she is teaching in a classroom."

Sandra took Eric's face in both of her hands and looked straight into his eyes. "Eric, I love you. I never want to hurt you in any way, most of all with words I don't mean." With a little laugh, she continued. "Furthermore, one of us has to remain sane in this relationship."

Sandra's equanimity, though it bothered him at times, had a stabilizing effect on Eric. He was draw to her precisely because of it. She was different from other girls. They began to discuss the possibility of marriage.

When Eric brought Sandra home to meet his parents, they were impressed. "She carries herself like a real lady," his mother said. Even his father in a surprised moment of friendship said, "Eric, you have good taste."

When Eric visited Sandra's parents, he was awed with them and their home. They lived in Lake Placid, New York, in a large mansion. They were cordial to Eric and seemed honestly please with him. At dinner, Eric was astonished at the entire family's behavior. His mother had always placed dishes of food on the table, family style, and everyone helped themselves. Here, the maid carried the serving dishes from person to person, and then took away the dish. Eric would have liked a second serving but hesitated to ask. The conversation at the meal was polite, and even though they complimented each other, there was a lack of uninhibited affection and emotion of which Eric was accustomed. "I guess this is the way very rich people behave," he thought to himself.

When Eric's and Sandra's families gathered at a meal at Eric's house, the atmosphere was more relaxed. Sandra's father, Dr. Bergenson, enjoyed Miriam's cooking with obvious pleasure as he helped himself to double portions of almost everything she served. "Haven't tasted food like this since my mother, may she rest in peace, used to cook for me." But he quickly added, "My wife, Muriel, constantly has me on a diet. She won't allow me this good old fashion food too often."

"I'm sure Muriel is an excellent cook," Miriam replied.

"Oh, she is," Eric interjected. "When I ate at her house, the food ws scrumptious!"

Muriel demurred, "I'm afraid the cook was responsible for the meal, Eric. But I will cook a special meal for you some time. I know some very unusual special recipes."

"I am looking forward to it," remarked Eric, a little embarrassed.

"I will lover every moment of it!" Sandra commented.

Six weeks later, Eric was married to Sandra in a beautiful wedding in the Bergenson's garden. As Eric walked up the aisle, he had a queasy feeling within his chest. "Do I love her? Why don't I feel more of a commitment towards her?" As he stood under the Chuppah and watched her come up the aisle towards him, he chided himself. "She's beautiful and graceful. She's highly intelligent and cultured. What more could I want?"

Alone in their hotel room later that evening, Eric wanted to open the door and run away from everything. He felt cornered. How did it happen so fast? Is this what he really wanted? He went to the window and pretended to look outside. He had read every book about physical intimacy he could get his hands on. He had even taken off his yarmulke and gone to a couple of X-rated movies, but questions still whirled in his head. Should he tell her that he has never been with a woman before? No! His pride could not let her know that. What should he do to appear experienced? He was never taught this part of life in the Yeshiva. Once when a fellow student asked the teacher, "What are the laws of the wedding night?" hoping to get more detail. The Rebbe had replied with a laugh, "They are the same laws which exist between man and woman. Don't worry about your wedding night, nature will prevail!"

"Well, I am worried," Eric quietly said to himself. "Should I get undressed in the bedroom or go into the bathroom? Should I leave some clothes on or come out naked?" The idea of coming out naked in front of a woman unnerved him. No one had ever seen him naked before except his mother when he was a little boy, and

CHAPTER 9

the doctor, who was a man. He sneaked a glance at Sandra. She was taking off her clothes and hanging them in the closet in a matter-of-fact manner.

Eric began to take off his clothes, piece by piece, and slowly hang them in the closet following her lead. The inadequacy which he had many times felt with Sandra began to overpower him. "Why am I following her lead; she should be following mine!" he thought angrily.

Eric turned to face Sandra. His open mouth never uttered a word. She was removing the last of her garments deftly without even disarranging her hair. There were no blushes or giggles as Eric had expected from a new bride. The expression on her face was the one she always carried, very methodical and purposeful. She turned and faced him full front.

All the cheap love novels Eric had bought with shaking hands in fear someone would see him and had read under the covers at night with a flashlight, had not prepared him for the woman who stood before him. Her ample breasts were perfect, her flat stomach and firm legs were picture beautiful. Her light brown pubic hair, softly accenting her slim hips, beckoned to him. There was a faint smile on her lips as she looked at his face.

All of Eric's shyness turned to passion. The rest of his clothes came off without hesitation and fell to the floor. He stepped back a couple of steps and let his eyes feast from her toes to her head. She stood still, her hands clasped behind her, her head slightly tilted. Her eyes never left his face.

He held out his arms to her. "My wife, my beautiful wife." She did not move. He came to her and took her in his arms. When he felt her soft firm breasts against his chest, a shiver of almost unbearable delight goose-bumped his entire body. He caressed her hair, letting his hand slide down her back to her buttocks. Her skin was firm, yet soft. He gently kissed her face; her eyes were closed. His hands caressed her slim hips, gently stroking their way up to her breasts.

"Oh God," Eric mumbled, "Thank you for this wife you have given to me." He felt tears of joyful emotion fill his eyes as he lifted her into his arms and carried her to the bed, gently kissing her face.

He snuggled his nose in her hair as his hands memorized her whole body. "Sandra, I love you. I love you so much," he whispered as his lips tenderly brushed down her neck.

Sandra took his head in both of his hands and brought his lips to hers. During a passionate kiss, she opened her mouth and let her tongue touch his. It was more than he could bear. Never in his wildest fantasies had he imagined such feelings of joy and agony. He could no longer control the passion consuming his body. He raised himself above her. For an instant he thought he saw a taunting, contemptuous smile on her lips as her legs opened, but in the excitement of the moment, he brushed it from his mind.

A myriad of colors flashed in his brain. A strange guttural sound tore from his throat. His loins felt on fire, "Oh, Sandra, my dearest beloved!" he cried as he exploded within her.

He dropped exhausted upon her with the heavy breathing of deep satisfaction. He missed her arms around him. He looked up at her. She had her hands behind her head.

"Are you finished?" she asked in a nonchalant tone. Eric was stunned. He quickly rolled off her.

"Are you all right? Did I hurt you?" Eric stammered, embarrassed.

"Of course, I'm all right," she answered with an amused laugh. "No, you didn't hurt me."

"Did you like it? You wanted it." Her hand motioned down her body. "Sure, I enjoyed you, Eric. I enjoyed watching you go through the various stages of passion, depending upon my response." She raised her head and cupped it in her hand, resting on her elbow facing him. "But to tell you the truth, I don't see why everyone makes such a fuss about having sexual intercourse."

"I like to call it 'making love.'" Anger and hurt crept into Eric's words as he covered himself with the sheet.

"That's a euphemism for sexual relations. It is an animal act designed to propagate the species. The pleasure which may be involved with the act is to promote the union."

"This is not your first time?" Eric asked.

"No," Sandra laughed again. "As a scientist I was curious, and I have experimented. But in all my experiments, I have discovered nothing of value that separates human sexual unions from the animal world."

"Why did you marry me, Sandra?"

"Because you are a very fine person. And I wanted to be married. Being a rabbi is an honorable position, and I shall receive recognition along with you. I know you will be good to me, and I will be able to work on my research. I'm a human being, Eric, and as such, I am gregarious. I desire the company of another human being."

"This couldn't be the woman I married," Eric said to himself. He sat up, reached over to her and took her hands in his. He searched her face desperately. "Sandra, do you love me?"

"Of course, I love you, Eric. I find you a very interesting person. Quite complex. I don't think I shall ever be bored with you."

Eric was trying frantically to remain calm. "I am not a specimen for observation. I am your husband. I am supposed to be your soulmate. We are supposed to share our lives together!"

"Eric, because we are married it doesn't mean that we cannot have individual lives. We are individuals. You have your way of life and I have mine. We are sharing a home, a bed together. We are companions. Sharing life doesn't mean owning the other person!"

Eric was beginning to feel light-headed. "Maybe after we have children, Sandra, and we share the experience of raising them together, you'll feel differently."

"Eric, I don't want to have children. It is a lousy world in which to bring children. Besides, I don't want to take time away from my research....my work."

Eric felt his insides churning. He thought he had reached a pinnacle of his desires....to have someone with whom he could be united, to share love, to have a family, to cultivate a meaningful, happy life of love and contentment. "Who is this woman I married? Am I now trapped?" Panic filled his mind. Stunned, he got out of bed and went to the bathroom, shut the door and vomited, running the water and flushing the toilet to cover the sounds. He knelt for a while with his arms on the toilet while cold sweat poured from his body. All the love he had felt for Sandra vanished. A stranger was in the bed in the next room, not the woman he had married in his mind, and now he would have to learn to live with this stranger.

Days passed. Life fell into a semi-routine that brought no peace to Eric and Sandra Froman. Contrary to Sandra's insistence that they each had their own individual lives, she constantly tried to control Eric's life, to manipulate his feelings and desires. Eric was just as insistent in maintaining his independence.

The tension between them often flared into conflict.

"Eric, dear," Sandra said one night. "You don't have to study now. Let's go to the movies."

"Sandra, please don't tell me what I have to do or what I don't have to do. If you want something, just ask me, don't tell me!"

"Why should I always have to beg you?" she hot back.

"You don't have to beg me. Can't you understand? Why didn't you ask, 'Do you have to study tonight?'"

Sandra burst into tears. "You never think of anyone except yourself! You have no consideration for me. I have feelings too. What terrible thing did I ask for? All I wanted to do was to go somewhere WITH YOU, and you jump down my throat!"

Eric softened his voice when he saw her tears. "Sandra, sweetheart. Please listen." He held her hands. "It's not what you say, but how you say it."

When Sandra saw he was weakening, she immediately regained her cool composure. "Now I have to watch every word that comes out of my mouth. Perhaps I should preface all my statements with 'Yes, my lord and master, if it so pleases you…'" She pulled her hands away.

Eric looked at Sandra with frustration. In his heart, he knew he could never reach her. He picked up his books without speaking, walked into the study, and slammed the door.

Finally, Eric received his ordination, and was offered a pulpit in a small synagogue in the city. He threw himself into his work with all his strength. By the time he came home at night, he was exhausted.

His working did not help his marriage as he had hoped. The relationship was steadily deteriorating. Though he begged Sandra to come to the Synagogue on Saturday morning to see him lead the services, she always managed to arrive at the very end. "I just can't seem to get myself out of bed and started on Saturday mornings,"

CHAPTER 9

she would say. He pretended not to notice the whisperings of the congregants about her.

One night, Eric was deeply depressed as he drove home from a particularly long and irritating board meeting at the Synagogue. He mulled over and over in his mind ways in which he could save his marriage. He had done everything possible. It takes two to make a marriage. They simply did not have enough in common. The strain of the marriage was affecting his work. The Board had complained about his lack of patience, and his irritability. He made up his mind that he would speak to Sandra about a divorce.

Again, Eric went over their problems. For six months he had tried to develop a warm relationship with Sandra like the kind he had felt they shared before they were married. They both tried to gain nourishment from the good times they had spent together as they sat for hours discussing their problems. He could not make her understand that her desire to dominate him, to have complete control over him always, prohibited his growth emotionally as a human being who wanted to love her as a partner in life.

"Men's emotional needs are different from women's, Sandra," he argued. "Men need to feel self-sufficient. Men need to feel a sense of dignity, a sense of pride. They need to feel adequate as a man, as a husband, and as a father!"

"Feelings of inadequacy come from inadequacy!" Sandra would argue. "You need to understand what your inadequacy is and admit to it. Then try to overcome it! If you felt adequate within yourself, then you would not feel intimidated by me!"

"But it is your obligation as my wife not to strengthen or add to my inadequacy by your behavior, but to help me overcome it."

"And what about me? Am I supposed to lower myself into an obedient, subservient wife because of your feelings? I have feelings too, you know! I lower myself to no one, not even you, Eric! I do love you, but you seem not to be considerate or interested in MY feelings. You don't want to understand ME!" Driving home in the rain, the many conversations whirled in his mind. He felt that they did have a special kind of caring for each other, but there was that wall between them. His heart cried bitterly. He had always promised himself that they would have a loving marriage, not a kind

THE SECOND GENERATION

of existence that his father and mother shared. He parked the car, turned off the lights and sat for a few minutes. Hot tears burned his eyes. "It's ironic," he said to the raindrops on the window, "I have the same marriage as my parents. Sandra and I may care for each other, but it is a marriage of toleration." Eric looked at his watch. "Well," he gave a big sigh, "it is almost 11:30. She's probably already asleep. Just as well, I'm too tired to talk tonight anyway." Eric wiped his face with his hands, straightened his hat and got out of the car into the rain.

When he put the key into the door to his home, he was surprised to see the door open automatically to him. Sandra was standing in the doorway. "Hello, sweetheart," she greeted him.

Sandra was wearing a light blue wrap-around skirt with large pockets into which she shoved her hands. Her white silk man-tailored shirt, with open buttons exposing part of her lace bra, clung seductively to her body. Her hair was in a ponytail and though she was wearing high-heeled house slippers, she looked like a very young girl.

"Well, are you going to stand out in the rain all night or are you going to come into the nice, warm dry house," she asked him with a light laugh.

Eric stepped back and pretended to look for the house number. "Am I in the right house? Is this the residence of Rabbi Froman?"

Sandra reached out and took his arm. "Oh, Eric, come on in. I want to talk with you. I've been waiting since eight o'clock for you to come home."

To his further amazement, she helped him take off his wet raincoat and hung it up for him.

"Well, this is a pleasant surprise!" he exclaimed. "To what do I owe this pleasant welcome?"

"Come, Eric, she took his hand, "Let's talk over a cup of tea and a piece of cake."

Eric was exhausted and did not feel like talking. He only wanted to go straight to bed; however, he was curious about Sandra's behavior. It was the exact way he had always dreamed of his wife greeting him. Maybe his marriage could be saved after all? The hot cup of tea and piece of cake also sounded tempting.

CHAPTER 9

"I baked the cake myself!" she said with pride. "Just for you!"

On a Bunsen Burner, no doubt!" He immediately added, "I'm sorry. That wasn't called for!"

"No, Eric, I deserved that! Come, sit on the couch. I'll bring in the tea and cake."

"That's the first time she has ever admitted she was wrong about something! Who said miracles still don't happen?!" he thought as he gratefully sat down on the couch, kicking off his shoes.

Sandra immediately came back into the room carrying a tray with a round coffeecake covered with nuts and brown sugar, a teapot and two cups. She put the tray on the table in front of him.

"Well, what do you think?"

"Sandra, it is simply beautiful!"

"I baked it just for you!"

"Sandra, I'm very appreciative of all this. It is truly the one bright spot in an otherwise shitty day for me. But there must be a reason for it all. What is it that you want to talk about?"

Sandra slipped off her shoes, stepped upon the couch an sat down, facing Eric, her legs curled back under her. She sighed, smoothed the wrinkles out of her skirt sighed again and then looked into Eric's eyes. For a second, the picture of his mother's cat jumping upon the couch, tucking her legs under her and then primping herself, flashed before Eric's eyes.

Eric rather enjoyed Sandra's discomfort. He leaned over and poured a cup of tea for himself and sliced a piece of cake for both. Rather than encouraging her to speak, he took a bite out of the cake. "Hm-m-m, not bad for a Bunsen Burner," he said with a laugh.

Sandra reached over and put her hand on Eric's knee. "Eric, I've been thinking. Our marriage hasn't been exactly the greatest in the world."

Eric put down his cup of tea and waited for her next words.

"I was thinking. I haven't exactly been the warmest wife there is. I've been so busy with my work. I guess I....I...uh," she gave another big sigh, "I have forgotten that a man needs more than a woman, he needs a wife, a partner."

Eric was surprised to see this side of Sandra. "What brought all this thinking about?" he asked more tersely than he wanted.

She shifted her position so that she was leaning against him. "I was in the lab today and I looked at all the glass, tubes, jars…all the chemicals; they were just objects, Eric, cold, inanimate objects." She began to loosen his tie and unbutton his shirt. "I felt very lonely, and then I thought of you," her hands began to softly stroke his neck and twist the hairs on his chest. "You're so warm, so gentle, so sweet…you put up with so much from me. 'What are you doing?' I said to myself. 'These things can't give you love. Eric can!' So, I put on my coat, rushed home, baked this cake and waited for you to come home!" Both of her arms slid around his neck and pulled his face down to her lips.

Eric was afraid to speak or move. It was all a dream. He was sure he would wake up if he moved.

Her hands were deliberate as she flung open his shirt, pulling it off with one hand and pulling up his undershirt with the other. She straddled his lap facing him. Leaning forward she rubbed her breast against his naked chest. The silk blouse touching his skin filled him with sensuality, but still he did not move.

"Who's unresponsive now?!" she demanded as she began to unbuckle his belt and unzip his pants. She backed off his lap, knelt on the floor and tugged at the legs of his pants. He lifted his hips slightly to assist her in sliding them off. Then he arose and took her in his arms. He reached behind her and pulled the ties of her skirt, letting it fall to the floor. Slowly he unfastened each garter tab from the stocking, gently rolling down her stockings as he kissed her legs.

He unfastened her bra and freed her breasts as she responded to his touch.

She reached for his shorts.

"No, not yet!" he took her hand and placed it on his inner thighs. "You owe me my wedding night, Sandra. If you truly love me, then give it to me now!"

Sandra stood up and very slowly, not taking her eyes off Eric, reached up and pulled the clasp out of her hair, letting it fall seductively over her shoulders. Very, very slowly she removed her lace panties and stood with her hands behind her, head turned to one side. Eric did not move.

She held out her hands to Eric. "Come, my beloved, come."

CHAPTER 9

Eric still did not move.

She came to him, pulled down his shorts and rubbed her body against his. "Please, Eric, don't punish me. I want you! I want you so badly!" Her lips pressed against his mouth.

Eric could no longer contain himself. He grabbed her in his arms and together they sank to the floor. He began to kiss her whole body as her hand gently stroked the insides of his legs, softly stroking its way to his groin. Her touch sent quivers of excitement up his body. How he had longed for this! Oh God," he moaned as he felt her hands caress him. "This is more than I ever dreamed of."

He pulled her up to him and began to kiss her neck as he rolled over onto her.

"Eric," Sandra barely whispered with a panting voice.

"Yes, my beloved, yes!"

"I have decided that I want a child."

Eric grew cold. He lifted himself and investigated her face. "Do you want me, Sandra, or do you want a child?" His voice was chilled.

Sandra's face turned red. "Of course, I want you, Eric, but I also want a child. I think it will help our marriage."

Eric got up and began getting dressed. "You are not a good liar, Sandra!" There was complete silence.

"You're right. Why do I have to lie to you?" Sandra was up on her feet facing him. "I want to have the experience of having a child. I want an extension of myself."

"Another experiment, Sandra?"

"You might call it that!"

"I am not a baby-making machine. I'm not available only to fulfill your whims and wishes. Have a child for the sake of the child, not to glorify yourself…or to satisfy your own curiosity and, above all, not to experiment with! No! You get someone else to give you a child. Not me!"

That night Eric packed his bags and moved out of the house. He slept the rest of the night in his car, and the next day found a small furnished room four blocks from the synagogue. Two weeks later he received a summons for a divorce hearing. The following month there was a letter from the Synagogue in the mailbox advising him that did not wish to renew the contract of a rabbi who was divorced.

"One who cannot settle his own marital problems, certainly cannot settle others. Signed, The Board."

CHAPTER 10

A WEEK AFTER Christina's funeral, Paul returned to school. He threw his whole being into his studies. Whenever Paul was diligently studying, his father would lessen his insistence on physical development. As he grew older, Paul learned how to trick his father into thinking he was into long-distance running, thereby lessening his father's insistence on physical development. Paul would dress for jogging and run out of the house on a routine basis to the great satisfaction of his father. He would jog to the library, sit and read for a couple of hours, and then return home panting and huffing as if he had run for miles. In warm weather, he would carry a runner's plastic water bottle in his pocket. When he rounded the corner by his home, he would spritz a few drops on his face and neck, wet the clothing under his arms and on his chest and back. Even the neighbors commented about his devotion to running long distances. He grinned in self-congratulations at fooling them all.

Paul matured into a clean-cut, tall, lean young man, but it was obvious that he would never be the athlete his father wanted. His slim fingers, with carefully manicured nails, were more suited for scholarly work than for playing football and wrestling. Paul sensed his father's disappointment with him even though he seemed blessed with his high scholastic achievements.

One night after supper, just after his sixteenth birthday, Curt Steiger said to Paul, "Son, do you like girls?"

Paul felt a twist in the pit of his stomach. "Of course," he replied as nonchalantly as possible.

"What do you like about them" Curt persisted.

"Oh, I like the way they look, the way they smell."

"The way they smell?"

"You know, like perfume. They smell good."

"How about their bodies? Don't you like their bodies?" asked his father.

"Why are you asking me all these questions, Dad?"

"Well, I never see you going out with any girls. Don't you have any girl friends?" "Yes, in school I'm friends with all the girls. We talk a lot."

"Talk?" his father's face registered disgust. "Don't you want something more than talk?" His sarcasm was obvious. He leaned back in his chair and crossed his arms in front of himself. "You know, son, you have to start building a manly reputation. People are going to begin whispering about you. When I was thirteen, I was already experimenting with girls." He put both hands down heavily on the table. "You don't like the company of boys more than girls, do you, son?"

"I like being in the company of both, Dad. But I like being with girls for a different reason than with boys," Paul lied.

"Yeah? What's that?"

Paul knew he would have to think quickly, make something up. He hated his father for putting him through this questioning and he wanted to shout, "Get off my back and leave me alone!" But he was too scared to defy him.

"Well, I have been meaning to talk with you about girls, Dad."

Pleased and flattered that his son wanted to talk about private female relationships with him, Curt rose from his chair and strode over to Paul, slapping him on the back. "Sure, let's talk, man to man!"

Paul wanted to make sure the conversation pleased his father. He chose his words carefully.

"Well, you see, Dad, there's this girl in school. About so high." He motioned with his hand to about five feet. "A slight bit plump. Well, she's been giving me the uh, uh, you know, 'come on looks. Well, the boys talk about her. It seems like she has sort of a reputation."

"So, That's the best kind of girl to start with."

"Well, I feel it would be just using her. I don't think that's fair."

"You wouldn't be using her, Paul. Apparently, she likes being with the fellows; otherwise, she wouldn't have that kind of reputation. You'd probably be doing her a favor."

"You really think that, Dad?" Paul felt disgust for his father.

CHAPTER 10

"Sure, what's her name?"

"Nancy."

"Is she pretty?"

"I think so. She's blond, with light blue eyes."

"Hounds have to run after foxes, son. That's the way God created them. Go get 'em, Paul" Again, Curt slapped his son on the back with great satisfaction.

Before the conversation with his father, Paul had never even noticed Nancy. All he ever said to her was a casual "Hi" in the hallways of the school. She wore heavy make-up and short dresses which were usually too tight. Her habit of punctuating every other sentence with "fuck" and "suck" was repugnant to him.

Curt arose. "Bring her home, Paul. I'd like to meet her. How about Friday night? I have to go to the Book Fair so I'll be leaving the house about eight o'clock."

"I don't know if she can come on such short notice."

"You won't know until you ask her. Today's only Monday."

"Okay, I'll ask her tomorrow in school. I have to study now." Paul arose and started for his room. Well, he had gotten himself into a mess now. He had to follow through with some sort of action, he thought as he closed the door to his room. He threw himself on the bed and pulled the pillow over his head. "Boy, oh boy! What am I going to do now?" He rolled over on his back and looked up at the ceiling. "Suppose I bring her home and she expects me to make love to her? Everybody says she's experienced, and I've never been with a girl. What if she laughs at me? I don't want to look like a fool! I've never even kissed a girl square on the lips. What if she expects French kissing?" The idea of putting his tongue in Nancy's mouth was repulsive to him.

He reached into his pants, held on to himself, closed his eyes and began to make pans as to what he would do. First, he would gently rub his hands down her back, ending with both hands on her buttocks. Tightly holding both cheeks in his hands, he would sling her down on the bed and let her have it. She would pant and scream with ecstasy, just like in the movie he had seen at his friend, Ted's, house. "You are the best man in the whole world, she would moan, as he left her in a whimpering heap upon the bed. His fantasy exploded with a knock on his door.

"Paul, can I come in?" he heard his father's voice.

Paul jumped quickly under the covers, even though he had his clothes on. "Yes, Dad, of course, come in."

Curt came into the room and threw a small package on the bed. "Don't want you catching anything, son. And you're too young to be a father. Have a good time." Curt turned and walked out of the room as quickly as he had come in.

Paul picked up the package and examined its contents. A feeling of nausea and excitement sept swept over him. He put the package under his pillow, got undressed, crawled into bed and tried to go to sleep. He was gently dozing when the thought occurred to him that he might forget the package under his pillow and the housekeeper would find it. He took the package and put it in his underwear drawer only to again rise in a few minutes and put it in his pants pocket.

The next day in school, Paul studied Nancy's face and body. "Of all the girls, why did I have to pick Nancy?" he said to himself. "Maybe I can switch to someone else," he mused as he examined every girl in class, but his eyes kept coming back to Nancy. For the first time since he was in school, the teacher's voice, rising and falling as she instructed the class, began to get on his nerves. He kept glancing at his watch, hoping each time that the slow hands would have miraculously shot ahead. When the bell finally sounded, Paul became even more uneasy. He felt his heart speed up its beat and sweat running down his sides from under his arms. He maneuvered himself between his classmates to walk behind Nancy in the hall. He gently touched her on the shoulder from behind, "Nancy?"

To his surprise, Nancy turned around with a big smile. "Hi, Paul, are you following me?"

"No..uh..yes. I'd like to talk with you for a few minutes, okay?"

"Sure, what's up?" She broke into laughter. "Sorry, Paul, I didn't mean that the way it sounded." Nancy slid herself into a little cove between the lockers and corner in the hallway, which left Paul appearing as if he had her cornered.

CHAPTER 10

"Way to go, Paul!" One of the fellows slapped him on the back as he went past them.

Paul felt himself turning red. He wanted very much to have appeared relaxed and casual.

"Well, Paul, we don't have too much time. The bell is going to ring soon. What's doing?"

Paul became fascinated with Nancy's bright red lips, painted to give her a pouting look. His eyes fell downward to her blouse. Three buttons were unbuttoned, allowing a plain view of her cleavage. There was a little mole on her left breast. He wondered what the whole breast would look like. He had a tremendous urge just to snuggle into that cleavage.

Nancy had noticed his eyes. "If you've been listening to gossip, Paul, then we have nothing to talk about," she said indignantly, and started to push him away so she could get out of her little alcove.

"No, Nancy, honest. I have something very important I would like to talk about with you. I haven't heard any gossip. I don't even know what you are talking about."

Nancy hesitated for a moment. She started to speak when the bell sounded. "Meet me in the cafeteria lunchtime, in the far left-hand corner as you walk in. We'll have more time to talk then." With a swish of her round backside, Nancy turned and disappeared around the corner.

Paul felt a tired relief come over his body, only to be replaced almost instantly with the tense anticipation of lunchtime.

After what seemed hours, Paul rounded the corner of the lunchroom to find Nancy already there waiting for him. This time the blouse was closed except for on button on the throat.

"All right, Paul, let's don't play game. What is this great important thing you have to tell me?"

"Well, it's to ask kind of a favor from you."

"Oh yeah, like what?" her voice was filled with sarcasm.

Paul gave a big sigh. "This is going to sound strange."

"Nothing I haven't heard, no doubt. Come on, spit it out already!"

"I would like you to meet my father."

"What!!??"

"Would you please let me bring you to my house to meet my father?"

"Meet your father? Wait a minute. Why do you want me to meet your father? What do you think I am?"

Paul realized that his request did sound unusual. He quickly interjected. "I want to have a date with you, but first I would like to take you to my house to meet my father."

"What the fuck! You mean your father has to approve your dates?"

"No, it's not that!" Paul had to think quickly. The request did sound strange, even to him. "I think you are a very pretty person, Nancy. You see, my mother died so when my Dad sees me go out with pretty girls, it reminds him of when he once dated Mom and makes him feel good."

"Sounds sort of kooky but logical."

Paul knew that Nancy though his mother died recently by the way he was talking. He saw a pleased look replace the skeptical one on her face. Confidence spurred him to continue. "My mom didn't wear much make-up and she wore her dresses a little longer and not quite so tight. Do you think you could dress that way too, Nancy? It would really make us very happy."

"Sure," Nancy replied, "It sucks, but I know what you mean."

"Oh yeah, one more thing?"

Nancy gave a big sigh. "What else?" He had begun to irritate her with his continuing list of requirements.

"These are a lot of demands, but what the fuck! It's something different. Okay, only sweet little words will flow from my mouth. When do you want this big event to take place?"

"Would Friday night be okay?"

"Sure."

"Thanks a million, Nancy. I'll pick you up at seven O'clock Friday night, okay?"

"Okay! Okay! Here's my address." She handed Paul one of the little address labels that come in the mail from the VFW. "Stick it to a book, so you don't lose it." She laughed.

When Paul picked up Nancy on Friday night, he was amazed to see the change in her. Her hair was neatly combed, and she wore very light makeup. He was a little disappointed to see that her lips

CHAPTER 10

were not the usual bright red but a soft pink. Her dress was long-sleeved with a high neck. "I can be a fucking 'lady' if I want to," she said when she saw the surprised look on his face.

It was apparent that Nancy was enjoying playing the role of the "real lady type." She put out her hand for Paul to help her down the stairs as she took delicate little steps.

When they arrived at Paul's house, his father was waiting by the door with his coat and hat on. "Hi, Paul, sorry I have to go but I got a very important call." His eyes swept over Nancy from head to toe.

"Dad, this is my date for tonight, Nancy. Nancy, this is my dad."

"You're a lovely girl, Nancy." There was a slight surprise in his voice. "Hey, I don't know what you two have planned for tonight, but you're welcome to spend the evening here if you want to. There is a nice fire going in the fireplace, plenty of food in the refrigerator and a damn good movie on TV. I'd loved to be here, too, but I must go. Don't wait up for me. I won't be home until after one a.m. With that, Curt Steiger left the house with a wink at Paul, firmly closing the door behind him.

A rush of hate swept over Paul ending in a blush Paul felt encompasses his whole body. Both Paul and Nancy noticed that all the lights had been turned off in the living room except one soft light in the corner.

"Hey, what the fuck is this?" Nancy suspiciously blurted out. Is this a set=up? Your father doesn't seem like a man mourning his dead wife? What was that wink he gave you?"

"Oh, come on, Nancy. Dad has had a lot on his mind lately. You want to sit down?" Paul motioned to a chair as he began turning on the lights. "We can go out if you want to. It's okay with me."

All his feelings of anticipation and excitement had dissipated, replaced by the anger he felt for his father. He even felt an anger towards Nancy because of her suspicions. At first, he had planned on introducing Nancy to his father, then taking her to a movie and then home. He would tell his father it had been a "successful" evening. This would get his father off his back and keep peace between them.

However, in making plans and speaking with Nancy, he had begun to enjoy a special kind of excitement. When he saw her, so nicely dressed, his anticipation had heightened. He had fingered the little package in his pocket until the print had worn off. In his mind he had created a scenario of their bodies together, his head resting on her soft, white breast."

"The fireplace is nice," he heard Nancy speaking as his mind struggle reluctantly to return to reality. "Let's stay here a while and talk, but no fucking funny stuff, okay?"

"Don't worry," he mumbled, his anger again rising towards her for interrupting his fantasy, as well as for her crude language.

"Listen, Nancy," he blurted out, "I don't want you to use that kind of language with me. It turns me off!"

To his surprise, Nancy turned red. "What are you, some kind of prude?" she retorted. "All the other guys like it. It turns them on. It's a sign of...." She hesitated, "freedom of spirit!"

"To me, it's a sign that someone doesn't have intelligence and must rely on four letter words for expression." Paul knew it was a stinging retort and he rather enjoyed the pained look that swept across Nancy's face. Not wanting to hear her reply, Paul said, "I'll get us something to eat," he said and went into the kitchen.

As he was making some chicken sandwiches, he became aware of Nancy quietly coming into the kitchen. He pretended he did not know she was there. He knew she was standing behind him waiting for him to acknowledge her presence, so he deliberately slowed down his pace in making the sandwiches.

"Paul?" she said in a low small voice.

"What?" he answered without turning around.

"I'm sorry, but you don't understand."

"What's there to understand?"

"When you asked me out, I thought it was why all the boys ask me out. But you seem different."

"I don't know what you are talking about." Paul lied, happy that Nancy was behind him and could not see his face.

"Yes, you do! You know exactly what I am talking about!"

"Why do you think the boys ask you out with only one reason in mind, Nancy? You ask for it."

Paul enjoyed hurting her because she was making him feel guilty.

CHAPTER 10

"How do I ask for it?" "The way you dress, the way you talk!" Paul turned around and looked at her. His anger turned to pity when he saw the tears glistening in her eyes.

"I want everybody to like me. I want to be popular with the guys."

"That's a hell of a way to be popular!"

Tears rolled down her face. "Every time a boy asks me out, I swear to myself that I'm not giving in. But I don't know what to do, how to stop them when they get started."

"What's the matter with a simple 'no'?"

But they seem to want me so much. It feels so good to be wanted. At that moment I feel I'm important. The guy's whole attention is turned to me. He wants me. I'm somebody!"

"Why can't you be liked for what you are, Nancy?"

"What am I, Paul?" Nancy suddenly burst out in loud sobs. Her mascara made little paths of black down her cheeks.

"You're a fine, intelligent, pretty young lady." Paul patronizingly replied.

"Bullshit!" screamed Nancy, catching Paul by surprise. Not receiving an immediately reply, Nancy began to apologize. "I'm sorry. I am so sorry. You just make me feel so damn inferior. Why did you ask me out? You, Paul Steiger, an 'A' student, always perfectly dressed and proper. Why would you want to be associated with me? Certainly not because I'm a 'fine and intelligent.'" She was mimicking him, "pretty young lady. Why? Paul, why? Admit it, you wanted to get fucked, didn't you?"

"I wanted to get my father off of my back!" Paul shouted back, startled at his own confession.

"What?" Stunned, Nancy's tears stopped abruptly.

"My father thinks I should be a macho man, and part of being macho in his eyes is having women. I thought once he saw you, he'd be satisfied."

"So, I look like a whore!"

"Damn it!" The feeling of hatred for his father and for Nancy overwhelmed him. Paul brought his fist down hard on a tomato, squashing it to smithereens.

"Squashed tomato sandwiches! Wow, what a delicacy!" Nancy stated, but her lips curved upward in a smile.

Paul looked at the tomato, seeing seeds and juice splattered all over the cutting board. picked up two slices of white bread, sopped up the crushed tomato and gently placed the sandwich on a dish with an olive on top. With a slight bow, he handed the dish to Nancy, "Special for the lady," he said with a bow. Both broke into laughter, with a feeling of relief that the crisis had ended.

"Let's talk truthfully with each other, Paul." Nancy began.

"Sometimes truth hurts." Paul replied.

"Good, then we'll know it's the real truth," Nancy answered.

"No use letting this good food go to waste. Sit down, Nancy." Paul motioned to the chair by the kitchen table.

"Why did you ask me to dress differently to meet your father, Paul?"

"I didn't want him to think that I was going out with a common whore."

"Is that what I look like? Really?"

Paul hesitated.

"Remember, pure truth, Paul."

"That is the impression you give. It does not mean that you are one." Paul quickly answered.

"But I get attention when I dress like that. No one would ever notice me otherwise."

"That's a bad way to get attention, Nancy. Think, what do you get the attention for? You just told me that's why so many boys want to take you out."

"But you asked me out. You could have asked out any other girl just to meet your father. Why me?"

Paul took the little package out of his pocket and put it on the table. "Maybe in the back of my mind, I had hopes, Nancy."

Don't you still want to, Paul? She asked, disappointment spreading over her face.

"No."

"Why? Don't you find me attractive?"

"Yes, I find you attractive. But I don't want to be like all the other fellows."

"Wow, I don't know whether to be insulted or flattered by that statement!"

CHAPTER 10

"Let's just be friends, Nancy." Paul put the little package back into his pocket. "Tell me about yourself." Paul felt good about himself.

When Paul dropped Nancy off at her home at eleven-thirty, he gave her a light kiss on the cheek. "Thanks for a wonderful evening, Nancy." Nancy grabbed Paul and gave him a big hug. "I think you have changed my life, Paul." She whispered in his ear. "Thank you."

Paul did not realize the full impact he had on Nancy until he saw her in school on Monday. To everyone's amazement, the heavy make-up was gone. Her hair was neatly pulled back with a ribbon. Her simple blouse was buttoned almost to the neck and her skirt was full, down to the knees.

Paul happily noticed how many of the students told her how nice she looked. After class she beamed at Paul, "Thanks" was all she said. Paul could not understand how he could have brought about such a change in so short a time to one human being, but he did experience a sense of power almost leading to exhilaration. He had help shape another person's life!

Chapter 11

A couple of weeks later, Nancy met Paul in the hallway of school, waving a piece of paper with great enthusiasm. Her eyes were excited, and she giggled as she handed him a xeroxed sheet.

"Look what I got!" She pushed her hands into the pockets of her brown corduroy skirt, and with a little twist of her body, stood back to watch his reaction as he read the paper.

It was an invitation. In the center of the sheet was a picture of a toy gun with a little flag coming out of its barrel on which was imprinted 'Bang." The wording read: "You'll get a 'great bang' out of a party at my house this coming Saturday night." Then her name was hand-written in, "so, Nancy, be sure to be there for the big surprise. Time: 8:00 p.m."

"It's an invitation to a party at Shawn Garrett's house this Saturday night." She bubbled out when she did not get an immediate response from Paul. "Did you get an invitation too?"

Shawn Gazrrett was one of the richest boys in school. He was also one of the handsomest, most popular and most arrogant students in the school. His father was in the importing business, which necessitated his taking frequent trips to all parts of the world.

THE SECOND GENERATION

Sometimes, Shawn's mother would go with his father, and when she did, Shawn would give a party at his house. Although Paul was friendly with Shawn, he never liked him. Shawn was too sure of himself, too macho, too ostentatious with his money. Most of all, Paul did not like the way he treated the kids who followed him.

Shawn, in turn, felt uncomfortable around Paul, so Paul was never formally invited to his parties. "I really don't think you would like this kind of party, Paul. I don't think it's your kind of fun, but if you want to come, you are more than welcome." Shawn would say to him if any mention of a party was brought up when they were together with others. Paul never accepted the half-hearted invitations. He had heard that the parties involved drinking, drugs and many bedrooms used for activities rather than sleeping.

Shawn was an only child whose parents considered mature beyond his years, giving him anything his heart desired. As a result, since he had money, he also had a sports car, and many parties and social events revolved around him. He was the hub of "the gang.,"

There was mutual respect between Paul and "the gang," however, Paul was not a part of it. Paul knew it was because he refused to "kowtow" to Shawn. "But you are left out of so many things," others would say to him, "Don't you feel bad?"

"I refuse to be subservient to anyone. If that is what it takes to belong, then I just won't belong!" Paul would answer them. He rather enjoyed the feeling of self-pity and loneliness he experienced when he was left out of big "goings-on." He felt his suffering was a cleansing of the soul.

"It says that I can bring a friend. Will you go with me, Paul?" Nancy asked.

"What?"

"Come on, Paul, come to the party with me."

"Well, I don't know," Paul answered. The old nagging feeling that he really wasn't wanted caused him to back away.

"Nancy, I didn't receive an invitation, nor has Shawn said anything to me. I am really not the kind of person for these big parties."

"Aw, come on, Paul. It says I can bring a friend. You're my friend, aren't you? Besides, I did you a favor and met your father. You owe me one!" She looked as if she was going to cry.

CHAPTER 10

"Sure, we're friends, Nancy, but...." Paul was thinking of something else. He knew Nancy had the reputation at school for being "easy" and if he were to be her escort, everyone might think that he was with her for only one reason. He had met with her a few times since that first night at his house, but no one had seen them together. He always took her where he was sure he would not be seen. Guilt overwhelmed him. He wondered if it was because he was ashamed of being seen with her, or because everyone might believe that he was making out with her.

"Paul, I'll level with you." Nancy lowered her voice and slightly dropped her head. "A lot of guys there I've been out with and well, you know, I want to change. I don't want to be like that anymore. I'd...I'd feel more comfortable if you were with me. Everyone likes you, Paul. Everyone respects you. Please, Paul, please?" She looked up at him. Her eyes were pale blue sapphires slowly being filled with tears.

Paul felt pleased that Nancy wanted him to act as her protector and he was curious about what went on at Shawn's famous parties. Here was a perfect excuse to go, as an invited friend of a guest. To hell with what anyone thought! Hus actions with Nancy would be proof enough that she was only a friend. Besides, everyone was talking about how she had changed lately, and he felt pride in having helped. She watched her words when she spoke, and he noticed that her actions and dress were deliberately lady-like. She wouldn't embarrass him. It would be interesting to see how she acted in a party atmosphere.

"Okay, Nancy, I'll go. I'll pick you up at 7:30 Saturday night." Nancy threw her arms around him and gave him a big hug. "Thanks, friend, thanks a million!" She caught Paul by surprise and before he could react in any way, she was gone. He stood in the hallway feeling proud and foolish at the same time.

On Saturday night when Paul arrived at Nancy's house, a full moon hung on the horizon, casting an eerie red-orange light. Paul couldn't throw off a nagging sensation that something was amiss. He straightened his tie nervously as he rang the doorbell. The door flung open immediately and there standing in the darkness of the hallway was Nancy in a light blue wool dress, teasingly form-fitting down to her thighs where it fanned out into a full skirt that fell to midcalf. The moon cast a spotlight on the thick ruffle around the neck and down the bodice, framing her face and pointing like an arrow to her attractive body. Soft blonde hair curled gently to her shoulders. Light blue strapped shoes accented her slim ankles and elegant, well-shaped legs.

Paul was overwhelmed. "Wow, Nancy, you look great!"

"Thanks, Paul." Nancy seemed to float forward as she gave him a brushing kiss on the cheek. Her soft scent of perfume was extremely pleasant, and the slight touch of her body against his excited him tremendously, but he did not in any way touch her or return the kiss. She laughed and ran to the car in a happy, excited and playful mood. She waited by the door for him to open it. As she slid into the seat, she let her dress come up to show off her leg, pretending that she was not aware of what she was doing. Paul, in turn, pretended not to see her thigh as he shut the door. As Paul put the key in the switch, he felt a soft touch on his hand.

"Paul let's not go yet. Let's talk a few seconds. Okay? Please?"

"Okay." Paul leaned back in his seat. The uneasiness he had felt earlier returned.

"Paul?"

"Nancy, we're going to be late. If you have something to say, please say it!"

"Well, excuse me! You don't have to bite my head off!"

"Look, Nancy, I'm sorry. I just don't like to play games." He hesitated, then turned to her, "Come on, speak up, girl. Tell papa what's bothering you!" He tried to assume control of the situation in a joking manner to break some of the tension. "Well?" Nancy was silent. He gently took her hand. "Nancy, we're friends, right?"

She nodded her head affirmative.

"Then talk to me. Don't be afraid."

"Promise you won't get mad?"

"Dogs get mad, people get angry! I promise you I won't be angry. Come on, what is it?" He gently moved a few strands of hair which had fallen over her face. Nancy kissed his hand and instinctively, he quickly pulled It back.

"Do you find me attractive, Paul?"

CHAPTER 10

Paul gave a deep sigh. "Yes, I do, Nancy."

"Then why haven't you ever tried to kiss me? When I kiss you, you don't return the kiss? You even pull away from me, like just now!"

Paul felt boxed in. He wanted to open the door and run away; however, he felt a responsibility towards Nancy. He would have to be careful with his words or he would lose all he had accomplished with her. Paul sighed deeply. "Nancy, I see more in you than just a beautiful body. I don't want to insult you by focusing only on MY desires."

" Oh, so you do have desires!?" Playfully and seductively she began to caress his face. "So-o-o, what's the matter with little old Nancy? Isn't she 'tractive to you?" She asked in baby talk, pink lips puckered out.

Again, Paul pulled back. "Nancy, please. We're right here in front of your house. Aren't you afraid your mother or the neighbors will see us?"

"Who's going to see us? It's dark here where we are parked. Why did you park under this tree? Did you have something in mind? Huh-h-h?"

"Nancy, please." Paul felt perspiration under his collar. "I told you I don't want to be like the other fellows you went out with. We're friends, Nancy, and there's more to a real friendship than just….just that! You don't have to use your body to have someone like you!"

"But you didn't want to take me to this party! I want to show you how grateful I am!"

"A mere 'thank you' will do. I told you, I like you as a person, and I'm proud to be your escort tonight!"

Nancy leaned back against the door, half facing Paul. "You're the only guy I've been out with who never tried to find out where my legs start or what's between them!!"

"Nancy, I don't like you talking like that. It sounds so…. so common!"

"I'm not a whore, Paul!" She suddenly flared angrily.

"I know that." Paul answered. "So, why do you act like one sometimes! ~ He immediately felt remorse when he saw tears inundate her eyes and slide down her cheeks.

"I'm not a virgin either, Paul," she softly muttered.

"Nancy, I am your friend. I see you as a good, decent human being. You can be whatever you want; you know that!"

In a slow, halting voice she spoke as if she had not heard him.

"My father broke me in at nine years old."

Paul was shocked, "Your father!?"

Nancy stared out of the front window, speaking to some unknown entity. "As far back as I can remember, he used to stroke my body, gently touching me all over and kissing me. He said that what he was doing would help me to grow more beautiful than any other woman. 'You want to be beautiful, like a model. You want to be so beautiful that everyone will look at you, don't you?' he would say to me."

"Yes, Daddy, I want to be very beautiful."

Paul had the feeling that she was speaking to her father, not to him. Her eyes were looking far beyond the car.

"You are my favorite little girl and I will help you to be very, very beautiful"

"I was nine years and seven months old. Mother went to the hospital to give birth to my baby brother. That night Daddy took me to bed with him."

"I want you to know, Nancy, my sweet, beautiful, little girl," he said to me as he held me in his arms, "that your baby brother is not in any way going to take your place. I still love you more than anyone else, even Mommy. But don't tell Mommy; we don't want her to be jealous, do we now?"

"No, Daddy."

Paul started to speak, "Nancy?"

"I knew it was wrong, but it was nice, in a way, to be in his arms, his warm hairy body next to mine." She was nine years old again as she spoke.

"Daddy, what are you doing?"

"Do you love me, Nancy?"

"Yes, Daddy, I love you."

"I love you, too, Nancy, and this the way two people show that they love each other. See how gently I'm touching you? That's a sign that I love you very, very much!"

CHAPTER 10

"Did you tell your mother?" Asked Paul.

"No, my father said she was too nervous because of the new baby and she would probably send me away if I did, and we would never see each other again."

"Oh, Nancy, Nancy," Paul instinctively took her into his arms and rocked back and forth with her.

Suddenly, reality enveloped him.

The enchantment was broken. Anger and embarrassment swept over Paul as his body covered with a cold sweat. He gently pushed Nancy back to her seat with shaking hands.

"What happened? What's wrong?" Her tone rose shrilly. "What did I do wrong?"

"Nothing! We're late for the party!"

"But our party was better." Nancy cooed. Paul tried to control his anger at himself and at Nancy.

"What's the matter with you, Paul? Have you got some kind of hang-up?"

"Let's change the subject, Nancy. I don't want to talk about it!"

"I think you're queer!" Nancy sat back with folded arms in front of her, looking straight ahead.

At that moment Paul didn't damn well care what she thought or who she was. They rode in strained silence while Paul tried to figure out his emotions. Why couldn't he have grabbed her, thrown her on the seat of the car and gotten it over with? God knows she was willing enough! His father was right. He was a weakling. He was feeling sorry and angry at himself, when he became aware of Nancy huddled against the door of the car, softly crying like a small child. His anger turned to compassion. He had rejected her. She couldn't take rejection when she wanted so desperately to be wanted, to be loved.

"Nancy?"

"I sometimes think that Daddy was truly the only one who really loved me."

"Where is your father now?"

"He's dead."

"Dead?"

"Killed in Korea."

"How old were you when you found out he had been killed?"

"Fourteen."

"Where is your mother?"

"In the house with my brother."

"Do you get along?"

"We tolerate each other. She never did care that much about me. I think Daddy was right; she was jealous because Daddy loved me and gave me so much attention."

"Boy, this is one sick, mixed-up kid," Paul thought to himself. "What have I gotten myself into?" The thought of counseling or helping Nancy became overwhelmingly too difficult. He didn't know what to do, what to say. He wished with all his heart and soul that he did know. On instinct, he began to talk to her.

"Listen, Nancy you are a very desirable person. People will love you for what you are, for the kind of person you are, if you will just give them a chance. You don't have to buy love with your body. I keep telling you that again and again that your body is worth more than just a bit of pleasure for men to enjoy."

"But, Paul, I really want you. I'm aching for your right now. I'm not a whore, Paul, honest. Just make love to me. I won't go with anyone else, promise." She raised her right hand as if to emphasize her vow. "I need you. Please don't throw me off like everybody else."

Paul realized she had not heard a word he had said. He regretted he had agreed to take her to the party, but it was too late now to back out. Shawn's house was in front of them.

"I'll tell you what, Nancy, after the party, we'll talk and well, whatever happens, will happen, okay?" He said to her as he parked the car. He reached over to her, took her face in both of his hands, and softly kissed each eye, the tip of her nose and lightly touched her lips.

"Really, Paul?" Her eyes searched his face.

"Really, Nancy." Paul gave her an affirmative shake of the head. Nancy burst out in little giggles, "Let's leave the party early, okay?"

"Okay! You've got a date!" He said to Nancy but to himself, he thought, "I'll cross that bridge when I come to it."

Paul had thought that the big house in which he lived was elegant but now when he walked over the threshold into the old mansion, he felt he had walked into a scene out of the movies. The

CHAPTER 10

parquet hardwood floors were accented with rich colored Chinese rugs. White furniture was set off by colorful pillows flower displays and a huge fireplace framed with beveled mirrors. Exotic oil painting decorated the walls. Nancy drew in her breath with stunned admiration.

Along the far wall, Shawn had arranged a serving table loaded with fruits, cheeses, several chafing dishes and all kinds of pastries and cakes. Opposite the food, a bar had been set up. Liquors and wines of all kinds were lined up behind the bar on a glass table.

Shawn appeared with a drink in each hand. "Hey, Paul, what a surprise!"

"Nancy's invitation said to bring a guest and I was the lucky fellow she chose." He spoke hastily.

"Hope you don't mind."

"Not at all, Paul," Shawn replied, as he downed the drink in his right hand. He looked at the drink in his left hand. "Oh, what the hell!" he said as he downed it too. "It's about time we added to your education – not that you haven't already started. Your zipper is open!" Shawn gave Nancy a nudge with his elbow and a wink.

"Damn!" Paul thought to himself as he impulsively looked down, only to find the zipper closed. Everyone around them began to laugh as Paul felt his face burn crimson.

"How about a reefer, Paul," one of the fellows called. "Keeps the face from turning colors." Again, Paul heard laughter.

"No thanks," Paul answered. "Not yet at least." He hated himself for having come to this stupid party. "I'll take a drink though," he quickly added, hoping to direct the attention somewhere else.

"Sure, Paul, come on over to the bar," Shawn invited him. "What'll it be?" The tension dissolved.

Paul did not drink hard liquor, but he could handle beer. His family always had beer in the house. "How about a beer?"

"Sure thing, one beer coming up!" Paul was handed a chilled mug of beer.

"How about you, Nancy, what'll you have?"

"I'll just take a coke for now, okay?"

"A coke? Come on, you can do better than that!"

THE SECOND GENERATION

Paul quickly intervened. "She'll have a drink later. How about just giving her a coke for now?"

"Sure, one coke coming up for the lady!" with a dignified bow, Shawn handed Nancy the glass.

"Thanks." Nancy took the drink with a little curtsy. "See why I needed you, Paul?" She whispered. She turned to Shawn. "Gee, Shawn, this place is really something! Mind if we look around?"

"Not at all, help yourselves!" Shawn extended his arm in a gracious invitation and then walked away.

"Look at the paintings, Paul. It's like being in a museum!"

A few minutes later, Shawn was again at their side; his eyes continually sweeping up and down Nancy. "Well, how are you doing?"

Paul answered. "Shawn, to be perfectly honest with you, we were admiring your artwork. Your home is magnificent. You have some unusual masterpieces, especially that Chinese sculpture." Paul pointed to a dark wood pagoda decorated with flowers on a stand in the corner.

"Well, well, a connoisseur of the arts! But you have the real masterpiece, Paul." Shawn answered with his eyes again taking in Nancy's body.

"Oh, cut it out, Shawn." Nancy teased with a pleased laugh.

Paul felt annoyed with Nancy's obvious pleasure.

"Do you have any more artwork? I would love to see it." Paul changed the subject.

"Yeah, it's all over the house. You're welcome to wander around and look for yourself. I guess I don't appreciate it as much as you because I see it all the time. But talk about appreciation of REAL artwork, that you will see through the hallway.," he pointed to the left, "in the room on the right towards the end. Go look and tell me what you think of MY kind of artwork!" H gave them both a playful push

Paul and Nancy smiled at each other. "Let's go see," said Nancy. When they turned right, they entered a room made of glass. A huge swimming pool filled the center of the room, surrounded by a flagstone patio laden with plants and flowers. Lit from underneath, the pool was occupied by several fellows and girls swimming in the nude. Shawn appeared behind them. "Now THAT is true

CHAPTER 10

art!" Shawn declared as he pointed to the nude girls. "Life-like in every aspect – looks like they just came off of the canvas, doesn't it?" Shawn laughed. "Want to join them?"

"No thanks," replied Paul, trying not to show his embarrassment. "Tell you the truth, Shawn, I have been wondering how this lady in blue dances. Do you have music?" "By all means," replied Shawn. "In the Blue Room. Turn right as you come out of the doorway."

"Thanks, see you later, Shaw." Paul quickly maneuvered Nancy out of the pool room into the ballroom.

For the next couple of hours, Paul enjoyed himself in Nancy's company. She was sparkling and witty. They ate, danced and talked with each other and others in a warm, friendly atmosphere, disregarding the many activities going on in different rooms of the house.

Around eleven o'clock, Nancy whispered to Paul, "Shall we go?"

"Yeah, I guess so," he answered. With the help of the four beers he had drunk, he felt he could handle any situation.

"Then, come on," she started toward the door.

"Wait, we have to thank Shawn and tell him we're leaving."

"Why?"

"Because it is the proper thing to do, Nancy. You just don't come to a party and walk away without thanking your host!"

"Gee, sometimes you are so old-fashioned! We can thank him Monday in school."

"No, it's not polite. It'll only take a minute. Come on."

They found Shawn in the living room at the bar telling jokes to his buddies. All of them had been drinking heavily.

Paul walked up to Shawn and held out his hand. "We want to thank you for a fun party, Shawn."

"You're leaving already?" Shawn blinked his eyes a couple of times as he looked at his watch. "It's only 11:05."

"Well, I had a rough day and I'm getting pretty tired. I had a real good time though."

"Aw, come on, we have a special activity planned for tonight. You don't want to miss it, do you?"

"Thanks, but I think I've had enough for one night."

"How about leaving, Nancy? We'll take you home Nance! Stay with us a little while longer. You are good scenery to have around!"

"I agreed to take her to this party, and I feel it's my responsibility to take her home." Paul turned to Nancy. "Unless you really want to stay. It's up to you."

"What would you like me to do, Paul?" Nancy asked him with a little smile.

"I want you to do what you want, but I would like to take you home."

"Thanks for the offer, but I want to go with Paul." Nancy said without hesitation. She gave a grateful look to Paul.

"Okay, okay, but how about one last drink for both of you before you go? Come on, one for the road!"

"Well, I've had quite a few already. I don't think I should have any more and drive."

"Aw, come on, just a little one. Hey everybody." Shawn shouted, "Paul and Nancy are getting ready to leave. Let's all have a drink with them before they go!"

The response was overwhelming. "Sure, fill 'em up!"

"No beer this time, Paul, this is a toast!" Shawn warned Paul.

"All right, surprise me, but make it light!"

"How about you, Nancy, what'll you have?" Shawn asked her.

"I'll have a Whisky Sour, if you don't mind." Nancy answered with great dignity.

"Oh-h-h, we have a real lady here tonight. One 'surprise' and one whisky sour coming up!" Neither Nancy or Paul saw the exchange of winks between the host and the fellows getting the drinks.

Fifteen minutes later, both Nancy and Paul were reeling between reality and a misty world of dreams, a world where there was no sharp distinction between objects, people or events. A huge, white bearskin appeared from somewhere and was place in the middle of the room on the floor. Shawn started to climb up onto the coffee-table, but misjudged his step and fell, to everyone's delight. He unsteadily picked himself up and stood upon the table to make an announcement.

"Ladies and gentlemen," he began. "I have a special announcement. Please gather 'round. In fact, I have two special announcements, one for a special lady in this room here tonight and one for you guys. Which announcement do you want first?"

CHAPTER 10

"The one for the lady!" They all shouted, pushing and shoving each other with giggles of delight.

"All righty. The lady first. I am very pleased to announce that tonight we're choosing a 'party playmate' – queen of the evening. By unanimous vote, she has been chosen. I am pleased to present to you, ladies and gentlemen, excuse me, I am pleased to present to you, gentlemen, our party playmate –

Miss Nancy Welham!"

Nancy, honored at being chosen for anything over all the rest of the girls, stood up and made a lop-sided courtesy while all the fellows cheered. Her face was flushed with excitement. As she tried to return to Paul, two fellows lifted her by the arms.

"A queen must have a throne," someone shouted, as they half led, half-carried her to the bearskin rug in the middle of the floor.

"I don't want to lie down on the rug." Paul heard Nancy wail.

"But you're a playmate and what are playmates for but to play with, right?" Two fellows began unbuttoning her dress.

"Please, what are you doing? Leave me alone!"

Paul jumped up. "Leave her alone! Enough is enough! She doesn't want to be your playmate. Get someone else!"

"Ole Nancy has always been our playmate. Don't get do excited. You'll get your chance!"

Paul tried to push his way to Nancy. He wanted with all his might to take her into his arms and protect her – to shield her from them.

"Leave her alone. Let me take her home!" he shouted.

"Sir Guahan is charging to rescue the fair damsel in distress! Ho! Ho! Ho! What do we do with knights in shining armor, friends?" Shawn demanded.

"We put them in the dungeon!" Someone shouted. Two chairs were placed front-to-front and Paul was tied to them. "Now back to the damsel, friends. Let us remove her distress."

Nancy cried, "No, please don't do this. Somebody please help me! Paul! Paul! Paul, where are you?!"

Rapidly the party became a sexual orgy, as clothes were strewn all over the room.

Paul head Nancy cry out, "please daddy, you're hurting me!"

The squirrel's head blew apart in front of Paul. His pants filled with warmness, and vomit belched up in the back of his throat. The laughter that filled the room seemed to Paul to be directed at him. "God, look what he's done!" he heard someone say. He tried to call out but only a garbled noise escaped his lips as the vomit sprayed out of his mouth.

"Puke on me, will you?!" The sound of the fist hitting bare flesh seemed to echo over the room as Paul collapsed into darkness.

 # CHAPTER 12

October 1979

ERIC FOUND A second position in a small synagogue of 173 families in a suburb of Albany, New York. The salary was minimal, but the people of the congregation seemed to be very pleasant and sincerely pleased to have Eric as their spiritual leader. Best of all, the synagogue had potential for growth. A large garden complex was being built several blocks from the synagogue, which was attracting young couples with small children. A new shopping center had recently opened only a mile away.

The Congregation gave Eric a small, yet wonderfully comfortable, three-bedroom house in which to live. In the living room was a stone fireplace, something he had always wanted. He converted the family room into his study, lining its paneled walls with books. There was a breakfast bar which divide the kitchen from a small alcove for dining area. The dining and living rooms were separated only by an archway spanning the width, which gave a feeling of space to the entire area.

The upstairs contained the master bedroom, with double windows facing the street, two small bedrooms and two bathrooms.

Eric thoroughly enjoyed cleaning and fixing up his home. At long last he had a place of his own which he could feel belonged solely to him. He delighted in leaving his books spread open on his desk, tables, chairs or wherever he was studying for as long as he wanted, without having someone reprimand him for his slovenliness.

Within a short time, his congregants began to love him, and participation in services and activities increased. The elderly ladies giggled with delight as he teased them about their beauty. Mothers

THE SECOND GENERATION

brought their single daughters to all services and events in hoe that the handsome, young, single rabbi would perhaps favor one of them. The men were attracted to his strong sense of purpose and dedication, and he had an immediate rapport with all the children. Everyone admired his knowledge of the historical and religious texts and writings, as well as his compassion and understanding of their individual problems.

For the first time in his life, Eri felt a measure of contented belonging. He had his own home, he liked his position, and his disappointment over his failed marriage with Sandra was beginning to fade.

Then the call to Jacqueline's deathbed came, and Eric's life began to change. He became aware of the emptiness of his house when he came home from work. He began to long for a stable family life with a wife and children. Why did Jacky's death trigger these emotions within him? Was he trying to recapture his relationship with Jacky in a fantasy of what could have been? Did he really want to get married? Could he happily give up the independence and individuality he so cherished? Could he tolerate someone in the house upsetting his lifestyle? He was never actually "comfortable" with Sandra and Jacky was too full of self-will.

"No, I am an individual. I must have my own space and identity!" He heard himself declare out loud, jolting himself out of his imaginary argument with Jacky. "Jacky is dead!" He said to himself. "Why am I arguing with her?" He walked over to the mirror and began to talk to his reflection. "Get hold of yourself, man! You can't afford self-pity and depression. Get hold of yourself. You are a rabbi. You must have more courage than anyone else. You are a leader, so lead!" He undressed, and stepped into the shower, turning it on full force as if to wash away the contradictions and confusion he felt within himself.

To keep from thinking and sinking into depression, Eric involved himself with constant work. In addition to his regular pastoral duties of sermons, counseling, comforting the sick and the bereaved, he organized and taught adult educational classes, wrote articles for publication, expanded the small afternoon Hebrew school and planned elaborate holiday celebrations. He accepted all

CHAPTER 12

invitations to speak and participate in community affairs for people of all denominations.

When Eric was asked to give the keynote address at the dedication of a new Holocaust Center at Albany University on May 8th, he was surprised and flattered. The coordinator of the dedication, Ms. Rachel Winograd, had been impressed with a speech he had given from the City Hall steps in honor of Veterans Day. She said she liked both his words and his delivery, and since she had found out that he was a Second-Generation child, it would be most appropriate for him to give the keynote address. Her voice over the found was deep and husky so Eric imagined her as being rather large and plump with short brown hair.

When Eric arrived at the University auditorium, he asked for Ms. Winograd as she had instructed. To his surprise, a slender, petite lady, with green eyes, peeping through long blond hair answered in the deep husky voice. "I'm Rachel Winograd, Rabbi Froman. I am delighted you are going to be our main speaker today."

Rachel read the surprise on his face. "Didn't expect to meet such a gorgeous hunk of woman, huh?"

"Well, your voice certainly doesn't fit your stature," Eric honestly replied. "I must admit, however, that such a deep voice from such a small woman is quite appealing," he was quick to add.

Rachel tossed her hair back in laughter, "Wow," what tact! You just made that up, didn't you?"

With head lowered, Eric answered sheepishly, "Yep!"

"Come on, Rabbi, let's give the world a laugh," she said. "Escort me to the stage." Eric was 6'4" and Rachel was 5'3". "Mutt and Jeff live again!" She declared as they walked down the aisle.

The dedication ceremony and Eric's words were warmly received by all in attendance and the activities progressed smoothly. After the event, Rachel and Eric went out for a cup of coffee in a nearby coffee shop. Eric found her animated and full of life. Her eyes twinkled with excitement as she spoke of her work as a professor of anthropology at the University. Although she was an Israeli, she spoke with a crisp British accent, which she said she acquired in learning English from a British teacher.

Eric did not find Rachel sexually appealing, but he was attracted to her quick sense of humor and vivid appreciation of life. He found her mysteriously enchanting with her mystical explanation of different cultures. Most of all, he was wonderfully comfortable in her presence because, despite her high position, she completely lacked any display of pretention. She did not flirt with him or try to impress him but treated him as someone she had known for many years. When Rachel invited him for a Sunday afternoon meal, he readily accepted, both out of a desire to develop their friendship and out of curiosity to see how she lived.

When Eric walked into Rachel's apartment, he was amazed at the beautiful simplicity of her taste. Braided scatter rugs of various colors lay on the highly polished wooden floors. To his unpracticed eye, the furniture appeared unusual, almost nonfunctional. The couch consisted of a wooden frame with high cream-colored pillows, smaller pillows of turquoise and rose, purposely thrown here and there. Three chairs of wrought iron were hung with lamb's hides, the woolly part forming a soft cushion. An olive-wood coffee table completed the arrangement. From the center of the ceiling hung a bamboo chandelier of curious design, casting a warm friendly glow on the room. The long wall of the living room was filled with books from top to bottom. The other walls, cream stucco, were hung with oil paintings of the Israeli countryside and water-color sketches of the villages and people of Israel.

Through a large open archway, Eric saw a dining room furnished in the same décor, simple yet elegant. On the glass-topped dining table sat a flat porcelain dish containing a variety of small, growing cacti, with tiny dried flowers tucked among them. White stucco walls were covered with numerous paintings and etchings. Large plants and vines added color and dimension, rounding out corners and windows. Instead of curtains, tiny blinds covered the wide windows.

"Like it?" Rachel asked Eric.

"I don't think I have ever seen anything quite like this!"

"Was that a positive or negative answer?" Rachel inquired.

"Oh, oh, I think it is very beautiful.… it's……it's very Israeli!" Eric replied.

CHAPTER 12

"Nearly everything in this apartment is from Israel. I can't go there to live now, so I brought Israel here to me...at least to live with in my home." Rachel had a wistful look in her eyes.

"Why can't you live in Israel, Rachel, if that's what you want?" asked Eric. "Is there someone here you can't leave?"

"No, I don't have anyone keeping me here, but I can't go now because I have obligations, and the delicious meal I prepared is going to ruin. So, let's eat!" Rachel skillfully changed the subject with a laugh.

Eric knew not to press her. "Well, if you cook as nicely as you decorate, I'll marry you right after the meal!"

Rachel threw up her hands, "Promises! Promises! That's all I get!" She laughed.

It was one of the most enjoyable times Eric ever had in his life. By the time he left at 11:00 pm, both Eric and Rachel knew it was the beginning of a strong friendship.

The next morning after services, as Eric was folding his prayer shawl, one of the ten men making the quorum, the minyon, called to him.

"Rabbi, there is a call for you in the office. A priest wants to talk to you."

One of the men joked, "We haven't been that bad to you, have we, Rabbi, that you are thinking of going to the other side?"

"I'll see what the other side has to offer before I give you an answer!" Eric retorted with a wide grin.

Eric went into the office and picked up the phone. "Good morning, Rabbi Froman speaking."

"Good morning, Rabbi," a man's voice replied. "I don't know if you remember me or not. This is Father Steiger. We met in the hospital one early morning a while back."

The penetrating blue eyes in the hospital chapel flashed before Eric's mind, as the pain of remembering why he was in the hospital also clutched at his heart.

"Oh yes. Of course. How are you?" answered Eric.

"Very well, thank you. And you?" replied Paul.

"Fine, thank God, but I'm sure you didn't call just to inquire about my health. Is there anything I can do for you?" asked Eric.

Here was a sigh on the phone. "Well, we have a little problem here. Maybe you can help us."

Eric was surprised that a Catholic priest would be calling him with a problem. " I'll do my best."

"I just received a call from one of my parishioners. His wife just died, and we have a dilemma."

Eric immediately knew what the problem was. "She was Jewish?"

"Yes," answered Paul. "The husband is quite upset. He wants her buried where he can be buried with her later."

"If she is Jewish, she should be buried in a Jewish Cemetery even if she was married to a non-Jew. Die she leave any instructions?" asked Eric.

No, not exactly. But she did have a cemetery plot at King Solomon Cemetery. You see, Rabbi Froman, her husband wants her buried in our church cemetery, but I feel since she was Jewish, she should at least have a rabbi officiate."

"I understand. Did she belong to any Synagogue or Temple?"

"No, at least her husband said she didn't. But she came to Mass with her husband sometimes. She just sat there. She never took part in the services."

"Where is she now?" asked Eric.

"Still at their home. She died in her sleep. Her husband woke up and found her dead beside him. Their family doctor certified the death. The husband's in pretty sad shape." Paul replied. "I have called Garland's Funeral Home to pick her up. They handle both Jewish and non-Jewish funerals. I thought it best to get her removed from the house until we can determine what to do."

"Good decision." Eric responded. "I'm in my study now. Can we get together and discuss it? Can you come now with her husband, uh, what is his name?"

"Magguin, James Magguin."

There was a brief silence at the other end of the telephone. Eric knew that the priest would have preferred that he go to the Church to meet with them, but e did not feel it proper. After all, if they wanted his help, they should come to him. Breaking the silence, he said, "I'll have fresh coffee waiting for you both. Do you know how to get to the Synagogue?"

CHAPTER 12

"It's the big building on the corner of Dane Avenue and Fairfax Road? Yes, I know where you are." Paul replied with a slight laugh. "Okay, we'll be over in a little while."

"Right, I'll be waiting for you." Eric was about to hang up but a deep sigh at the other end caused him to hesitate.

"Oh, by the way, Rabbi……"

"Yes?"

"Mr. Magguin is a working man. He does plaster for a living. Not much money there. A good man. Hilda was all he had. People are always cheating him out of his money." Paul spoke softly.

"There will be no charges for my services." Eric responded without hesitation.

"Thank you, Rabbi." Paul's voice was barely audible. Eric heard a click as the phone connection was ended.

Eric went out of the office and called to the men who were just leaving. "Gentlemen!"

They stopped and turned around. "Yes, Rabbi?"

"Would one of you mind bringing back some coffee and donuts? Father Steiger is coming over with one of his parishioners." Eric reached into his pocket. "Here's money."

An elderly gentleman named Mr. Berger, replied with a wave of the hand. "Don't worry about it, Rabbi, I'll be right back."

When Father Steiger arrived with Mr. Magguin, Rabbi Froman greeted them at the door of the Synagogue, escorted them into his office and seated them on the couch. He sat on a chair next to the couch rather than behind his desk, to relieve their possible discomfort at being in a Synagogue. The aroma from the fresh, hot coffee and the sweet smell of donuts filled the small office.

Eric immediately felt great compassion for Mr. Magguin, a short, stout man with pink swollen eyes. Rough, red hands held tightly to his tattered cap, stained with perspiration. "Do I put this on or leave it in here?" he nervously asked the priest as he held up the cap.

Paul looked at Eric.

"Doesn't matter. Leave it off, put it on – however, you feel most comfortable," Eric said. "Please have a cup of coffee." He motioned to the tray on his desk.

Mr. Magguin held onto his cap as he muttered, "Thanks" and softly continued. "My Hilda was a good woman, Rabbi. She was a good wife and I want to give her what's due her. I want to do right by her! But I want to be buried with her. She's all I had."

Eric touched the man's hand. "I am truly sorry for your loss, Mr. Magguin. I know you loved your wife very, very much and this is a terrible time to have to discuss something like this and decide what to do. I don't want to hurt you, but I also want to do what is right before God. Do you believe me?"

Mr. Magguin looked up at the rabbi and then to his priest. Paul nodded his head. "You can trust him, James."

Mr. Magguin pulled a crumpled handkerchief out of his pocket, mopped his eyes and gray stubby beard and with a big sigh, turned to Eric. "Will you bury her, Rabbi? She was Jewish. Father Steiger said she has to have a rabbi."

"Yes, I will perform the service, but only if she is buried in a Jewish cemetery. I am not permitted to perform burial services anywhere else."

"But she has just one grave in the King Solomon Cemetery. Can I buy another one to be next to her?"

"I'm sorry, Mr. Magguin, but you will not be allowed to be buried in a Jewish cemetery." Eric did not wait for Paul to speak but immediately began to talk to Mr. Magguin. "Mr. Magguin, have you ever visited friends or relatives and stayed at their homes for a few days?"

"Yes, many times." Responded Mr. Magguin with a questioning look.

"Did they treat you nicely and make you feel like you were home?"

"Oh, yes." Mr. Magguin replied, simply.

"After the visit was over and you came back to your own home, how did you feel?"

"Good to be home. I always told my Hilda that the nicest thing about going away was coming home. Why…?"

"It's the same with your Hilda, Mr. Magguin. She has enjoyed her visit with other people very much, but now she wants to be home. That is why she bought her plot in the King Solomon Cemetery. She bought only one plot because she knew you could

CHAPTER 12

not be buried there. You will have your own home to go to many years from now."

"But Rabbi, why didn't she tell me all of this? We were so close!" Mr. Magguin lamented.

"She probably didn't want to hurt you. She loved you and didn't want to worry you or ask you to change for her sake." Eric tried to comfort him.

"But how can she be buried in one place and me in another? In life we were always together…..in death we have to be parted?" Mr. Magguin's eyes filled, and slobs jerked the heavy shoulders.

The priest investigated the rabbi's face, anxiously waiting his reply. "Mr. Magguin, once the soul leaves the body, the body returns to the earth from which it came. That is no longer your Hilda. The soul…. the soul flies up to heaven back to God, that is your Hilda! When your time comes, Mr. Magguin, many years from now, your soul, too, will fly up to heaven and back to God. It is then you will be reunited with your beloved Hilda. Why, she is probably watching you right now. If she could speak with you, now, she would surely say, 'my dear husband, please don't be sad! We will meet again! We will be together again. Everything will be all right. You'll see.'"

Mr. Magguin looked at his priest. "That sounds like my Hilda. Think that is true, Father?" The priest shook his head in reassurance.

Eric spoke softly. "There are more rules which must be followed, Mr. Magguin, if you wish to do what is right for your Hilda."

The husband slumped in his chair. "What else?"

"No embalming, no flowers, no open coffin. And she must be buried tomorrow." Eric said firmly, a sound of command in his voice.

"You're not just going to put her in the ground like that?" Mr. Magguin asked in alarm. You are not going to buy her like you would bury an animal?"

"No," Eric reverted to a soft tone. "There is a sacred process. Special ladies called *Chevra Kaddish*, Holy Guardians, prepare the body for burial."

"What'll they do?" Mr. Magguin asked suspiciously.

"They will wash her, trim her nails, and place her body in a special white gown called a 'shroud.'" Eric quickly continued. "Hilda is going to meet God, face-to-face, so she must be prepared to meet the King of all Kings. She was a good woman, you said. She doesn't need any make-up or falseness. And, Mr. Magguin, would you want people staring at her as she lies helpless? She has left the human world. We remember her the way she was in life, not in death. This gives her dignity and honor as we accompany her home."

Mr. Magguin rose an extended his hand, wanting to end the conversation before the Rabbi could add more stipulations. "Whatever you say. Thank you, Rabbi, thank you so much." He stuffed his damp handkerchief into his back pocket.

Father Stieger also extended a hand. "Thank you, Rabbi," he said with a little smile.

When they were at the door, Mr. Magguin turned around. "Rabbi, one more thing?"

"Sure," responded Eric, "What is it?"

"Can I come to the funeral, and can Father Stieger also come?"

"Most certainly. Everyone can come to a funeral. In fact, it's considered a holy deed to do so."

"Can I also visit her at the cemetery sometimes?"

"Of course. You may go any time you want."

"Thank you, Rabbi." He turned and went out of the door.

The priest turned to face Eric. He put out his hand. "Thanks." Eric shook his hand, nodded his head with a smile as he walked Paul to the door.

"Eric sat down in his chair behind the desk. As he sipped the coffee, he thought, "Very nice guy, that priest, very sincere. He could have buried her in their cemetery, and no one would have known the difference. Mr. Magguin obviously would have preferred to follow familiar custom, but the priest had him convinced to 'do the right thing.' Interesting," Eric said aloud, as he took another donut.

The next day, after the burial, when the priest was about to go back to his car, he noticed the Rabbi, standing alone at the grave, watching as it was being filled with soil Why was he still there? Paul returned to the grave.

"Everybody else is gone. Why are you still waiting here?" Paul asked Eric. "Something wrong?"

"Out of respect for the deceased. Someone must stay until the grave is covered." Eric answered in a matter-of-fact voice. "We

CHAPTER 12

should accompany our brethren as far as we can…right up to the Gates of Judgment."

"Nice thought." Paul remarked.

"More than a thought." Eric said. "It is a custom of thousands of years. It links the dead together with the living…. generation with generation…those who have gone to Eternity, those who live on earth…and those yet to come." Before Paul could respond, Eric asked, "By the way, why didn't you just bury Hilda in your cemetery? Wouldn't it have been a triumph for the Church to have gotten a Jewish person? No one would have known!"

"No," replied Paul. But there is right and wrong. Hilda never converted, nor took part in the Mass. She bought her grave in a Jewish Cemetery. I was obvious what SHE wanted, or I wanted, or what the Church wanted. I believe in respecting people's wishes, Rabbi, as long as they don't harm anyone else."

"That's most honorable," Eric responded with admiration.

"As long as we're talking, I'd like to discuss something else with you." Paul said.

"Sure." Eric answered.

"I want to tell you how I admired your sensitivity with Mr. Magguin. You gave him a lot of comfort." Responded the Priest.

"Thank you. It's all part of the job. I'm sure you've done the same thing many times." Eric answered.

"I guess so. We are all employees of God." Paul quipped.

Eric laughed. "I never quite thought of it that way."

"But don't ask the boss for a raise! Doesn't work. I tried it!" Paul laughingly told him.

"How well I know!" replied Eric.

"Would you please answer a question for me?" asked Paul. "Sure, if I can. If not, I'll make something up!" Eric responded to Paul's humor.

"Why couldn't Mr. Magguin be buried here besides his wife? The earth doesn't make any distinction between religions. Mother Earth takes us all!"

"When the distinction is made on top of the earth, then it must be made under the earth as well." Eric replied.

"But isn't it the Jew who separates himself from all the other peoples? You make yourselves different. If you were like everyone else, there wouldn't be that distinction on earth." Seeing an irritated look on Eric's face, Paul immediately added, "Please, Rabbi, don't be annoyed with me. I am genuinely interested, and I want to understand."

Eric looked at Paul's face. Little beads of perspiration formed on his brow above the clear blue eyes. He knew that the strong rays of the sun must be creating a lot of heat under that black robe he was wearing. Eric touched Paul's arm. "Come on, let's sit on that bench over there in the shade."

"Thanks. It is getting warm here in the sun."

The bench under the weeping willow tree felt several degrees cooler. "Ah, this is better." remarked Paul.

Eric spoke. "Now, to answer your first question. It all stems from Abraham when he bargained with the Hittites to buy the Cave of Mach pela in which to bury his wife, Sarah. They offered to let Abraham bury his dead among them, but Abraham refused, buying instead a separate place. Jacob, Joseph, all our ancestors requested to be taken to the special place to be buried with their people. The Bible tells us that when each died, 'they slept with their fathers' which we take literally to mean 'to be buried with their people.'"

"But once life has left the body, as you simply told Mr. Magguin, there is nothing left but the dust which returns to the earth. What difference does it make?" Paul asked.

"There is a difference in the preparation of the body. We do not, in any way, tamper with the original natural state of the body – no embalming, no autopsy, no make-up. The body is washed from head to toe, the hair is combed. Even the nails are pared. Then the body is dressed in a white should. Nothing earthly goes with the body to meet God except the person's good deeds."

Paul opened his mouth to speak, but Eric continued. "Tell me, Father Steiger, would you perform services on Christmas or Easter in jeans and a tee-shirt? Everyone dresses certain ways for special occasions. One would be uncomfortable wearing a bathing suit to a wedding or a fancy garment to a beach party. In the Jewish cemetery,

CHAPTER 12

everyone is equal, dressed in the same way. There is comfort and peace in the sameness of tradition. Wouldn't you agree?"

"Yes, I guess that is true." Replied Paul.

"If you don't mind," Eric said, "there is another issue I would like to clarify for you, Father." Eric had an animation about him that intrigued Paul. There was excitement in his eyes, and he radiated enthusiasm.

"Not at all, please go on." Paul answered. "Strange person," he thought to himself.

"Do you know Hebrew, Father?" Eric asked.

Paul was surprised at his question. "I am not fluent in it. I studied Hebrew in the Seminary and learned to read the Bible and maybe carry on a quite simple conversation. Why"

"Do you know one of the Hebrew names for a cemetery?" asked Eric.

"No." replied Paul.

"*Beit HaEmet* – the House of Truth. Can we speak truthfully with each other?"

"By all means!"

"When I spoke of distinctions being made on earth, it was not negative. There is a distinction between a Jew and a non-Jew, but that distinction does not lie in the person. The Jew is a human being like all other human beings on earth. We have minds, ears, noses, faces, feelings of happiness and feelings of pain like everyone else. We are born, we love, we marry, and we die like all other peoples. Our differences lie in our reason for existence, our reason for living, but not in our human qualities."

There was a determination in Eric's voice that caused Paul to feel uneasy. "I'm not aware that most people consider the Jew more or less human," Paul replied. "to me, the difference between Jew and non-Jew lies in ideology. The Jew does not believe that Jesus Christ is the only Son of God, and….."

Eric interrupted, "Therefore he is condemned to eternal damnation?" His dark eyes flashed.

"Oh, no!" Paul hastily replied, "Those words are so terribly harsh." Ephesians 1:7 flashed through his mind: "It is in Christ and through his blood that we have been redeemed and our sins forgiven." Should he or should he not confront the rabbi with them? He decided he did not want to debate with this Rabbi. There was something about him he liked, a certain strength he admired. He felt he would like to know him better first.

"Please don't be sensitive to my every word. I mean no disrespect. I'm truly interested in your way of thinking. After all, our Lord was a Jew."

Eric grimaced. "Now you are going to tell me one of your best friends is Jewish?"

"Only when you agree to become one of my best friends!" Paul quickly retorted.

"Touché!" replied Eric, putting out his hand.

Paul responded with a slap to the hand. He looked at his watch. "Ach! I must go. Could we talk again?"

"I'd like that very much." Eric responded warmly.

"Rabbi, I don't want the words 'let's get together sometime' to be a polite way of parting. I really do want to talk further with you. Let's set a date right now." Paul pulled out his little appointment book from an inside pocket.

"Fine with me. Two weeks from Sunday is a Holocaust Commemoration at my synagogue. Would you be so kind as to be our guest, to say a few words on behalf of your congregation? Afterward, we could meet and talk."

Paul hesitated. He had never spoken before a Jewish group or in a synagogue, and he wondered how qualified he was to speak about the Holocaust on behalf of his Church.

Eric noticed his hesitation and held up his hand with the peace sign. "It's a peaceful commemoration. I do promise we won't crucify you!"

Paul turned red and laughed. "That's not it. I just do not know much about the subject. You'd be taking a big chance in having me speak."

"Maybe," Eric answered. "But I like your honesty. To med, that is the most important thing."

"Where can I read up on it?" asked Paul.

"I could give tons of information to you, but I don't want you to think I'm brain-washing or propagandizing you. I suggest you

CHAPTER 12

go to the library at Albany University. They have recently opened a very extensive section on the Holocaust. There you'll be able to read all about it."

Paul appreciated Eric's attitude. He arose and put out his hand. "Thanks, Rabbi."

Eric also arose and took Paul's hand with a firm shake. "Please call me Eric."

"Paul will be easier for you to say than Father." Paul responded.

As they got in their cars, Paul called out, "Eric!"

"Yes?"

"Shalom!"

"Shalom, *u'vraha*! Peace and God's blessings." "You'll need it if you are going to study the Holocaust." Eric said to himself as he drove away.

CHAPTER 13

THE NEXT MORNING after Mass, Paul went to the University Library. He loved the feeling he had whenever he was in a large library. The quietness, the smell of books, the awareness of all the knowledge stored on those shelves. He even enjoyed the feeling of insignificance it gave him because it stirred his desire to learn.

Behind the desk he saw a petite, blond-haired girl sorting through some books. The face of Christina flashed in his mine. He was only seven when Christina died, but he did remember she had had the same face, though not pretty, it glowed with the love of life.

The blond lady looked up with a surprised smile when he asked her where the Holocaust section was located.

"What's so funny?" He smiled pleasantly back at her.

"Well, we don't get very many priests in here wanting to know where Jewish Studies are located."

"Since when is the quest for knowledge limited by religion?" He questioned her with a laugh in his voice.

Seeing the puzzled look on his face, she came from behind the desk. "No offense meant. Come with me, Sir, I'll show you where it is."

As she passed him, he was aware of her soft scent barely detectable, yet extremely pleasant to his senses. The rustle of her full cotton skirt seemed to keep time with the soft tapping of her sandals as she led him to the far left-hand section of the library. She put her hands on her hips, gave a big sigh and said, "Now, let's see what we have here for you." She turned to him. "Do you have any background on the Holocaust?"

"No, not really." To Paul's surprise, a longing for Christina welled up in him. He had not had that feeling in many years.

THE SECOND GENERATION

"Okay." She began pulling out several books. "I would suggest you start with these, in this order." She placed them on a nearby table. "Good luck, Father, I hope you find what you are looking for."

"Thank you very much," Paul replied. "I'm impressed with your knowledge of what you've got here in the library. Can I call on you for more help if I need it? Paul desperately wanted her to stay, to sit with hi.

"She looked at her watch. "Sure, I'll be here for another couple of hours if you need me." She turned and disappeared behind the stacks.

"Wow, is he cute!" she said to herself. "Why are so many handsome men behind those collars?"

A couple of hours later, engrossed in his reading, Paul did not notice the blond lady standing beside him until his nostrils picked up her special scent. He looked up. "Hi there!" He felt he was grinning sheepishly.

"Sorry to bother you. But I must leave now. Anything I can do for you before I go?"

"Yes, thank you. As a matter of fact, there is. Do you know if you have anything on the Catholic Church during the Holocaust?"

The smile left her face. She turned and went to the further end of the stacks and then returned with a fat black book. Her face was serious. "I suggest you take this book home and read it. It contains both sides, together with many copies of documents."

"Both sides of what?"

"Read it and you'll see." Her face was solemn.

Paul took the book and stood up with an extended hand. "Thanks again for all your help. You've really been most kind."

"You are most welcome. Glad I could be of assistance." She took his hand.

"I hope I have the pleasure of seeing you in here again. May I ask your name?" Paul realized he was still holding her hand and let go of it abruptly.

The bright smile returned to her face. "Rachel Winograd," she replied. "And I certainly hope we meet again too, bye." With quick steps, she walked away.

CHAPTER 13

Paul felt uncomfortable. Had he made a fool of himself? He sat down as images of Christina flowed through his mind. The walls of books began to move closer to him, closing him in. His heartbeat quickened as he gasped for air. Paul quickly gathered an armful of books and rushed to the desk to check them out. The tall, dark-haired girl at the desk smiled warmly. "Did you find everything you were looking for, Father?" She asked.

"Yes, replied Paul, hoping the panic he was feeling did not show in his face. "Miss Winograd was kind enough to guide me."

"She's the best. You were in good hands." The girl replied.

"Thanks." Paul rapidly took the books and rushed to the door. Outside, he took a deep breath, closed his eyes and waited a few moments until he felt the panic abate.

Paul felt himself enter a new sphere of life as he read the material on the Holocaust. What he read about the Holocaust was too overwhelming for the human mind to comprehend. The more he read, the more there was to read; it was unending. He felt he was reading horror stories, crazed drug fantasies, figments of the imagination. How could something like this have happened in a modern world? Six million Jews, all the gypsies of Europe, thousands of them, two million Russians, political enemies – "sub-humans" the Nazis called them. All were exterminated in Hitler's "ultimate solution." No wonder the Rabbi was so sensitive at the cemetery last Sunday!

Paul began thinking back to his own childhood; how his father forced him to sleep in the cold wet woods, the heavy straps of the backpack cutting into his shoulders, the humiliation, the squirrel's head exploding in mid-air. He felt a tremendous kinship to the people in the Concentration Camps. "No! No!" he cried aloud. "It is not the same! My father loves me! He was only trying to make me be a man!" He covered his ears, closed his eyes, and desperately tried to make the collage of thoughts leave his mind.

The following Sunday afternoon, when he was at dinner in his father's house, Paul questioned Curt Steiger.

"Dad, were you in Germany during the war years?"

"Which war, son?"

"The Second World War."

"Oh yes, some of the time."

"What do you mean by 'some of the time'?"

"Well, you know in my job I had to travel a lot."

"Who took care of the store while you were away?"

"Your mother."

"Where did you go?"

"All over the world. In the rare book business, you must travel to find rare books. Why are you asking all of these questions?"

"I've been studying about the Holocaust."

"You what?!!" His father sat back in his chair abruptly, his steel blue eyes shooting through Paul.

Childhood fear of his father welled up in Paul, but he refused to give in to it. "Studying about the Holocaust. You know, when Hitler had all the so-called 'undesirables' killed, especially the Jews."

With controlled fury, his father demanded, "What in the hell do you want to study that garbage for? Half of it is lies anyway." He picked up his knife and sliced the meat on his plate with such strength that the knife cracked against the plate.

"Lies?"

"Of course, lies made up by the Jews to get the Land of Palestine away from the Arabs. Didn't you know that?" Curt put down his fork and looked at his son.

"Dad, I saw pictures of skeletons, of the crematories....."

"Of course, you saw pictures of skeletons. The relocation camps were full of disease – diphtheria, typhus. God knows what other diseases. They had to burn the corpses to stop the epidemics. Furthermore, there wasn't any food during the war, much less nutritious food. We were all starved to death. Why, me and your mother, we only had a bit of bread and even grass to eat at times. God knows, maybe that's why she died giving birth to you. Her body was so ravaged by malnutrition."

"But the pictures...," Paul insisted.

"Those pictures were doctored by the Jews to serve their purpose. You were in photography for a while. You know you can do anything with pictures. The whole thing has been blown out of proportion! Eat your dinner, son, before it gets cold!" Curt picked up his knife and fork and began to eat again.

CHAPTER 13

"But Dad, why did all the Germans obey Hitler, rather than follow their own conscience?

Couldn't they see he was wrong?" Paul persisted in his questioning.

Curt pointed his knife at Paul. "Son, they say 'hindsight is 20 – 20 vision. Look at what Hitler did for Germany! Our industries were rebuilt; there were jobs for everybody. We got our pride back. You know how we were cheated with the Versailles Treaty, where Germany had to take the full blame for World War I. We were forced to pay most of the reparations! How we were humiliated!" Curt slammed his knife down on the table. "Can't you understand what it means to have your pride restored after such a terrible thing has happened to you?!! After having been betrayed!"

"Betrayed by whom, Father?"

"Betrayed by the Jews, son. The Jews sold out the Germans. What's the matter with you? When did you become a Jew lover?"

"How did the Jews betray Germany, Dad? To whom did they 'sell out' Germany?"

Curt ignored Paul's question and continued with his tirade. "They are greedy, blood-suckers, Paul. They prey on beautiful German children. They pollute the populations!"

Nancy's gang rape flashed in Paul's mind. There wasn't a Jewish person at that party. In fact, there were only 'white' Americans, all good Christians. He remembered the compassion of Eric with Mr. Magguin.

"How can you say that, Dad? How can you say that any people pollute other people? There are good and bad in all people. I am a priest; I see it every day."

"You are a sorrowful weakling who hides behind a priest's frock. Why don't you have the guts to stand up with convictions, for what you know is right?" Curt's face was red with anger.

Curt's words cut through Paul with the violence of a razor. Paul answered, pronouncing each of his words with deliberation and distinction. "I do stand up with conviction for what I think is right and what I think is wrong. I can see what is not ethical or what is not moral. Can you? Where were you when all those horrible things were being done to innocent people – men, women and children?"

THE SECOND GENERATION

Paul realize he was standing and shouting. It was the first time he had ever confronted his father with such loud anger.

His father was as shocked as Paul was as he glared momentarily at him, then sat down heavily in his chair. "First of all, I didn't do anything. I told you I was out of the country most of the time, trying to keep my little business going, trying to put food in my family's mouth. But I understand the ones who did. They were only following orders!" Curt sat forward in his chair facing Paul. "Now think, Son, if every soldier, each person did what they thought was right, what kind of army would we have? What kind of people would we be? There would be only chaos. People need a strong leader. They need to be disciplined!" Curt pounded his fists on the table. A glass of wine turned over. The wine looked like blood creeping across the white tablecloth.

Until that last word, Paul wanted to believe his father, but when he heard the word, "discipline," his head reeled as the room moved around him. He heard his father's voice from afar.

"What's the matter son? Don't you feel well?"

Paul took a deep breath. "I'm okay. Guess I'm tired. Haven't been getting enough sleep lately." He held the arms of the chair tightly to steady himself. "Would you mind if I went back to my room at the rectory? I'm tired."

"Not at all, son. Are you sure you're, all right? Maye I should call the doctor to have you checked out?"

Paul felt better. He stood up. "No, Dad, I'm fine. Honest." He felt sorry for the concerned look on his father's face. "But if you don't mind, I would like to take my steak back to eat later."

His father's face relaxed. "That's a good sign. Sure! I'll pack it for you."

Paul sat down and waited while his father went into the kitchen. When he returned, he examined his father's face. "No, my father may have been strict with me, but it was for my own good. He meant well. He would never have killed anyone. He could never have done what they said the Germans did." Paul thought, consoling himself.

"When did you come to America, Dad?"

128

CHAPTER 13

His father hesitated. "Oh, now let me see…right after the war, with all the other refugees. Your mother and I, we had it tough in Germany. Our house was bombed out. We had no place to live, nothing to eat. We had nothing except the clothes on our backs and one trunk of rare books. Yes, we were able to save one trunk of rare books, and with that we started our lives all over again here, in this wonderful free country of America."

"I thought Hitler had all books burned except those that espoused his philosophy. How were you able to save them?"

"Oh, we hid them in the cellar. You know it was dry down there, thank God. We were against the burning of books, but what could we do? They would have killed us. We were victims of Hitler like everybody else." He slumped in his chair, shaking his head as memories flooded through his head. Suddenly he looked up. "Enough of this talk! Go on, son, here's your supper. Go home and rest. You work too hard. You take everyone's problems too seriously." He placed his hand on Paul's back as he walked him to the door. He held out his hand, "Goodbye son, take care of yourself!"

"Thanks, Dad," he took the hand. "I'm worry I raised my voice at you." His father brushed off his apology with a sweep of his hand. "You take care of yourself too! I'll see you next Sunday."

As the door closed behind him, Paul felt both hatred and love for his father. He was his father's only son – why couldn't his father have given him a hug instead of a handshake? Was he still disappointed in him? He had thought his profession as a priest would bring pride to his father. His father's words bothered him. Was he right about the concentration camps? His father had never lied to him; in fact, he did not even try to soften the truth regardless of how it hurt him.

Paul started the car. He felt a tightness around his heart that spread throughout his chest. It was the same fear he had felt as a boy when he had to make a difficult decision. "I don't have anything to decide. What's the matter with me?" He drove progressively faster towards his Church. When he entered the private lot assigned to clergy, he quickly parked the car in his numbered space, and ran up the steps to the side door entrance into the Church. He pulled out his keys and dropped them. "Damn! Damn! Damn!" he muttered as he reached down to pick them up. He felt he was on a merry-go-round that would not stop, that he could not get off. He unlocked the door with shaky hands and hastened to his seat behind the altar with a feeling of sanctuary against some pursuing evil. He sat quietly looking over the empty seats, his eyes stopping at each Station of the Cross. The brilliant light of the setting sun shining through the stained-glass windows caught his attention. Pouring like blood across the pews and floor, it spread in a pool at the foot of the Savior. Paul's entire body bean to shake uncontrollably as the blood seemed to pulsate closer to him with every loud beat of his heart. He thought he heard himself scream in the cold blackness that enveloped him.

 # CHAPTER 14

SUNDAY AT 6:00 p.m. Paul walked into the synagogue with mixed feelings. He had never been alone in the presence of this many Jews before. They are our Lord's people, he reassured himself. Eric was waiting for him at the door, talking with some of the congregants, but immediately extended his hand when he saw Paul.

"Welcome, Father Steiger. We are pleased you could join with us today."

"Thank you, I am pleased to be here," Paul responded as warmly as he could.

Eric introduced him to the people with whom he was speaking, and then led him to the pulpit. "Would you please sit here," he pointed to a chair, "next to me." He handed him a booklet, "Here's the program. You can see where you have been scheduled to speak."

Paul was listed among the beginning speakers. He was to follow three representatives from the city and state governments. A Protestant minister was to follow him. The Holocaust ceremony was to begin with a speech by the Chairperson of the Holocaust Center of Albany University. Ms. Rachel Winograd. "Rachel," Paul said half aloud to himself. "Wasn't that the name of the girl in the library?" He became aware that Eric was speaking to him. "Beg your pardon, what did you say, Eric?" he asked.

"I said we put you after the politicians, Paul, because we thought our congregation could use some spiritual guidance when they finish with us." Eric joked. "Is that okay with you?"

"Oh sure," Paul laughed. "What are spiritual leaders for, if not to add to the confusion of the people?"

THE SECOND GENERATION

"Joking aside, I must admit that these are rather good guys, especially the mayor. He really works for the people – pretty fair-minded too."

Before Paul could reply, a man come to Eric and whispered in his ear. Eric turned to Paul. "Excuse me, I'll be right back."

Paul replied with a nod. He began to examine the booklet Eric had given to him. On the front of the pamphlet was raised arm and fist. Across the arm were numbers burnt into the flesh. In flaming letters below the arm was written:

"I believe in the sun even when it is not shining."

"I believe in love even when not feeling it."

"I believe in God even when He is silent."

In very small letters in the right-hand corner of the pamphlet was written, "Inscription on the walls of a cellar in Cologne where Jews hid from the Nazis."

Paul stared at the arm in the picture. The fingers in the fist appeared to be tightening. The numbers on the arm appeared to be burning deeper into the flesh. "I believe in God even when He is silent," rang through Paul's head. He felt the program burning his hands, as he quickly dropped it to the floor.

The Protestant minster picked up the program and handed it back to Paul. "Impressive picture isn't it?" he remarked.

"Thanks," responded Paul. "Yes, it is." He was relieved when the mayor engaged the preacher. He did not feel like talking with anyone at that moment. He saw his hands shaking as he quickly began to examine the rest of the booklet. There were prayers and responsive readings. On the last pages were the names of the relatives of people associated with the congregation, who had died in the Holocaust. His last conversation with his father rang in his head.

"Half of it is lies anyway."

"Lies?"

"Sure, lies made up by the Jews to take the Land of Palestine away from the Arabs."

Paul looked at the congregation. He closely examined their faces. They looked normal. He saw no indication of the horrors of which he had read, engraved on their faces. Maybe his father was right.

CHAPTER 14

"What am I doing here?" He thought, panic stricken. "Are they using me too?" All the noise became condensed into one din-like thousands of bees buzzing in his head.

"Paul, Paul," he felt a hand on his shoulder and looked up. Eric was speaking to him. The noise stopped abruptly.

"Oh, sorry," Paul jumped up. "I guess I was mentally working on my speed," he said with a nervous laugh. Eric searched his face curiously but said nothing.

Paul noticed that the blond lady he had met in the library was standing beside Eric. She was smartly dressed in a dark blue suit with a large white collar. Her sandy hair was swept up in an attractive twist at the back of her head. High heels gave her the appearance of being taller.

"Well, hello!" Paul greeted her.

"How do you do, Father," she responded, extending her hand. "I didn't know you were a friend of Eric's, I mean Rabbi Froman."

"I didn't know you two knew each other," Eric said.

"This young lady was on duty in the library and helped me in my research on the Holocaust."

Eric laughed. "You've been had, Paul. This young lady is the Chairperson of the Anthropology Department at the University."

"Oh, I'm sorry." Paul immediately said in a stunned voice.

"Well, I'm not. I like being the Department Head!" She answered with an upward lift of her head.

"Oh, no, I didn't mean that. I meant that I made the mistake…"

"Oh, I know." She touched his arm smiling broadly. Her special scent swept over him.

"Rabbi, Rabbi," a voice was calling from in front of the pulpit. "It's past 6:15. Don't you think we should get started?"

"My public is clamoring for me." Eric said with a shrug of his shoulders. "Sorry, I have to go."

Eric had seated Rachel in the chair on the other side of his seat, so he was sitting between her and Paul. Paul whispered across the empty chair as Eric walked toward the podium.

"Yes," she whispered back. "What's your name?"

"Call me Paul. I am Paul Steiger."

"Pleased to see you again, Paul."

133

"Me too!" Paul sat back in his chair, suddenly feeling light-hearted and securely in control of himself.

"Ladies and gentlemen, we wish to welcome you to this Commemoration….."

Paul looked at Rachel's face and saw it transform into Christina's face. He could not take his eyes from her as he heard Eric speaking from a distance.

"……..of the souls who have passed on to eternity…."

Paul's dizziness returned. He was relieved when Eric came back to his seat because he blocked Rachel from view. Paul forced himself to listen to the two politicians. One more to go, and it would be his turn. His pulse began to race. He was not ready to give his speech. He whispered to Eric, "Could you please let me speak at the end of this program instead of the beginning?"

Eric was puzzled. He looked at Paul's pale face. "Are you okay?"

"Sure, I just want to hear the entire program before I speak. I'm working on some new ideas up here." He said, touching his temple.

"Fine, I can arrange it."

Paul felt a sense of relief. He sat back in his chair to relax and regain his composure.

When the scheduled time came for Paul to speak, Eric arose and said: "Ladies and gentlemen, Father Paul Steiger has requested speaking time at the end of our program. I guess he wants to leave the best until last! He is not aware that I always have the last word." The people laughed with polite acceptance.

When a film on the Holocaust was shown, Paul watched it with the words of his father ringing in his ears. "The pictures were doctored by the Jews to serve their purpose. You know you can do anything with photography!" A cry drew Paul's attention to the people sitting in the first several rows. Many had covered their eyes with their hands, others were crying openly. Some were rocking back and forth, shaking clenched hands in front of them. He studied the rest of the congregation. They were watching the film with solemn faces, but few showed the emotion of those sitting in the first several rows.

After the film, Paul tried to concentrate on the words he heard Rachel speaking…."downtrodden for thousands of years, weeping, suffering always, yet clinging to their God tenaciously, loyally, as

CHAPTER 14

no other under the sun…and yet there are those who claim the Holocaust never happened…that the Jews have invented a fiendish lie to help them grab the Land of Palestine. What will be when these survivors, these witnesses, no longer exist? Now we can say, 'Arise, survivors, arise and bear witnesses!'"

Paul watched in a trance as the people in the first several rows stood up in unison, pulled up their sleeves, and held their arms high with clench fists. On each arm was tattooed a number.

Paul did not hear the words that were spoken, or the song that was sung. His eyes filled with tears; frustration immobilized his whole body as he wanted to go down from the pulpit to the people, erase the numbers from their arms, and take away all that they had suffered.

Ironically, the hated discipline his father had taught him lifted him from his seat with cool calmness, and brough him forward to speak.

"Ladies and gentlemen, I know it is not my time to speak, but I have something to say."

A deadly silence fell upon the crowded room.

Never had Paul felt such a calm sureness descend upon him. He felt overwhelmed with purpose to reach these people and show them that all the world was not against them. He spoke his words with great deliberation. His mind seemed to be detached from his mouth and yet was in complete control of the words that came out of it.

"For the past week I have been studying the Holocaust. I admit to you that I knew very little about it until Rabbi Froman invited me two weeks ago to come here and speak. What I have read and studied in a mere few days is so unbelievable, so incomprehensible, that my brain does to have the ability to realize, much less understand, the…the….the THING that brought humanity down, down to its lowest pit of inhumanity. I see the numbers seared into your flesh. I hear the accounts of your violently shattered lives. I know it is true, yet, my mind, my mind…how can it bring together and rationalize such irrationality without……without bursting apart! Through it all, though, one theme shines forth with its ugly reality. I, and many like me, are guilty of ignorance, true, but the world, the world is guilty of apathy. I can be cured of my ignorance, but can the world be cured of not caring? Yes, it can be IF, I and people like me, reach out to the world. No! No! It is no longer 'if.' It is something we must do; otherwise humanity will surely doom itself to destruction!"

Paul hesitated and investigated the faces of his audience. There was complete silence, yet on their faces he saw acceptance of his words, perhaps surprised hope, but it was still hope. "I see you have planned a candle-lighting ceremony. I ask you, please may I light the first candle to the hope, to the burning desire, to the pledged that I, and all that I can reach, will dedicate our lives, not to only right a wrong, but to try to eradicate all wrongs which have been or are being perpetuated against any human being created by the God of us all!"

Paul reached down, picked up the matches and lit the first candle. Applause filled the room except from the people in the first several rows who sat stoned faced. He noticed that Rachel's face showed concern. She was not smiling. Paul felt their lack of acceptance for his act as he sat down in his seat.

Eric quickly came forward and let another candle saying, "Thank you, Father Steiger. Let us pray that the candle you so valiantly lit will be a source of light to all who seek the knowledge of truth that you have so eloquently proclaimed this day." Eric turned and began the planned candle-lighting ceremony.

After the Commemoration was complete, Eric walked back to Rachel and Paul. "How about you two staying here after the crowd leaves? Then maybe we can have a drink together in my office. In fact, both of you go on ahead to my office and wait for me. I'll be right there as soon as I see our guests to the door."

"It would be my unique pleasure," replied Rachel with a smile.

"Hey, don't tell me you're falling for a priest?" Eric said jokingly.

Rachel was fast on the retort. "Well, I wouldn't have to worry about him running around with other women!"

They all laughed as Eric disappeared into the crowds. Many people came to the pulpit to congratulate both Paul and Rachel on their speeches.

CHAPTER 14

When the crowd was almost gone, Paul asked Rachel, "Did I say something wrong?" The old feeling of insecurity was returning. "I didn't intend to."

"No, you spoke beautifully….right from your heart. Everyone knew it and appreciated your words. Didn't you hear the compliments you got?"

"Then what was the problem? Something was wrong with some of the people. I could feel it."

"Let's wait 'til Eric comes back. After all, he is the Rabbi. It is his job to answer all questions. Hey, here he is now. Well, friend, how did it go? What were the comments?"

"It will certainly be a Commemoration that will be long remembered."

Paul faced Eric. "What did I do wrong? What did I say that wasn't right?" His voice as anxious and sincere.

Eric looked straight onto Paul's eyes. "You did absolutely nothing wrong, Paul. You were magnificent!"

"Then what is it? I feel that something was not right. I am a man of God, too, I can feel the moods of my audience."

"Some of the congregants resented that you lit the candle."

"Why?"

"They believed you and they believed what you said, Paul. They believed in you as an individual, as Paul Steiger. But standing there in your vestments, you represented the Church. Your Church was the one institution that could have done the most, yet it was guilty of the greatest apathy where the Jews were concerned. They did not even issue an official protest! To the people here, you lit a candle in the name of one that could have done the most but did the least!"

"But, Eric, I just read that many Jewish lives were saved by Christians who hid them! Convents took in Jewish children. Priests risked their lives to save Jews in the onslaught of the Nazis!"

"That's true," answered Eric, "but study further, Paul. Those were INDIVIDUAL Christians of good will, of righteous hearts. We even have a pathway in Israel to their honor called 'The Pathway of the Righteous Gentiles.' It leads to the Holocaust memorial in Jerusalem. However, they did not act in the name of the Church, but in the name of their own consciences. The Church was silent!"

THE SECOND GENERATION

Paul heavily sat down in his chair and with a great sigh asked, "Where's that drink you promised me? Let's talk over a drink."

"Not here, you don't!" Rachel butted in. "How about you two coming to my place for some coffee? I think I even have a piece of dried-up cake that the dog didn't finish eating."

"Would you mind talking with Rachel hanging around, Paul?"

"I would enjoy it!

"I'm glad you said that." Responded Rachel. "Paul, you get the freshest piece of cake. Eric, you get the piece the dog was chewing on!"

Rachel was thirty-five years old and had never been married. Her five-room apartment was the frequent meeting place of many of the intellectuals of the community. She was good friends with everyone but intimately close to none. "Intimacy ruins good friendships," she frequently said. She was fiercely independent and sometimes would go out of town for a couple of days at a time without telling anyone where she had gone. When questioned, she would reply, "A girl has to be mysterious or she loses all of her charm," and that would be the end of the subject.

When the three arrived at Rachel's home, Paul was just as amazed at the beautiful simplicity of her apartment as Eric had been. He was particularly impressed with the artwork on the walls. He was especially attracted to one painting which had terraced gardens, with olive trees on hills in the foreground and a wall with a citadel in the background.

Noticing Paul's interest in the painting, Rachel explained it. "That's Jerusalem; the wall around the old city and that is the Tower of David."

"I've always wanted to see Jerusalem." Paul said longingly. "I understand it is very mystical."

"Yes, it is." Rachel answered. "I always go there when I feel deeply depressed. The very air seems to revive me and raise my spirits."

Contemplating the picture, Paul spoke softly, almost to himself. "I would love to see the city of our Lord, to walk in his footsteps along the Via Dolorosa."

"Yes, I guess that would be nice for you." Rachel said matter-of-factly. "Would you care for tea or coffee?"

CHAPTER 14

The words, "for you," made Paul feel uncomfortable. He sensed a separation from the warmness he had previously felt in her presence. "Tea, please." He replied with a large smile.

Trying to re-establish the closeness he had experienced, he added, "I guess we both share a common longing for Jerusalem, the Golden City."

"That's true, but for much different reasons." Rachel replied.

The uncomfortableness grew in Paul. "What do you mean?" Rachel looked at Eric. "Well, if we're about to get down to some nitty-gritty stuff. We might as well be at ease." Eric took off his jacket, tie, and unbuttoned the collar on his shirt.

"Good idea!" responded Rachel, kicking off her heels and removing her suit jacket.

Paul reached to the back of his neck, unsnapped his collar and pulled it off. H also slipped out of his robe.

"Ah, that's better." Eric said as he flopped down on the couch.

Paul settled into one of the fleece-lined chairs. "Wow, this is terrific. I never realized one of these things could be so comfortable."

Rachel disappeared into the kitchen.

"Everything about Rachel Is terrific." Eric said.

"Eric, am I imagining things, or did I detect a trace of irony in her voice before? Have I made her angry for some reason?"

"No," Eric replied. "Rachel is a historian of religions. She probably knows Christianity as well as you do, Paul. She resents any other religion laying claims to Jerusalem except Israel."

"Why? It is the birthplace of three great religions. Why can't all three share it?" Paul asked.

"If there had been peace between the three of them, there would be no objections to sharing Jerusalem. But Israel founded Jerusalem and laid claim to it for thousands of years before Christianity and Islam ever came along. Along came Christianity and claimed it for its own, slaughtering all the Jews and Moslems in the name of Christianity, followed by Islam who also tried to claim it for its own, slaughtering Jews and Christians. The Jews lost on both accounts, being branded as infidels by Christians and Moslems.

"Eric," Paul replied, "I certainly don't condone the actions of the Crusaders. The Church certainly did not intend for them to be looters and murders! Maybe the lure of bounty and plunder did unfortunately overrule their glorious ideals."

"Glorious ideals?" Rachel asked as she came into the room. "Who gave Christianity the right to claim that the Holy Land belonged to them?" Sparks of anger flashed in her eyes as she put the coffee and cake down on the table.

Paul felt the same guilty fear he had felt the day Christina had caught him in her underwear drawer. Rachel had stood up with her hands on her hips. Christina had been in the same position, and for a moment he saw Christina standing before him.

"I missed you. I just wanted to feel close to you," he stammered as he quickly slammed the drawer closed. Christina's anger vanished as she bent down and took him in her arms. *"Gentlemen never go into a lady's private things!" She warned him as she kissed him on the forehead. "You must be strong and not let your emotions overwhelm you. Do you understand, Paul?" she asked in a stern voice. "Please don't be angry with me, Christina. I promise I won't do it again!"*

Eric's and Rachel's laughter awaked Paul to reality. He realized he must have spoken aloud in the voice of a child, and they thought he had done it on purpose.

"It is I who am sorry and should ask you not to be angry with me, Paul. Anger will certainly inhibit constructive discussion," Rachel apologized. "By the way, who's Christina?"

Paul also laughed as if it were a joke. "Christina was my sister who used to reprimand me the same way you did. By the way, you look a lot like her."

"Oh, really? I'd like to meet her sometime," said Rachel.

"She died when I was seven—a horse threw her."

"Oh, I'm sorry." Rachel reached out and touched his hand.

Paul nodded his head. The touch and the scent of Rachel brought a lump to his throat. He wanted to ask Rachel to put her arms around him and hold him.

"Maybe we should drop the whole subject," Eric said as he closely watched Paul's face.

"No! No!" Paul almost shouted. "Let's just realize that we've learned different views. Only if we can discuss these views together, will we be able to find a common ground of understand between us."

CHAPTER 14

"Do you really want that understanding, Paul?"

"Yes, I do, Eric." He looked straight into Eric's eyes. "Yes, I so, very, very much!"

"Why?" Eric asked.

"The true Christian spirit is one of love and peace. We're supposed to abide by Jesus' teaching, 'Loved thy neighbor.' There are no reservations as to who that neighbor should be. Jesus was born a Jew. Should I not love the people who gave Him to me? How can I love them unless I understand them?"

Rachel gave Eric a diabolical look. "Spoken like a true Christian. Let's convert him! There are two of us against one of him!" She snickered.

"Lord no!" cried Eric. "Haven't we Jews got enough troubles already?"

"Watch yourselves," Paul warned, "I may just wind up converting both of you instead!"

"It's been tried for centuries by greater experts than you," Rachel answered, "and they all failed!"

"Aw, a gentle hand and soft words can accomplish more miracles than the mightiest weapon!"

"Oey!" Rachel leaned back in her chair, her hands on her head with her eyes rolled upward.

"All right! All right!" conceded Paul. "Let's get back to our discussion. Where were we?"

You were going to justify your claim to Jerusalem," Eric reminded him.

"Oh yes, the New Covenant with God, of course!" Paul answered.

"Do you actually believe that God has taken the Covenant away from Israel and given it to the Christians?" Eric asked.

"The New Covenant is not the same as the Old Covenant that the Hebrews had." Paul began to explain.

"Had?" interrupted Rachel.

"Well, Jeremiah 31:31-34 says, 'Behold the days come, saith the Lord, that I will make a New Covenant with the House of Israel, and with the House of Judah; not according to the Covenant that I made with their fathers in the day that I took them by the hand to bring them out of Egypt, which My Covenant they broke…' From this, you can easily see that God told Jeremiah that He would make a new set of laws, a new contract with man!"

"But, Paul, you just quoted that God told Jeremiah that He would make a New Covenant with the House of Israel, with the House of Judah, not with the gentiles!" "Of course," Paul replied to Rachel, "and who should stem from the House of Judah but a descendent of David – Jesus! Jesus is the founder of Christianity; therefore, Christianity is now the bearer of the New Covenant!"

Eric motioned to Rachel to let him speak. "Paul, the Jewish people do not object that the Christians say they have a covenant with God. If each of the peoples of the world had their own covenant with God, perhaps we would have a better world in which to live, but it does not mean that the Christian covenant has to obliterate the Hebrew covenant!"

"No, of course not!" Paul passionately responded. "Every Jew can be a part of the New Covenant. They would be most welcome!"

"Paul, to the Jew, the New Covenant has not taken place yet."

"How can you say that, Eric?"

"Because if the birth of the Christian religion really did introduce the New Covenant, then there would no longer be any need for anyone to teach the word of God."

"Why not? What about the masses who know not yet our Heavenly Father?" Paul almost demanded to know.

"It is also written in Jeremiah, same verse, that God says, 'for they shall know Me.' Since it is obvious that the whole world does not recognize God, then obviously, at least to the Jew, the New Covenant has not yet taken place."

"But we're teaching the world to recognize God," Paul refuted Eric.

"They shall teach no more every man, saying, know the Lord." Eric quoted from Jeremiah. "Paul, for you maybe it's fine, for the Jew, it is not acceptable."

"But that verse...'and they shall teach no more...' refers to the second coming of Christ. This will be fulfilled when Jesus returns once again to visit mankind!"

CHAPTER 14

"I sincerely respect our thinking, Paul, however, this is a matter of interpretation, and since Judaism does not recognize Jesus as being their God, we cannot accept the interpretation."

"Why can't Jews accept Jesus as the son of God?" Paul pleaded.

"Because we are forbidden by God Himself. The first Commandment says: 'I am the Lord your God, you shall have NO OTHER gods before me!' As to believing Jesus is the son of God, we believe that we are all children of God. Paul, you and I are both sons of God and Rachel is a daughter of God. For a Jew to forsake the First Commandment would be to forsake all the rest of the Commandments as well."

Eric continued. "According to Jewish belief, if God gave the laws in front of the entire nation of Israel, then shouldn't God have abrogated them also in front of the entire nation? Exodus 19 explicitly points out that the entire nation was present when God gave the Torah, the Bible, to the Jewish people at Mount Sinai. We are warned time and time again, as in Deuteronomy 13:1 and 4:2, 'Ye shall not add unto the word which I command you, neither shall ye diminish from it, that ye may keep the Commandments of the Lord your God which I command you...that it might be well with you and your children forever.' Deuteronomy 5:26. The examples you gave are for teaching purposes only."

"But the Jews didn't keep the Commandments!" Paul interrupted.

"No, please let me finish this thought. Now, if the Christian claim is correct, that the laws of the Torah no longer have to be obeyed, because Jesus fulfilled them for us, then wouldn't it make sense for God to cancel His original Commandments in the same manner he gave them, in front of all the people, in order to avoid confusion, if nothing else?"

"But He revealed Himself in the body of His son, Jesus."

"Jesus revealed himself only to two women and eleven disciples, not to the whole world, most of all, not to the Jewish people as a whole assembly. If you wish to believe that God changed His laws through Jesus, then I have no quarrel with you, but it is not for the Jew. To us, our Father, our Creator, has commanded our loyalty in person and He shall have it until the day He personally tells us He no longer desires it!"

THE SECOND GENERATION

"Even if the Jews broke the Commandment, the laws?" asked Paul.

"Yes, there were and are, and probably will always be, Jews who break the law, just like there are Christians who have not followed the Christian way of love and peace. But there are many who do, and since we are all one people responsible for each other, God has promised that He will not fail us, neither destroy us completely, nor forget the Covenant of our fathers which He has sworn unto us. Deuteronomy 5:31 says 'there shall always be a remnant.' God promised us that!"

"And I promised you coffee and cake! Enough of this heavy stuff. The coffee is probably cold. Here, have a piece of cherry cheese cake I found in the refrigerator. Guaranteed to put on five pounds!" Rachel began to pour the coffee and serve the cake.

"She's just made because she got squeezed out of the conversation, remarked Eric to Paul.

Paul looked at his watch. "Wow, it's after eleven. I have a 6:00 o'clock Mass tomorrow morning and I'm rather beat. It has been a big day for me."

Eric joined him. "Early prayers for me too. I really have enjoyed myself. I hope you were not offended in any way, Paul."

"Not at all," exclaimed Paul. "In fact, I was thinking the same regarding both of you."

Rachel rose. "Enough with the niceties. Would you like to meet again to continue our discussions?"

Paul quickly grabbed at the invitation. "Yes, I've enjoyed myself immensely. I don't know when I've felt so stimulated and so relaxed." His heart did feel light and happy. Rachel's presence had a definite positive effect on him.

"How about Friday night? Come for a Sabbath dinner. Eric, is that okay with you?"

"Sounds good to me. It's quite a walk, but I'll be here."

"I'll pick you up," Paul said. "What time?"

"I don't ride on the Sabbath, Paul. I'll have to hoof it over here after services.

"Uh, what time is that?" Paul asked.

"Around 8:00 pm" Eric told him.

CHAPTER 15

PAUL COUNTED THE days until Friday night with great anticipation. Rachel was bringing a flood of memories to him about his childhood. He used to feel the same anxiety when he would wait for everyone to go to sleep so he could slip into Christina's room to talk with her.

The Friday night dinner turned into ongoing sessions of discussions and debates. Each respected the others' private convictions and beliefs as well as their need for freedom of individuality.

Rachel had a way of balancing herself between the two men to neutralize their disagreements. Once in a particularly heated discussion, Paul arose from his chair, slammed his fist on the table and shouted, "You Jews have a martyr complex. You enjoy suffering."

"If we do," retorted Eric, "it is because people such as you, who have persecuted us throughout the ages, have given it to us!"

Rachel immediately defused the tension. "And I am suffering from both of you. Now sit down and shut up before I get a complex!" Both men laughed at the contorted face she made, and the tension was broken.

Within the ensuing year, the three single people found a bond, a security in the family atmosphere they had created. They were comfortable with each other with a feeling that, regardless of their arguments or what might happen to any one of them, the other two would continue their friendship without any strings attached.

"We ae so different, the three of us. Why do you think we have become such good friends?" Paul asked one evening as they were sharing a meal together at Rachel's home.

"I think it's because you are both clergies," Rachel answered, "of different religions. For your own people, each of you must act the part of a spiritual leader, strong and wise. But with each other, you are allowed to let down your act and be plain human beings. And, of course," she added, "I am so intelligent and knowledgeable, not to mention understanding of all religions, that I'm able to get along with anyone." She flipped her hand through her hair with a sigh.

Eric leaned over and whispered loudly to Paul. "Don't tell her that we only tolerate her because she's a good cook and we get a good meal once in a while at her home, and we don't have to do the dishes."

Paul responded also in a loud whisper, "Yeah, don't wake her up out of her dream-world. She may flip altogether!"

"Oh, that's all right!" Rachel calmly arose and walked to the refrigerator. "I didn't think you fellows would care for the chocolate cream pie with the whipped cream topping any way. I'll just give it to my neighbor!"

There was a rush toward the refrigerator as both men struggled to take the pie away from Rachel. Paul was trying to pull the pie out of Rachel's hands and Eric was holding Rachel when she suddenly let go. Paul tried to regain his balance as he went flying backwards, desperately holding out the pie in front of him. As he fell, he threw the pie onto the table and it slid forward. Eric lunged forward and grabbed the pie as it fell off the table.

Rachel leaned against the refrigerator, holding her stomach in laughter. "I think you are good friends because you once were clowns in the circus together!" She choked out between her laughter. "That was very nice of you, but you didn't have to put on a special show just for me!"

Both men glared at her.

"Okay, okay! You earned your piece of pie." Still laughing, she took a serving knife out of the drawer. When they finished the pie, Eric said to Paul: "Shall we retire into the living room to be out of her way as she does the dishes?"

"By all means," responded Paul. "Except, maybe this time, since she did cook an excellent meal, maybe we should do the dishes and let Rachel retire to the living room?"

Lifting a large wooden spoon, Rachel threatened to hit them. "Get out of my kitchen, you klutzes, you would probably break every dish I own! Out! Out!"

CHAPTER 15

When they were sitting in the living room, Paul said to Eric, "I've been wanting to ask you something for a long time, Eric."

"Yeah? What is it?"

"Well, it may not be any of my business, but I've always wondered something."

"What is it, Paul, you're driving me crazy with this preamble."

"Rachel's Jewish and around your age. Did you ever have ideas of maybe marrying her, Eric?" Paul asked.

"Naw, she's a great girl to be with, but definitely not my type."

Paul was amazed at the relief he felt. "What do you mean, not your type?"

"Well, first of all, she's so intelligent, she makes me feel like a fool sometimes," Eric said.

"Does she know that?" Paul asked.

"Hell no! She thinks I'm smart. I guess it would be some sort of blow to my ego if she knew she intimidated me."

"I would think her intelligence would be an attraction to you. It is to me."

"Oh, it is. I enjoy her company exceedingly. She's just not my type."

"What is our type, Eric?"

"Oh, I like tall, slim women. She is far too short and pudgy. Then there's one more issue."

"What's that?" sked Paul.

"She's the best friend I have ever had in my life. I'm dreadfully afraid that if our marriage didn't work out, I would lose a friend as well as a wife."

"Do you know what her feelings are toward you?"

"She doesn't want to get married. She is one hundred percent Zionist. She lives, breathes and loves Israel. She hopes to live there some day. I think that is why she became a Professor of Anthropology, specializing in religions. Israel is the well-spring of three of the great religions on earth, as you well know."

"Do you know anything about her life?" the priest asked.

"Her father is a professor and her mother's a teacher. Her father is considerably older than her mother. She was a student in his class."

"How sweet. Where do they live?"

"They live in Israel. They are also Zionists. When the State was created in 1948, they went there to live. Rachel came here on a scholarship to study for her Ph.D. When she got it, she was immediately offered this position. In Israel she would not be a rarity, but here in America, she is. There are plenty of Professors of Archeology in Israel. In fact, everyone there considers himself a mini-archeologist."

Paul felt a sense of relief when he heard there was no romantic relationship between Eric and Rachel. He was a priest; he had no romantic intentions toward Rachel himself, but he felt that he did not want to be the odd man in a threesome. He refused to admit to himself that the thought of Rachel and Eric making love, a thought that came to him many times in the dark of the night, bothered him.

CHAPTER 16

IN LATE SEPTEMBER, Eric was sitting in his office working on his sermons for the High Holidays when his secretary, Judy, buzzed him on the intercom.

"Yes?"

"You have a funeral."

"Who?"

"George Fieldstone."

"George Fieldstone? His is only in his late 50's! What happened?"

"Heart attack."

"When did he die?"

"Rabbi, I think he just died."

"Who notified us?"

"Nobody. His family is here."

"Here? Right now?"

"Yes. His family was with him at the hospital. He got pains in his chest; they rushed him to the hospital where he had a heart attack and died immediately. So, they just all came over here instead of calling. They are all here, waiting in the lobby."

"Send them right in." Eric began shifting papers on his desk hurriedly to give an appearance of order. Then he quickly put on his jacket and was straightening his tie when there was a soft knock on the door.

"Come in." Eric walked to the door to welcome them.

"Judy just told me. I'm so sorry. What exactly happened?"

"Rabbi, I don't know what happened. He was here one minute and the next minute, he was gone. No warning, no sound. Nothing. He was just gone! We were sitting in the living room talking, planning a trip to Israel after the Holidays. There was nothing I could do. I called the police. They were there within minutes with an ambulance. Maybe if I knew CPR, I could have saved him! I had been planning on taking lessons." Mrs. Fieldstone's eyes were filled with tears, yet she held herself with composed dignity.

"No, I have had many cases like this, Mrs. Fieldstone. CPR would not have helped." Eric did not know if it would have helped or not, but her husband was dead, nothing would bring him back. He had to say something to comfort her.

"You know my son, Marc, Rabbi?"

"Yes, of course. I'm very sorry, Marc." He put his hand on the eighteen-year old's shoulder. "I am truly sorry."

"I know." Was all Marc could say. He was trying very hard to hold back tears.

"Please sit down," Eric motioned to the couch and chairs as he went back to sit behind his desk, when there was another knock on the door.

"Oh, that's my daughter. She was parking the car. Come in, Dawn." Mrs. Fieldstone said before Eric could get to the door.

The door opened and a very tall, slim woman stepped into the room. Her light blonde hair was pulled back to the nape of her neck with a clasp. She had an olive tanned complexion with striking almond shaped eyes. Large golden rings hung from her pierced ears. She was dressed in a form-fitting dark brown leather suit with a light blue kerchief around her neck, accenting her blue eyes.

"I thought I'd never find a parking place! It's as bad here as in the city."

Eric rose to meet her. "I am really sorry about your father, Dawn."

"Thank you." She turned and sat on the couch with only a glance at Eric. Her presence made Eric feel uneasy.

"I got home only yesterday," Dawn continued talking. "at least I got to spend some time with Dad before…" She bit her lip, took a deep breath, and turned her head to the window.

"Dawn's been away in Europe for some time, Rabbi. She just returned to spend the Holidays with us."

"Oh, were you studying in Europe?" Eric asked, feeling stupid over the question.

"No, just traveling around with some friends."

CHAPTER 16

Eric nodded his head in reply and began to discuss the funeral and the kind of eulogy they wanted. Throughout the entire time, he had difficulty keeping his eyes off Dawn.

As the Fieldstone family was leaving, Dawn lingered behind. As she started to walk out of the office, she suddenly turned around and faced Eric, looking directly into his eyes. He had walked the family to the door and was standing right behind Dawn when she turned around. She took step forward and placed her hand on the lapel of his jacket. "Oh, Rabbi," she barely whispered in a soft voice, "please," she hesitated, "please try not to make us cry at the funeral. I don't know how much more I can stand." Eric instinctively knew she wanted him to take her in his arms to comfort her, but he stepped back. Her slim fingers with the long, red nails commanded his attention. The almond eyes and long nails reminded him of a cat stalking prey.

During the Shiva period, the days of mourning, Eric was at the Fieldstone's home both morning and evening to lead the prayers. Mr. Fieldstone had owned a leather factory and had been a long-time community leader. Many people were coming and going to pay their respects to the family. Mrs. Fieldstone, Marc and Dawn were kept busy constantly greeting and thanking all those who came. Dawn, however, made a special effort to be the one to always greet Eric at the door with a warm smile. She also always sat close to him wherever he was. He had an uncomfortable but rather pleasurable feeling that her eyes were always on him. He enjoyed the little game that was going on between them, which each pretended didn't exist.

On the last day of mourning, Eric gave his usual speech of how the family must now turn to their own lives. They could not bring back the past, but they must now look to the future, fortified by memories. "If any of you need me, if only to talk, I'm as close as the telephone. Please don't hesitate to contact me."

During the following week, Eric made an evening 'phone call to the Fieldstone home to inquire about them. He had hoped to get Dawn on the 'phone, but Mrs. Fieldstone answered. "Yes, Rabbi, thank you so much for calling. You have been a great comfort to us all. George had prepared for everything. He was a highly organized person. Everything has already been arranged for our care. The only problem I have now is trying to fill the terrible hole in my heart. I feel as if a part of me has been torn out of my soul. I miss him so much!" She began to sob.

"Tim is a great healer, Mrs. Fieldstone. Just try to believe each day will be easier."

"Why did God take him away from me, Rabbi, why?" He was just 58 years old. He was in the prime of his life!"

"I can only answer your question with a question. Why did God give him to you for 35 years? Why did God give you so many years of happiness, of love, of sharing contentment? The soul belongs to God. He only took back what he had lent to you. Try to be grateful for the time George and you had together. I know it is exceedingly difficult now for you. I know you are suffering, but in time, things will be better. Just hold onto your strength. Your children need to see that strength in our now."

"You're right, Rabbi. Thank you very much. Thank you for calling. I will be at services Saturday morning."

"I'll look forward to seeing you, Mrs. Fieldstone. May God comfort you and bring you peace."

"Thank you. Goodbye."

Eric gave a sigh of relief as he hung up the 'phone. It always irritated him when people cried. "Why did God do this to ME?" They think they should be excluded from all sorrow. How slow they were in thanking God for the good things they had in life! He looked at his watch. 9:47 pm. "I think I'll take a shower and get to bed," he said to himself. Wearily, he stood up from his desk and headed towards the bathroom when the doorbell rang. "Who in the hell can that be?" he muttered with annoyance.

When he opened the door, he was surprised to see Dawn Fieldstone standing before him.

"Dawn, what is it? Are you all right?"

"May I please come in, Rabbi?"

"Of course." Eric stood aside and motioned her to come in.

"Oh Rabbi, I'm so sad and lonely. I miss my father so much!" Dawn stood close to him. Caught by surprise, Eric did not respond immediately. Then professional integrity guided him to move away.

CHAPTER 16

"Come, Dawn, sit in the living room and let's talk. Would you like a cup of tea or a cup of coffee?"

"No," Dawn sobbed. "I want to just talk, please?"

"Dawn, I can't take the place of your father. I'm sure your father would have wanted you to be strong enough to face this adversity in your life. Come, please sit in the living room." Eric again motioned for her to move.

She sat on the couch, taking off her shoes, and folding her legs under her. Eric sat on a chair near the couch with an uncomfortable feeling that Dawn was taking control of the situation.

"Why won't you sit beside me? Don't you find me attractive?" She pouted.

"To the contrary, Dawn. I find you extremely attractive. That's why I'm sitting on this chair and not next to you," he responded with a grin.

Dawn laughed. "Thank you. You're quite handsome yourself!"

Eric instinctively pulled back. "I don't think you came here tonight for us to complement each other." He felt he was again gaining the upper hand.

Dawn stiffened. The tears had abruptly stopped. "Why are you so formal with me, Rabbi? Why

Can't you be as warm toward me as you were during Shiva?"

Eric reached over to the couch and took one of Dawn's hands. "I'm sorry if you misinterpreted my expressions of compassion and sympathy for you and your family. I did not mean to give you any special ideas," Eric lied convincingly.

"Oh Eric. Do you mind if I call you Eric?" She did not wait for his reply. "Your old-fashioned principles are adorable." She placed her hand on his. "I have been married before, and it's not like you would be seducing me!" Eric felt the ball of control bounce back onto Dawn's side of the court.

Eric extracted his hand and leaned back in his chair. "How long were you married?"

"Only two years. I made a big mistake. He was a real jerk. He was probably after my money!"

"I'm sorry," Eric said without any feeling of regret.

"Don't be. I'm not."

"How long have you been divorced?"

"Only a couple of years. That's why I spent a year in Europe. To get away from it all," Dawn responded with a sigh.

"How do you feel now? Have you been able to get over it?"

Dawn suddenly arose. "I really don't want to discuss it. I think I'd better go."

Eric also arose and began to walk her to the door. "Are you okay now? You were pretty upset when you came in."

"Yes, I feel better now. Thank you so much." Suddenly she turned around, kissed him on the lips with an open mouth, at the same time, pressing her body against his. Eric, again caught by surprise, did not push her away or respond in any way, but stood stunned. Just as quickly, she backed away from him with a mischievous grin. "Just a wee sample of something good, in great appreciation for all your kindness." She was gone, closing the door behind her before he could answer.

Eric did not sleep well that night. In fact, he did not sleep well for the next few nights. The aroma of her perfume lingered with him and the thought of her warm, wet kiss aroused him."

Thursday night at dinner in Rachel's house, Eric told Paul and Rachel of his experience with Dawn. To his surprise, neither of them laughed or teased him. Rachel frowned, evading his eyes.

"What's the matter with you two? Are you jealous that gorgeous women fall for me?" he laughingly asked. "Paul, I bet you wish it could happen to you. Your collar probably chases them all away from you."

"To the contrary, I'm considered a challenge for women. You would be surprised at the hints and passes I get!"

"Really?" Eric acted amazed, but he wasn't. He had heard numerous stories about women attracted to priests.

"And remember," Paul continued, "I also listen to confessions. I'm not going to say that some of them don't make me sweat under the collar, and many times I've been glad there is a partition between us."

"But aren't you ever really temped?" Eric asked seriously.

"Yeah, sure, but when I look in the mirror and I always see the white collar, then I am able to regain my composure."

CHAPTER 16

"That's what the *tzizies* (fringes) are supposed to do for Eric, but Eric tucks them in so he can't see them," Rachel teased.

Eric turned to Rachel, remembering her earlier look of reproof. "Why are you against Dawn? You don't even know her!"

Rachel lowered her eyes. "She was at the University for almost a year."

"So?"

"She flunked out."

"Sol? Her marriage was souring. Maybe that was the reason she couldn't keep her mind on her studies."

"She couldn't keep her mind on her studies because she had her mind on the men."

Eric responded with anger in his voice. "I can't believe I am hearing this from you, Rachel! She told me she just spent a year in Europe with her friends to try to get over her divorce."

"She spent a year in Europe with Dr. Patrick Fitzgerald who was on a sabbatical to write a paper on literature. She paid for the trip for both of them."

"How do you know all of this?" he demanded of Rachel. He felt a knot in his stomach.

"It's the scuttlebutt of the whole faculty. Eric, I'm truly sorry. I hate to be the one to tell you, but you are my friend." Rachel reached out to put a hand on his arm, but Eric pulled away from her.

"Eric," Paul began, "No one is telling you what to do. Rachel is just warning you of a possible dangerous situation. It is up to you to make your own decisions. Rachel would never hurt you. You should know that. She's only trying to warn you of potholes before you fall into them. In fact, this is the first time I have ever heard Rachel say anything derogatory about anyone."

"Why am I so angry? I hardly even know Dawn," Eric thought to himself. He took a deep breath and forced himself to smile. "I know you both are just thinking of my welfare. I appreciate it, really, I do. Sorry if I blew up. It really wasn't fair of me." His mouth spoke words that his heart did not feel.

"Oh, come now! Rachel responded with a full smile. "You're not getting married! What are we so concerned about? If you want to have a little fun, Eric, you are certainly entitled to it. None of our business, right Paul!"

"Right!" Paul lifted his coffee cup. "Here's to your friend, and here's to you, Rachel. Wonderful meal, kosher food is not so bad after all, but when are you two going to try a big ham steak for a change of pace?"

"At your wedding, Father!" Rachel and Eric replied in unison, bursting into spontaneous laughter.

CHAPTER 17

THE FOLLOWING WEEK, Rachel telephoned Eric and Paul and told them, without explanation of her destination, that they were on their own for their weekly meal together because she would be gone for a few days.

"Where does she disappear to every couple of months?" Paul asked Eric.

"I don't know, I really don't. It used to drive me up the wall. In fact, it still bothers me, but I guess she is entitled to her privacy."

"I guess so, but I always wonder if she's all right," Paul said. He did not want Eric to know how very much he missed her.

"Oh, she comes back, spirited as ever. I think she just needs to get away by herself occasionally," Eric said. "She hates being taken for granted."

"Boy, that is some independent woman!" responded Paul.

"You don't know the half of it, Paul."

Eric invited Paul to his house for the usual weekly dinner, but Paul insisted on bringing the food. He bought falafel, chummus, and various salads from a kosher restaurant. "Not as good as Rachel's cooking," Paul said, "but it's something different."

"My favorite kind of meal," Eric truthfully answered. He missed Rachel too, but he enjoyed eating alone with Paul. He enjoyed the male companionship as well as the discussions they had regarding their philosophies of religion and world events. This night Eric found himself talking with Paul about Dawn.

"Have you ever had a personal relationship with a woman, Paul? I mean before you became a priest?"

"Oh sure," Paul replied as he thought of Nancy with a feeling of revulsion.

"I mean," continued Eric, "having a woman get under your skin, where you think of her a lot."

"Oh, yeah, I sure have," Paul answered in a matter-of-fact way.

"I mean like a fulfillment of the Biblical commandment, 'Man shall leave his father and his mother, and shall cleave unto his wife and they shall be one flesh.' You know, a woman is supposed to make a man feel whole, complete, to be his other half. I think when a man marries a woman, there should be a sense of that completeness."

"What are you driving at, Eric?" asked Paul. "Are you talking about Dawn? Does she give you a feeling of completeness?"

"No. I mean yes. Yes, I'm talking about Dawn, but no, she doesn't give me a sense of completeness." "What is it that attracts you to her, Eric?"

"Well," Eric hesitate and looked at Paul. His face was sincere without any trace of anything except genuine interest. "Well, to be truthful, there is a sexuality about her that causes my blood to rush to my temples and pound."

"Uh HU!" Paul responded with a smile.

"Oh, cut it out and be serious!"

"Sorry, Eric, it was too good to let pass without comment. So, what is it that bothers you? Is it what Rachel told you about her?"

"No, even if it's true, I sincerely believe in giving a person another chance. We all make mistakes. I know you fully understand the conception of forgiveness."

"Of course, you're right. What is it then that bothers you?"

Eric gave a big sigh and sat back in his chair. "I feel a certain tension between us."

"What kind of tension? What's causing it?"

"I think it's a power struggle. Each of us is trying to control the other one. But you know what? I even find that tension attractive. When I feel I am in control, that I have control over her, it is like I get a 'high.' Do you understand me?"

Paul thought of his father. All his life, he had tried to fight the control his father exercised over him. He did not like Eric at that moment.

CHAPTER 17

"Do you actually think it is right for one person to try to control another?" Paul tried not to let his disdain sound in his voice.

"No, of course not. It's not that kind of control, like a master over a slave. I guess it is more like not allowing her to control me."

"Oh?" Paul responded with a shake of the head.

"I could see in Dawn my whole world. She could be my perfection. She is beautiful, extraordinarily so, has social graces, dresses like a million bucks, which by the way, she has. And I really don't think I would be such a bad catch either. At least she seems to think so. She has told me that she thinks I am good-looking and so on." Eric sounded as if he were trying to convince himself rather than Paul.

"Eric, compliments and beauty do not make a mutual completeness. Each person has a different kind of need for completeness. What does she want from you? What do you want from her? Do your spirits blend? Do your souls unite as one being? Paul felt as if he were counseling a couple contemplating marriage.

"I don't know. I am very stimulated and excited when I'm with her."

Paul continued. "Do you feel an inner peace? Do you feel you can be yourself without any feelings of rejection, or do you feel you always have to please her?"

"That's one of the things that bothers me, Paul. Yes, I have feelings of peace, but not inner peace. I don't know what it is. I think maybe I'm being extra cautious because I was so hurt by my first wife, Sandra. I thought she was all I ever wanted in life, too! Maybe I'm scared to start over again!"

"Are you thinking of marriage? You just met her, you really don't know Dawn that well, do you?" Paul felt sad without knowing why.

"Paul, I really don't feel like playing the dating games. Whenever I go out with a woman, I immediately think whether or not she could be right for me."

"I can understand that. But don't you think you should get to know Dawn a little better, especially since you have all these doubts and hesitations... right?"

THE SECOND GENERATION

"I guess so, Paul. You know, you're lucky. Priests don't get married. You don't have to worry about choosing the right girl or having a failed marriage."

"I sometimes think about it, Eric. I am only human. It would be nice to come home to a loving wife, children… to have all the everyday worries of a family, as well as all the joys. I look at the families who come to church, and sometimes I envy them."

"Paul, you will always be part of my family. If I marry and have children, you will come to my home and share my family with me."

"Thanks, Eric, you're good to say that. I really hope you mean it – that it is not just a sympathetic expression of pity."

"Shut up and eat your falafel!" Eric responded, as the sound of the doorbell echoed through the house.

"Damn!" said Eric. "That damn bell always rings when I am eating, sleeping, or in the shower! I wish sometimes they would leave me alone!" He got up to answer the door.

Paul heard a female voice. "Oh, Eric, please forgive me for not calling first, but I just had to see you!"

"It's okay, come on in. I have a guest, but you're welcome to join us." Eric said in a light, happy voice.

"Maybe I should come back later? I'm sorry to have butted in on you." The female voice was soft and breathless.

"Not at all, please come in." There was pleading in Eric's voice.

"Okay, if you really don't mind."

Paul was surprised to see Dawn. Her light blue eyes perfectly matched the glistening light blue silk dress she was wearing. Her blonde hair caressed her shoulders and framed the cleavage of her olive-skinned breasts. She was a picture of perfection down to the tiny ankle bracelet between her graceful leg and tiny foot. Paul jumped up and said "Hello" without waiting for an introduction.

"Why hello," Dawn responded with a polite nod of her head. "I am pleased you are not a female!"

Paul was thrown off guard. "I beg your pardon?" He felt stupid.

Dawn flipped her hair back with a laugh. "I am just happy I don't have any competition with Eric."

"I don't think any woman could compete with you," Paul answered, feeling uncomfortable. "I think I ought to go."

CHAPTER 17

"No," Eric quickly answered, "please don't go. Stay a while longer."

"But, Eric, maybe the gentleman has things to do. It isn't nice to keep him here against his will." Dawn's words were light and faintly teasing.

Eric's face reddened. "No, Dawn, this is my very good friend, Paul Steiger. He is a priest, and we have dinner together every week. Today is the day we meet to eat and talk together. You are most welcomed to join us, but Paul stays!" Eric's voice was definite.

Dawn immediately apologized. "Paul, I am SO sorry! I didn't mean to say you had to leave because I was here! To the contrary, I would love to talk with you. I just thought that maybe you were ready to leave and out of... uh... manners, Eric did not want me to think you were leaving because of me so I thought I was giving you a way out... oh dear, am I rambling?" She put her hand to her mouth.

Paul felt uneasy... as if he were the ball in a tennis match over which he had no control. Their contest for dominance began to jangle his nerves.

"That's okay." He heard himself speaking. "I really do have to go." He registered a little smile on Dawn's face and the grimace on Eric's face. "I'll just take my falafel, if you don't mind." He reached over and rewrapped the sandwich, placing it back in the bag. "See you tomorrow, Eric. Okay? Dawn, nice to meet you."

"Likewise," Dawn replied, smiling with satisfaction.

At the door, Eric put his arm around Paul's shoulders. "Please, Paul, I don't want you to go. I really look forward to and enjoy our dinners together."

As Paul stepped out of the door, he felt the uneasiness leave him. It was a sense of freedom. "It's okay, Eric. I don't feel comfortable." He leaned towards Eric and whispered, "And I don't think she is making a business call. Be careful, my friend."

"What do you mean?" Eric asked, visibly embarrassed.

Paul shrugged his shoulders and placed his hand over his heart, "Aw, sweet love, I adore you!" he clowned.

Eric laughed lightheartedly, "Don't worry! I have everything under control."

Paul went down the steps as the door closed behind him. Sitting in the car, he opened his falafel and began to eat as he started the car. He was annoyed with Dawn's interrupting his time with Eric. "I should have taken a drink too," he thought as he drove off.

Eric returned to the room in fury to face Dawn. "It is MY home!" he thought to himself. "She has no right to come in here and take control!" Dawn was not in the kitchen. He went to the living room – not there either. "Where in the hell did she go? Maybe she went to the bathroom?" He waited a moment and then called out, "Dawn, are you in the bathroom?"

A voice came from the bedroom. "No, I'm in here."

Eric's temples began to pound as he walked to the bedroom. Anger was fueling every nerve in his body. Dawn lay curled up on the bed crying. "I'm so sorry, Eric. Please don't be angry. You just don't understand. I'm not really like this. I just can't stand it anymore! I'm going crazy!" She began to shake all over as tears flowed down a face contorted with misery.

Eric's anger disappeared. "What's the matter? What has happened?" She was like a scared little girl, terrified of some evil approaching as she lay helpless. Eric, with a feeling of a brave knight in armor saving the beautiful maiden from the fierce dragon, gently wrapped a blanket around her and held her in his arms. "Everything will be all right. Don't cry. Sh-h-h." He rocked back and forth, holding her to his chest.

Dawn's head snuggled under his chin. "You are SO good, so kind, so wonderful, thank you, thank you so much!" she burst into tears again. "It's okay, it's okay." He patted her hair. The aroma of her perfume was intoxicating, and as he comforted her in his arms, he felt good… better than he had felt in a long time. The bed was soft and made a little squeaky sound as they rocked. It reminded him of the squeaky sound the old rocking chair had made when his mother rocked him in her lap when he was a little boy.

A deep sigh from Dawn brought his thoughts back to the bedroom. He moved back, raising Dawn to a sitting position facing him. He took both of her hands into his one. With the other hand, he brushed the hair out of her eyes.

"Now tell me, what is the problem!"

CHAPTER 17

"Eric, I'm sorry. I was rude to Paul. Do you think he like me? Can you forgive me?"

"That isn't what you are crying about."

"No, I am crying because something made me act in such a deplorable way!" She looked like she was ready to dissolve into tears again.

"Hey, don't cry," Eric said. "I can't stand to see tears. It tears me up. Please don't cry!"

"I'll try," Dawn whispered in a little voice. She swallowed hard, took a deep breath and began to talk as she looked straight into Eric's eyes.

"Ever since the first day I met you, I think I fell in love with you. If you remember, I didn't look at you that day in your office. I was afraid to! I know this is love because I have never felt this way in my whole life, not even with my husband. I never loved him. I know now because I love you, and what I felt or him was nothing like what I feel for you. You are everything I ever wanted in a man and you are a MAN, a true man, and I so admire you for that. I can't sleep. I can't eat. I think of you day and night, every minute you're in my mind and in my heart. Without you, I am a half a person, with you, I am a whole person. My soul cries to mate with your soul!"

Eric could not catch his breath. Her face looked so pure, so fresh, so innocent, like a child. He wanted to speak but he did not know what to say. "Dawn…" he began.

"Sh-h-h, don't say anything," she whispered as she took his hand and laid it just above her left breast. "Feel my heart… feel my heart speaking to you, begging for your love. " She took his other hand and placed the fingers against her lips. "Feel my lips quivering for your kiss." Her eyes were half-closed, her cheeks were flushed with excitement. "My body is aching for your love. Please I need you. I want you." She whispered as she unbuttoned his shirt, sliding her fingers inside, she began to lightly kiss his neck, lips trailing down his chest. A fireball exploded in Eric's brain, spreading throughout his body. The timing of their love making was perfection, and every muscle and nerve in his body tingled with ecstasy. With her warm body in his arms, he fell into a dreamless slumber.

When Eric awoke, all the lights were out. Soft candlelight on the night table and dresser reflected in the mirror, giving the room a warm, cozy, mysterious atmosphere. Dawn was kissing his cheeks, eyes, his lips. Her beautiful body softly reflected the candlelight. "Come, my love," she whispered.

Eric did not resist but allowed her to lead him as she glided towards the bathroom. Soft candlelight reflected from a bathtub filled with perfumed water. She motioned for him to get in the bath, stepped in after him, and kneeling astride is legs, she began to rub his shoulders and chest with something pleasantly creamy, forming little circles on his skin.

"In all my lifetime, I never dreamed there could be a man as perfectly satisfying as you are," she said in a soft, low voice. "Your timing was perfection, all your movements anticipating my ever need. I feel like a virgin who has experienced her first taste of love, granted by an Apollo of love, the epitome of masculine strength. My body tingles still with desire for you." She eased forward as Eric pulled her to him, the warm water rippling around them.

When Eric awoke the next morning, Dawn was gone. His first thought was, "Was I dreaming?" He looked around. Melted candles were on the night table and dresser. He got up and went to the bathroom. When he opened the cabinet over the sink to get his razor to shave, there was Dawn's perfume bottle. He took it in his hand and smelled it. Memories of the night somersaulted through his mind. He crawled back into bed, drew her pillow close and dropped into the abyss of sleep.

CHAPTER 18

TO ERIC'S DELIGHT, Dawn wanted to study Hebrew, all the great books, the Torah, the Talmud, and the Midrash. She wanted to learn everything. In the ensuing months, between sessions of love-making, they would sit for hours together, Eric teaching her commentaries and thoughts of the great sages. She was a brilliant student, eagerly learning with expressions of admiration for Eric. Several times, she brought up the idea of marriage. Eric confessed that he also was thinking of the same thing, but that he felt he was not quite ready for such a commitment.

One day when they were studying the laws about keeping a Jewish home, Dawn again brought up the subject of marriage. "Eric, I have a biological clock ticking. I know I am still young, but I want to live to see my grandchildren. I don't want to be changing diapers when I'm in my late 40's. And I don't think it is fair to children to burden them with older parents at young ages. You aren't getting any younger either, you know."

"I know, Dawn, and I understand what you are saying. But every time I start to think about marriage, I get the jitters. I've had a pretty bad experience once, and I just don't know if I could bear to go through another one."

"I feel the same way, Eric. Remember I also had a bad experience and, furthermore, I think everyone gets the jitters before they get married. But just look how happy we are together! I would be a good wife and a good mother."

"I have no doubt about that, Dawn. But to be truthful, I am not comfortable with you when we are with others. When it is just you and me together, it's heaven and everything I have ever dreamed of, but I'm a Rabbi, and that means I must be with other people. They depend upon me; I must be available whenever I am needed. I can't just be with you."

"I feel the same way when we are in public together. It is because we are, in a way, living together and we feel guilty about it in front of people." Dawn said.

"I think we've been very discreet," replied Eric.

"Of course we have! But don't fool yourself. People know I spend nights here. They know we certainly have something going between us. They are just being very nice because they think we are made for each other, and they fully expect us to be married. Once we're married, those feelings of guilt and discomfort will go away."

"I don't know, Dawn. I would like to work it out before we get married, not afterwards. Please be patient a little while longer. It'll be better for both of us, and we will have a more solid marriage."

"I'm sorry, Eric, I live you very much. I will always love you. I'll never love anyone else the way I love you, but I can't wait any longer. People may not judge a man by the same standards in a situation like this, but they see the woman as a person of questionable character and morals."

"That's not true! No one is saying anything! But if you feel this way, then maybe we ought to part for a while and not see so much of each other?"

"No, not just to part. I'm going to start looking for someone else, someone who's not scared to get married."

"Wait a minute. You mean that after what we have shared together, you want another man touching you?" Eric felt sick.

"What you mean is that you could not bear for another man to make love to me, Eric. It's none of your business what I could or could not want. That is not what we are discussing. I am telling you right now, either we make plans to get married soon, or I'm out looking for someone else. I cannot afford to waste any more time with you, regardless of how enjoyable and satisfying it may be." With those words, Dawn arose from her seat on the couch, picked up her coat, and went out, slamming the door behind her.

Eric sat stunned. He thought of her in bed and in the bath with another man. His heart palpitated, and sweat poured from his body even though the room was quite cool. "Maybe she's

CHAPTER 18

right," he thought, "maybe I'm not comfortable with her in public because I am a Rabbi, and we are sleeping together." At the same time, he felt anger flow through his body. "How could she do this to me? How could she love me as much as she says she does and still do this to me? She's bluffing... yes, that's what she is doing... she's bluffing... give her a few days without calling her and she'll be back. She'll call me, begging to come back!"

That night Eric rushed home after minyon and waited for the phone to ring. He definitely wasn't going to call Dawn. He tried to study but his eyes kept lifting to the clock. Finally, at 10:00 p.m. the phone rang. Eric's heart jumped with happiness. "It's Dawn," he thought. He picked up the phone and tried to say hello without betraying his feelings.

"Hello, my Erickale, how are you?" It was his mother. He tried not to sound disappointed.

"Just fine, Mama, how are you?"

"Could be better, but at my age, I'm happy to be as well as I am."

"Come on, Mama, you're still a young chicken."

"More like an old soup hen," she replied. "But I didn't call to talk about me. I want to know how you are and what's doing with you?"

"Ma, how would you feel if I got married again?"

"Is she Jewish?"

"Of course she is! Have you forgotten I am a Rabbi! Come on!"

"I mean are BOTH her parents Jewish? Is one a convert?" asked Mrs. Froman.

"Ma, cut it out. No, both of her parents are Jewish. They are members of my congregation. Her father died about a year ago."

"Do I know her?" asked his mother.

"I think you met her. Remember when you and Papa were here for the Chanukah party?"

"Yes."

"Remember there was a tall blonde girl wearing a brown leather suit standing next to me?"

"That's one's not for you, son."

"Why not? What do you mean she's not for me. You don't even know her!" Eric's words were sharper than he intended.

"I didn't survive the concentration camps for no reason. I can look at her and know what kind of person I am seeing and I say she is not for you."

"But Ma, she is intelligent, she's beautiful… she's everything I have ever wanted in a woman and I love her!"

"So why aren't you comfortable with her in public?"

"What makes you think I'm not comfortable with her in public? Where did you get that crazy idea?" Eric always hated it when his mother was able to see the things he felt. It made him feel like a little boy who got caught with his hand in the cookie jar.

"Even a blind person could see you don't like her trailing after you all the time. Being comfortable with her in bed is not enough for marriage!" Mrs. Froman said without hesitation.

"Ma, I hate it when you condemn somebody you don't even know!"

"I don't have to know her. I know YOU and that's all that is important to me."

"Then you should know that this is a woman who will make me happy!"

"She will not make you happy. She will only cause you grief and give you a lot of sorrow. She's a very selfish, jealous woman!"

"How do you know that?!" Eric was curious now.

"I watched her face when you talked to other people, especially other women. She didn't like it at all!"

"Ma, that is only insecurity. After we are married and she feels secure, she won't be like that!"

"Oh no? Listen to me, son, she'll be worse. These kind never understand. They have a sickness, a need to control, and when you speak to other women, they are afraid of losing their control over you."

Eric's impatience was returning. "Ma, please do me a favor, let me bring her to dinner and let you talk to her. You'll see she is really a wonderful person."

There was a big sigh at the other end of the phone.

"Please, Ma, give her a chance… give me a chance."

CHAPTER 18

"Okay, come this Sunday about 5:00. We'll have supper together and see what happens. I'll invite your brother and sister and we'll see how she fits into the family."

"Thanks, Ma. Thanks a lot! How's Papa?"

"Okay, thank G-d, Okay… I'll hang up now. I know you want to call her. Goodbye son." She hung up before Eric could reply.

As he replaced the receiver, the phone rang. It was Dawn, and she was crying.

"What can I do, Eric? I can't live without you. You're all I have in life. You are my life!" she stammered between sobs.

Eric, astonished at this about-face, thought, "What a change from the cold attitude Dawn had when she walked out of the house leaving me with an ultimatum." Her pleading and helplessness gave him a satisfying feeling of power.

"I don't get this. Why the big change-of-heart?" Eric was surprised at his own question.

"It's frustration from loving you and not being able to be a part of you. It's tearing me to pieces! I can't bear to lose you!"

Eric felt a need to punish her for the way she had made him feel when she threatened to leave him for someone else.

"Dawn, tell me something… does it bother you when I talk to other people… other women, when we are out together?"

"I don't know why I can't be with you, standing by your side when you talk with others. Why do you have to break away from me and leave me standing by myself all alone?" The tears had stopped. "Because I am a Rabbi and people want to talk with me, not with us. If we're going to be together, you must accept the fact that I must be a part of other people' lives, sometimes with you, but a great deal of the time without you."

"Does this mean you have changed your mind about getting married?" The excitement in Dawns' voice excited Eric.

"Can you come for dinner at my mother and father's house this coming Sunday… about 5?"

"You're damn right I can!" and again, she burst into tears.

"Now, why are you crying?" Eric asked.

"Because I'm so happy!"

Eric hung up the phone without the expected feeling of happiness. He had thought that when he made up his mind to give Dawn an engagement ring, his uneasiness about her would disappear. Instead he felt an even greater tension, an apprehension.

"Just the jitters because my last marriage failed," he tried to reassure himself.

"Dawn's intelligent, she certainly is attractive, and most of all, she dearly loves me." It was the first time in his life that he felt someone truly loved him. "The nervousness will go away once we are married," he told himself.

CHAPTER 19

AS THEY GATHERED around the dinner table at his parent's home, the conversation was reserved and deliberate. Everyone, including his brothers and sisters were unusually quiet. Dawn was the center of attention. Eric dismissed her open display of affection as evidence she did not know the customs of a Jewish orthodox family, where men and women do not touch each other in public. "She will learn," Eric thought to himself. He fingered the engagement ring in his pocket.

When the time came for dessert, Eric went into the kitchen. His mother had prepared a chocolate cake with chocolate icing. "Let me help you serve, Ma," he said to his mother. She did not reply but stepped aside, turning away.

Eric cut a portion of cake and on it, he placed the ring, standing up so that the stone was on the top. He covered the slice with a paper napkin. His mother did not see the ring. When she turned around and saw the napkin covering the cake, she asked, "What are you doing?"

"Ma. Go sit down. I have a surprise for you. I'll serve the cake. Come on, Ma, don't argue! Please do what I ask." He gave her a little boy look with pleading eyes. She laughed, pulled him down and kissed him on the cheek. Without speaking and with a deep sigh, she went to the living room.

Eric covered the other slices of cake, too, and placed them all on a serving platter. Returning to the dining room, he announced. "Mama has made her famous chocolate cake, so luscious. So scrumptious, even the eye must devour its beauty with one gulp, as if unveiling a masterpiece.

They all applauded and laughed, as Eric served the cake, slice by slice, each draped with a napkin.

"Do not uncover your plate until I give the word," he ordered.

As he sat down, with a twist of the hand, he announced, "Now! Uncover Ma's masterpiece!"

The napkins came off with a flair. When Dawn uncovered hers and saw the engagement ring, she shrieked with joy and tears streamed down her cheeks.

There was a dead silence at the table. Eric felt his heart fall.

"Well?" he demanded. "Aren't you going to wish us *mazel tov* – good luck?"

"Why of course!" said his sister, recovering first. "Mazel tov!" She raised her glass. "To many years of happiness and health!"

A ragged chorus of "Mazel Tov" followed her words.

Eric could not understand why he had a sense of panic and consternation, rather than the elation he had expected.

The next day, Eric phoned his mother. "Well, Ma, what do you think? What is your opinion of Dawn now?"

"Eric, you gave her a ring before you gave us a chance to get to know her. Our opinion doesn't matter since you have already made up your mind! Your father and I love you and, of course, we wish the best for you. If you are happy, we're happy. You are my child; I only wish the best for you."

"Is that all you have to say?" Eric asked with great disappointment. He wanted his mother to say how much she liked Dawn and how happy she was the Dawn was coming into the family. He wanted his mother to reassure him he was doing the right thing.

His mother, instead, turned the conversation to problems she was having with his father. Eric became impatient and angry with his mother. "I'd would like to listen to you, but I just don't have time now, Ma. Take care, talk to you later," he said as he hung up the phone.

The following Sunday during dinner at Rachel's house, Eric announced to his friends that he was going to marry Dawn. Instead of the congratulations he had expected, he was met with solemn faces.

"I don't understand you two!" He looked at them with anger rising within him. "Shouldn't friends be happy for me? What is wrong?"

CHAPTER 19

Paul responded first. "Sorry, Eric. Of course, you are right. Congratulations! I would be happy to perform the ceremony," he tried to joke with a wide smile, "free of charge."

"Thanks, Paul. And you, Rachel," he asked softly between clenched teeth. "Aren't you going to give me your blessings?"

"I'm sorry, Eric," she said as she lowered her eyes. "I cannot give my blessing on what is doomed to failure from the start, but I will wish you good luck." She hesitated for a few seconds and then added, "You are certainly going to need it!"

Eric became conscious of Paul's intent gaze. He suddenly felt estranged from them both. "Well! Thank you for that, Rachel!" He said more tartly than he had wanted. "It has been a long day. I am tired. I think I'll go home." As he arose, he motioned with his hand. "Don't get up. Finish your coffee. I'll let myself out." He grabbed his coat and left without saying goodbye.

Outside in the cool air, he took a deep breath and stood still for a few moments. The night was reminiscent of the time when he was called to the hospital the morning Jackie died. "Was it a premonition of impending disaster," he thought to himself. He felt a longing to return to his friends upstairs as he looked up at the lighted window. He needed to feel safe in the security of their friendship. He shrugged his shoulders. "This is stupid. Rachel is just jealous!" he told himself as he hunched up against the wind. He got in his car and turned towards home where he knew Dawn was waiting for him.

Up in the apartment, Rachel and Paul sat gloomily over their coffee. Paul laid his hand over Rachel's hand. She did not pull away.

"I'm sorry, Rachel."

Rachel looked at him, fighting to hold back her tears.

"What in the world for?" She tried to make her voice sound normal.

"You love him, don't you?" Paul asked, hardly above a whisper.

"Of course, I love him! He's the best friend I have ever had," Rachel replied, tears now streaming down her cheeks.

"I'm your friend too, Rachel," Paul said softly.

Rachel looked up at Paul, wiping her cheeks with the back of her hand and then placed her other hand on his. "Of course, you are, and I am truly thankful for your friendship." She had regained control of herself as she smiled at Paul.

"He loves you a lot, Rachel," Paul responded. "He told me once he would marry you, but that he would be afraid of losing his best friend also, if the marriage didn't work out."

"I believe that," Rachel responded with a laugh. "A wife you can dump any time. A good friend is harder to find."

"Would you want to marry him, Rachel?" A lump lodged in his throat when he asked the question.

Rachel looked at Paul with a queer little smile that made him uncomfortable.

"My God, no!" Eric is not my idea of a husband. He is a good soul, highly intelligent with a lot of untapped potential, but I would not want to live with him day in and day out the rest of my life. But then again, I really don't think I would like to live with anyone day after day the rest of my life."

Relief dissipated the lump in Paul's throat. "Then why are you so upset about his marriage to Dawn? Don't you think it is really his business? 'He makes his bed – he has to sleep in it', as the adage goes."

Rachel looked straight into Paul's eyes. "Paul, it's caring! It is like watching a moth fly into the flame of a candle. No, Paul, I don't intend to try to stop Eric from marrying Dawn, but don't you believe it is only right to warn a friend when we believe he is heading into disaster? I would do the same for you, Paul."

"For me?" Paul did not know why he was surprised to hear Rachel's words.

"Of course," Rachel answered. "If I thought you were heading into something that would be harmful to you, would you not want me to tell you or at least try to warn you?" She hesitated. "Wouldn't you do the same for me?"

Rachel's face was sincere. Warmth spread throughout Paul's being. He gently brushed back an unruly wave of hair from her eyes and let the back of his hand softly stroke the side of her face.

"Rachel, I would do anything to help you, to protect you, to make you happy. I would never let anything hurt you!"

CHAPTER 19

Rachel responded by touching Paul's face with her fingertips, ever so gently.

"Eric is so stupid," Paul said, But I'm glad he is." He pulled Rachel towards him and brushed her lips with his. At the touch of her lips, a pang of utter joy swept through his heart, and he shivered with delight. Fearful of her reaction, he quickly took her face in both of his hands. "I will always be here if you need me."

She smiled a light, bittersweet smile. "Thank you, Paul, you are a good friend." She pulled back casually, sitting up straight in her chair, and raised her shoulders with a deep sigh.

"I don't mean to chase you, Paul, but I am tired, really."

"I understand; so am I." He stood up, taking Rachel by the hand as she got up from the chair, slightly turning her so he could take her into his arms. He stroked her hair as he paced her head against his chest, under his chin. "Everything will be all right," he whispered. "Everything will be all right."

"Paul?" a small voice sounded from under his chin.

"Yes, precious one?"

"Ding, ding, ding, ding!" Rachel said sharp and clear. "That's a danger signal.......as they say in the old country.........we would hate ourselves in the morning." She pulled out of Paul's arms with an uncomfortable laugh. "You are really a wonderful person, Paul, and I am extremely appreciative of having you as my friend. Come on." She tucked her arm in his and led him to the door. As Paul went out, she pinched his cheek. "Thanks, Paul, for being here when I really needed a friend."

Rachel closed the door and walked to her bedroom. "Maybe I am jealous," she said to herself. "Maybe I am afraid of losing Eric." Within herself, she knew she did not really want to marry Eric, and even if she did, she couldn't. It would not be fair. It would be too much to ask of any man. Eric deserved better.

Paul walked to his car with a happy gait. Rachel was so easy to be with, so comfortable to hold. It was true. He had wanted to spend the night with her, just to hold her in his arms.....just to feel a female body next to his, without pressure, without tension, just a sharing...maybe, just maybe he could feel like a man again. Flashes of Nancy's naked body on the bear-skin rug flashed before his eyes.....he heard himself starting to breathe loudly..... his mind zoomed in on Nancy's naked breasts.....then he heard her cries. He felt helpless as her cries grew louder and the male voices counting pounded in his brain. He was having difficulty breathing. He leaned heavily against a tree, gasping for air. He tore at his throat as dots swam before him. "Please God, please help me," he begged, looking upward towards heaven, searching desperately for G-d. As he looked upward, he saw a small squirrel sitting on the tree limb above him, peering cautiously down. All was quiet again. He heard only the sound of the wind. "Squirrels don't come out at night. What are you doing up so late, little fellow? Your girl kick you out, too?" Suddenly, he saw the squirrel's head explode into a myriad of pieces. Paul heard a cry rip out of his throat, and he waited to hear the thump of the little body hitting the ground. Where was the sound? "Fall, damn you! Fall! Get it over with!" With rage he hammered the tree with his fists. A sharp pain tore across his check and he was startled to feel a wet warm oozing onto his fingers. A broken twig on the side of the tree had cut a gash in his face. "I must be going crazy," he mumbled to himself. In desperation, he again looked up to heaven, "Oh, Mother of Mercy, help me!" he begged. All he saw was the squirrel scampering up the heights of the tree. It wasn't dead! It was still alive! Exhilaration filled his heart. "It didn't happen! It is alive! Thank you! Thank you!" he cried in ecstatic happiness, tears flowing from his eyes. "It's alive!"

"Are you all right, Father?" The man's voice jerked Paul back to reality.

"Yeah, Yeah, I'm okay. I'm sorry. I guess I got sort of carried away.... I...... I.... was so happy to find out someone was alive whom I thought was dead. I guess I acted a little foolishly. I didn't know anyone was listening."

"Oh, that's okay, Father. As you always say, God is listening. I guess maybe you were talking with God?"

Paul did not hear any mockery in the man's voice. Blinking his eyes, he looked up and recognized an elderly man from his parish.

"Are you sure you're okay, Father?" The man handed Paul a tissue.

CHAPTER 19

"You know, Mr. McMillian, sometimes I just get tired, very tired. Maybe I should not tell you this, but my emotions get the best of me."

"Oh, that's all right, Father. I know what you mean. We all think of you as a man of God, but we know you are human too! You have a right to have emotions, especially of joy in finding out that someone is alive. Why, I think that's wonderful!"

"Thank you. Can I give you a lift home, Mr. McMillian?"

"Oh, no, thank you. The doctor says I must get exercise. I must walk. Good for the old pump, you know." His hand patted his chest. "I love to walk alone at night. It's quiet and I enjoy my memories."

"Okay, be careful. See you at Mass tomorrow."

"Sure thing, Father. You go on home and get some rest. Feel better."

"Thanks, Mr. McMillian." Paul got into his car, started the motor and drove slowly off, waving goodbye to Mr. McMillian.

"I can't go on like this. I have got to do something. I cannot go for therapy. If someone finds out, they will think I am crazy. And what would I tell a therapist? I am a priest. I am supposed to be strong, to help people with their problems. It is my father. He made me kill. Why did I have to kill that squirrel? Why did I have to go with Nancy to that party? Why did I have to become friends with Nancy?" It is my father's fault! He made me do it!"

Rage began building in Paul. His foot pressed stronger on the accelerator. "I tried to be a man, like my father wanted, and I lost my manhood. I will never know what it feels like to make love to a woman." Every time thoughts of a woman came to Paul, Nancy on the rug flashed before his eyes. Harder he pressed on the accelerator. Stronger became his rage, and the car zoomed down the street. He felt his face burn with heat of rage. The red flashes of the police car enraged him even more as his foot became heavier and heavier. Suddenly, a large white dog ran into the street in front of his glaring headlights. Paul instinctively jammed on his breaks, spinning the car completely around, the back-end smashing against a fire hydrant. Water shot up into a spray as Paul's head smashed against the steering wheel.

When Paul awoke, he was in the hospital emergency room. His head was aching, and he reached to feel for a wound. "What happened?" he asked the people around him.

"Suppose you tell us what happened?" one of the doctors said, as he looked into Paul's eyes with a small flashlight.

Paul closed his eyes and tried to think back. "A big white dog ran in front of my car and I jammed on the brakes to miss him."

"Why were you trying to outrun the cops?"

Thoughts began to filter back into Paul's mind. "I wasn't trying to run away from the police. My accelerator was stuck. I couldn't slow down," he lied. "How long have I been out?"

"About thirty minutes. How do you feel? The doctor held up a finger. "How many fingers do you see?"

"One. I'm okay. I just a headache. My head is too hard to crack. I'm okay. I want to go home." Paul swung his legs off the bed to get up. The room spun around him.

"Wooo....just let me rest for a few moments more."

"Maybe you had better spend the night here and let us make sure you're okay."

"No, I want to go home. Where is my car?"

"You can't drive. Is there someone we can call to come and get you?"

Paul immediately thought of Eric and Rachel, then dismissed the idea. It would not be appropriate for a priest to call a rabbi or a girl to come and get him.

"What time is it?" Paul asked.

"It is past midnight. Whom should we call?"

"No, no one please. I do not want to bother anyone this time of night. Maybe a cab. Where is my car?"

"We don't know. The policemen who brought you in are outside. Maybe you should talk to them."

"Yes, thank you." Paul slowly got off the bed. With all his strength he tried to act as if nothing happened. "Where are they?"

"That way." The doctor answered, pointing to the swinging doors on his right.

The police bought Paul's story of a stuck accelerator since there was no alcohol in his blood. They took him home in a police car and told him to pick up his car the next day at the impound lot.

CHAPTER 19

Paul felt completely drained as he let himself into his room. He looked in the mirror. The face that looked back at him seemed haunted. He pulled the bandage off his forehead, exposing a small cut on a large bruise. "Maybe it will knock some sense in my head." He smiled at the face in the mirror, but tears transformed the smile into a grimace.

Paul turned away from the image and fell upon his bed. "Oh, shit!" he mumbled as his eyes closed in exhaustion.

CHAPTER 20

WHEN ERIC ARRIVED home, Dawn greeted him at the door. She was wearing a soft white blouse and a long black skirt, both of silk, giving the illusion of clinging to her body and yet, flowing free. The house was lighted only by candles, which accented the sensuousness of her body. Bottles of chilled champagne were on the table in a large bowl of ice decorated with red rose buds. Cheese and grapes were attractively arranged on a platter with various kinds of crackers.

"Come, love," she purred, "let's make this a night to remember."

"I'm all for nights to remember," Eric responded as he took her into his arms. She began kissing his neck with slight licks of her tongue.

Eric reached for the buttons on her blouse. "You are so sexy; you drive me to utter madness!" he mumbled.

"Not yet, sweet darling," she stepped away. "Let's first have some champagne to celebrate. I have a special night prepared for you. Just for you, my sweet lover." Her half-closed eyes glistened with desire. "Leave everything to me, my precious. Let's just take off this naught shirt." She began to unbutton his shirt, slowly and deliberately.

The next morning, Eric did not go to minyon – the morning prayers. When he awoke, Dawn was dressed in a long white, form-fitted gown with colored flowers delicately embroidered on the sleeves, around the neck, and down the buttoned front. When Eric opened his eyes, she was sitting beside him, stroking his head.

"Wow," he said, "A beautiful angel awakes me from my earthly slumber. Am I in heaven?"

"Have you ever made love in the morning sunlight?" Dawn asked in a dreamy voice.

"No, I never cared for six in the morning," Eric frankly replied.

"We must cure that illness," Dawn cooed. "We begin with a glass of champagne!"

The champagne tasted cool and refreshing to Eric's dry throat. Dawn's steady, soft hands stroking his body brought a consummate pleasure.

After Dawn left the house that morning, Eric made up his mind to go through with the wedding. The nagging feeling of doubt, he told himself, would dissipate with time. "I am just afraid of marriage because of my past experiences. Everyone has these feelings of doubt before marriage!" he reassured himself.

Three months later, Eric married Dawn in the synagogue. The congregants had happily insisted on having the wedding in the sanctuary as a gift from the synagogue to their Rabbi and his new bride.

The Ladies Auxiliary catered the affair with bustling excitement, and the Men's Club arranged a special wedding canopy in his honor. Gifts filled his study.

As the ceremony began, Eric was disappointed that doubt still nagged him. He looked at the pale face of Rachel sitting next to Paul in the back role of the pews and his heart ached. Paul was dressed in a dark blue suit, white shirt, and stripped tie of all shades of blue. Jealousy tugged at Eric's heart as he realized that Rachel and Paul made a striking couple. A fury enveloped him as he imagined them in bed together. Something that belonged to him was being taken away.

"Eric, Eric, what is the matter with you?" His father's strong whispers brought him back to reality. He looked up. Dawn was coming down the aisle toward him, a magnificent picture in her cream-colored lace gown with its long sleeves and high neck, veil flowing from a small golden crown on top of her head. Through the veil, he saw her smiling at him.

Eric became aware that the people were whispering to each other. He wondered what they were saying. He looked again a Dawn. She looked like a beautiful princess. His eyes flashed to the seats where Rachel and Paul were sitting. He was sure he would see their approval of this wonderful woman he had chosen for his wife. Their seats were empty! Gloom and apprehension settled over Eric as tears welled in his eyes. For a split second he hated Dawn. Then he took her hand to lead her under the canopy. Surely, he loved her!?

CHAPTER 21

THEIR HONEYMOON IN Mexico was an affirmation, a reassurance, of their wedding vows. Mornings of breakfast on the balcony, of swimming side-by-side in the sea, of her glorious body stretched beside him on the sand. Afternoon siestas when their darkened room enclosed their passion, followed by blissfully sleeping in each other's arms. Dancing under the stars, candlelight dinners and whispered love words ended their days. But it was not to last.

When Eric and Dawn returned home and settled into married life, those honeymoon days retreated into a far-off and unimaginable distance. It would never be that good again. Though Eric loved coming home to a wife, he was not completely comfortable living with Dawn. She has a quick, sharp tongue that lashed out at him whenever he did or said something that did not meet with her approval. As a result, Eric was always on guard, as if a guest were in the house, and he had to be on his best behavior to make a favorable impression.

He tried to work out their disagreements, but in the end her tears would fill him with guilt and pity. She was able to turn situations around so he would feel it had been his actions or words that had caused the friction. Then she would cry and whimper, "You try so hard to please me, yet I continually embitter your life. Please forgive me."

"Everything will be fine," Eric would assure her. "These are little difficulties all married couples have. We'll work them out together. You'll see, we'll work it out." Many times, he held her in his arms as she sobbed, petting and cuddling her like a child. At those moments, Eric loved the sensation of being her protector.

Eric tried to include Dawn in his friendship with Rachel and Paul, but whenever she was with them, an uneasy tension was

THE SECOND GENERATION

created. The quiet comfortableness was gone. Conversations were strained as the four tried to mind a common ground.

"Why don't your friends like me?" Dawn cried one night as she sat on the bed.

Eric sat beside her and dried her tears. "Of course, they like you, Dawn, how could anyone help but love you? You're so lovable." He enfolded her in his arms. "You are just new. It takes time."

"It is Rachel's fault," sobbed Dawn.

"Rachel?" Eric sat back in surprise. "Rachel has never done or said anything bad to you! Why would you say such a thing?"

"She is your good friend," Dawn said. "I don't want to say anything about her."

Eric took Dawn by the shoulders. "What did Rachel do?" he demanded. "It seems to me she treats you very nicely."

"She acts nice to me in front of YOU, but when we're alone... like in the kitchen tonight..." she hesitated.

"What happened?" Eric's voice was rising with anger.

"Well, she was very nasty. She only talks to me in short, tart sentences. She hates me! She's jealous of me because I have you. I just know it, Eric! She wants to take you away from me! She wants to break us up!" Dawn's voice was near hysterics. Tears were flowing again. "I love you, Eric, please don't let her break us up! Please!"

Eric pressed Dawn close to him. "Nothing is going to happen. No one and I mean NO ONE will ever take me away from you or break us up! I love you, Dawn, I love you so much!"

"Hold me, Eric, hold me tight. I love you so much too."

Eric held Dawn, rocking back and forth with her on his lap. "Now, now, my precious soulmate, everything will be all right. Everything will be fine." Against Eric's chest, Dawn smiled to herself as she quietly whimpered.

The next day Eric went to see Rachel. As they sat drinking coffee, Eric searched Rachel's face. It was hard to believe that she would be rude to anyone; however, where jealousy is concerned, even the gentlest person could become a shrew, he thought to himself.

"Rachel, why is there always tension when Dawn is with us?"

"Eric, how long have we known each other?"

"Five, six years?"

CHAPTER 21

"In that time have you ever known me to lie to you, to fool you, or to play games with you?" Rachel asked.

"No. In fact, that is one of the reasons why I like you. There has never been any of the male-female shtick between us. We have always been honest and open with each other," Eric admitted.

"Do you trust me, Eric?" Rachel asked.

"With all my heart," Eric responded.

"You promise you will not be angry with me if I tell you the truth about the tension between us when Dawn is around?"

"I may not like what I hear, and I may not agree, but I promise not to be angry."

"Okay, there is tension when Dawn is around because she has an overwhelming desire to control. She does not know how to share in relationships, to be part of something. She wants to control and manipulate."

"Why do you say that? She is trying so hard when we are all together. I never heard her say anything I could call controlling." Eric was defensive.

"Think, Eric. When we are together, think of how she hangs onto you like syrup on a pancake. She extends no hand of friendship to either me or Paul. She spreads a net of possession around you which says, 'This is mine, keep your hands off!'" Rachel spoke in an even voice with no emotion.

"Don't you think it is just because she is insecure, that she hangs on to me? Are you sure all of this is not something you are reading into the situation?" Eric's defensiveness was increasing.

"Is that why she told me in the kitchen last night that you no longer need Paul or me because you have her now?"

"Are those your words or her words?" Eric demanded.

"Her words precisely." Rachel replied.

"What did you say?" Eric asked.

"I told her that you would make a lousy husband if your loyalty to your friends was so shallow that you could, with a flick of a hand, swap them in for someone else. How could she be sure of your loyalty to her if you had no loyalty for your friends?"

"What did she answer?"

"Nothing. She changed the subject. Eric, I don't want to interfere or make trouble between you and your wife. I will always be your friend. The choice is yours, whether you want to continue being my friend. In all the time I've known you, I have never given you ultimatums or made any demands on you, and I don't intend to do it now. I will try to get along with Dawn for your sake, but one cannot force friendship. It must be desired and cultivated by both parties. Just because I am your friend, doesn't mean I have to subordinate myself to your wife or to take any abuse from her!" Rachael's words were emphatic.

"Absolutely not! I certainly agree with you. But, please, let's keep trying to include her. I think it is still just because she is new and insecure. You don't understand. You have never been married and then divorced. To have a failed marriage is devastating. She is worried that this marriage won't work either. Please, give her a chance!"

"Fine, but I won't take any insults from her. If you try to force me to, then our friendship can't continue."

"Rachel, please, I value our friendship and I want it to continue. I need it. You are the only person with whom I can be myself and talk out of my heart." Eric did not plead but spoke in a statement of fact.

"Let's don't discuss it anymore, Eric. I am your friend. I shall always be your friend. If you ever need me, I am here."

"Thanks, Rachel. I know that." He put his arms around her and held her close to him. He felt a sense of warmth and contentment he never felt with Dawn. Dawn was exciting, beautiful, highly intelligent, and extremely satisfying sexually. But there was something missing he could not quite put his finger on, and he wasn't sure if he really wanted to know what it was. His attraction to Dawn was strong, but his peace and contentment was with Rachel. He gave Rachel a kiss on the nose and left.

"Where have you been?" Dawn asked as he came into the door.

"I stopped by to see Rachel," he replied nonchalantly.

"Why did you have to see her?" Dawn demanded. I'm here waiting for you are you are off with another woman!"

"I was not with another woman. I was with my friend!" Eric's annoyance was building.

CHAPTER 21

"What do you mean, YOUR friend? Who in the hell do you think I am?" Dawn's anger was building as well.

Eric tried to keep his voice controlled. "You are my wife and yes, you are my friend, too. But you cannot displace I have had for several years. I need to talk with her also!"

"And what about ME?" Dawn's voice rose, shanking with intensity. "You don't need her anymore. I am your friend. I am smarter than she is. You can talk to me! What secrets do you share with her?"

"No secrets. I just wanted to talk with my friend!" Eric shouted. "You cannot separate me from my friends. It is a different relationship!"

Dawn's hand smashed Eric across the face. Without hesitating, Eric slapped her back. Dawn fell to the floor, her lip bleeding.

Eric knelt instantly, appalled that he had hit her that hard. Guilt flooded over him. He picked her up and held her as he sat on the floor, kissing her eyes, checks and head. "I'm sorry, Dawn. Oh, my precious, I'm so sorry."

"Why are you so mean to me, Eric?" Dawn whimpered, tears streaming down her face. "I love you so much and I try so hard to please you."

"I'm truly sorry. But don't ever slap me. I will not allow anyone to slap me. I react without thinking. I cannot stand to be slapped?" Eric closed his eyes as the sting of his cheek brought back memories of the sting of the slaps his father gave him when he was a child. The words, "Little Nazi, I'll get you for disrespecting your father!" rang in his ears. From far off, he heard Dawn speaking.

"Eric, please try to understand. I am your wife. I want to be the only one, the most important person in your life. I want you to trust me with all your feelings, with all your secrets. Let's share everything just between us. Just you and me. We don't need anyone else in our life. You fill every need in my life. Let me fill your needs. Give me a chance."

"Dawn, don't you understand? I am an adult, a rabbi, and I cannot have only one person dictating my life, even though you are my wife. I am an individual. I want my individuality. I must interact with other people, and I need my friends. You are very special to me. Because you are my wife, I love you differently than anyone else.

You give me great joy and pleasure for which I am grateful, but I need to be my own person. I need my sense of individuality. I need a feeling of independence."

"I can't be fulfilled or happy if I know am not the ONLY important person in your life; the whole focus of your life!" Dawn's voice began to rise again.

"That's your problem, Dawn, something you will have to deal with. You cannot expect me to be subservient to you and your every whim. We are to share life together, not one to be the servant of the other."

"You made love with Rachel?" Dawn's question was demanding.

"No, I did not! What is the matter with you???"

"Have you ever made love with Rachel?" Dawn's question was demanding.

"No! What difference does it make?" Eric's answer reflected his impatience.

"I can't bear the idea of anyone else making love with you. It makes me feel inadequate." Dawn spoke more calmly. "Who were your lovers in your lifetime?"

Eric was resentful of her questioning. He felt his private life being violated. "Have I ever asked you the people you made love within your past, Dawn?" he replied. "You did not come to me as a virgin. What difference does the past make? It is the here and now, and the future that we will share together, that is what counts. Maybe I had 50 women and you had 50 men. I don't care. It is now and what is between us that is important!"

"Of course, you are right." Dawn answered. "As always you are sensible, and I have the brain of a twit. I just want to feel that you want me and that you desire me and that I am important to you in your life." Tears again began to flow.

"You are the most important person in my life, Dawn. I married you and no one else. Doesn't that make you the most important person over everyone else? We will work out our problems." Eric hugged, then kissed Dawn.

CHAPTER 22

ERIC WAS UPSET when Dawn hired a cook and a maid. "I don't cook," she said, "Neither do I clean. I like to keep my hands looking beautiful."

"All right, if you want to have a woman in a couple of times a week to clean, I don't mind. But a full-time maid and a cook? On a rabbi's salary, how can we afford such luxury?" Eric questioned.

"I have plenty of money, Eric. My father always kept me comfortable. You don't want me to lower my living standards, do you?" Dawn wheedled.

"But what will the people think? I am a rabbi of the people. My wife should also be one of the people, not a prima donna. People must be able to feel comfortable with you. You are raising yourself above them. That's not good for me or for you. I don't look right."

"Nonsense," Dawn retorted. "Warmth comes from within the person. They will just admire you for having a beautiful highly cultured wife. We'll make a good impression on everyone, not just your congregants. You will become great, and I will help you. After all, my love, we must appeal to the upper class too, the professionals, not just to the poor peasant of your congregation."

"Dawn, those so-called poor peasants are good people. They made a beautiful wedding for us. Have you forgotten?"

"Of course not! And I am certainly appreciative; but after all, we are THE Rabbi and THE Rebbetzen. We deserve their respect. Be realistic, my dear, the power lies with the rich. You don't want to be associated with 'poor nobodies' all of your life!"

Eric was angry at Dawn's words. He loved his congregation. "I don't like discriminating between people, separating the rich from the poor, or favoring the rich. Above all, I don't want to be an arrogant snob. I am a rabbi of ALL the people, not only of the rich!"

"Oh, come now, love. People judge you by whom you are associated with, you know that. Get in with the rich, and you'll go far. Hang around the poor, and you will remain unknown all your life. Is that all you want to be in your life – an unknown nobody? I certainly don't!"

"My congregation is different from my personal friends." Eric retorted.

"Your personal friends? Ha! A Catholic priest and a pudgy little whore! That's not exactly high society!" Dawn spoke with tight lips, chin jutting forth with defiance.

"Rachel is not a whore. She happens to be a professor at the University. She is not only educated but highly intelligent!" Anger was boiling over in Eric.

"Eric, she could have all the degrees in the world and have the encyclopedia memorized, but personally, she is so…so common. She is not exactly one of the 'beautiful people.' Sometimes I think all your taste is in your mouth, Eric."

"I married you, didn't I?" Eric shot back.

"To both our good fortune. Come, love, give me a kiss." She held out her arms to Eric, tilting her head to one side with a slight, tempting little smile. "Come, sweetheart, come to your Garden of Eden."

Eric's anger still burned. "Leave me alone." He turned his back to walk away. She encircled her arms around him from behind. "Gotcha," she laughed. He turned around and gathered her in his arms. "I don't know what you have, Dawn, but if you can charm everyone like you charm me, then there is nothing beyond our reach." Eric knew he had lost the argument, but what the hell, sex was best after they argued.

The next day in the late afternoon, Eric sat in his office thinking. Why wasn't he content? He could not get rid of the restless feeling that gnawed at him. He never knew there could be such ecstasy as when he was with Dawn. The chemistry between them was more than mere imagination. But their mundane, everyday life was not whole. Something was missing. "I'm just not accustomed to married life," he tried to tell himself. "I'll get used to it. It is just a matter of

CHAPTER 22

adjustment." The ring of his private phone broke his thoughts. He picked up the receiver. "Hello."

A familiar voice answered. "Hello there, Eric, are you busy?" It was Paul

"In fact, I am," answered Eric. "I am counselling a man here who is going to stab his wife with a dagger. Their son also is here, and he is having delusions from too much crack. He thinks he is a fly and keeps trying to walk on the ceiling. And their daughter, a beautiful, no, gorgeous hunk of female is begging me to make love t her. She finds me irresistible!"

"Game's up! I just spoke to Judy, and she said you were alone. Secretaries know everything."

"Damn, I thought I would impress you with my interesting cases of counselling and make you jealous," Eric laughed.

"No luck. Those people sound mild compared to some I get in the confession booth. How are you doing, Eric? How's married life? Must be good, 'cause we haven't seen you in a long time. Have you forgotten your old friends?"

"Nah. I think of you all the time. Uh, uh, who did you say was calling?" Eric teased. He was very happy to hear Paul's voice. How long had it been?

"Hey, Eric, it's been a long time since you and I have been over to Rachel's home. Rachel called and asked if we could come for an old-fashioned discussion, and I agreed. How about it? Supper, and a good old argument, like we used to have. Okay?"

Eric had deliberately stayed away from Rachel and Paul for the last few months, hoping to stabilize his marriage and relationship with Dawn. The invitation to be with his friends beckoned like an open door from a cage. His restlessness disappeared and a happy anticipation returned. "Sounds good to me. Sure, I'll be there! When is it?"

"Right now, unless you have some appointments."

"No, I can come now. See you in a little while."

"Great! Goodbye!" Paul sounded as happy as Eric felt, which added to Eric's cheerfulness.

Eric dialed his house. The maid answered the phone. "Froman's residence. Could I help you, please?"

THE SECOND GENERATION

"Matilda, please! I've asked you not to answer the phone that way. A mere 'hello' is sufficient!" Eric tried not to sound angry.

"But, Rabbi, Ms. Dawn said I should," insisted the maid.

Eric felt his patience ebbing. "Matilda, I don't think my wife yet realizes the importance of a clergyman being close to his people. That way of answering the phone is cold and indifferent. I'll speak with Dawn about it when I get home; but from now on, please just answer the phone with a simple 'hello.' Is that clear?"

"Yes, sir."

"Good. Tell my wife that I'll be late for supper." Eric hesitated. "Better yet, tell her I will not be home for supper. I will see her later."

"She will want to know what time she can expect you, sir, and she will want to know where you are going."

Eric held his temper with great restraint. "Did she tell you to ask me these questions, Matilda?"

"Yes, sir. She gave me instructions that in case you call with this kind of message, to find out where you are going and what time you plan to be home."

"Thank you, Matilda. Please tell Mrs. Froman that when I come home, she will see me."

"She won't like that, sir."

"Goodbye, Matilda." Eric hung up the phone in a fury. The walls of his study were closing in on him. He grabbed his coat and ran out of the door, slamming it behind him as if to lock in the stifling feeling that was choking him. For the last few weeks, he had been reporting to Dawn where he was, what he was doing, how long he would be there and when he would be home. He had thought at first, "What is the big deal? If it makes her happy and keeps peace in the house, so what?"

Etic went into the lavatory and splashed cold water on his face. He looked in the mirror as Rachel's words swam in his head. "She wants complete control, Eric. The tension comes from her inability to control."

Eric looked in the mirror at the black rings under his eyes. He had not been able to sleep well in the past few weeks. The feeling of relentlessness swelled up in his chest. "No!" he said with

CHAPTER 22

determination. "I will not let her control me! I don't have to get her permission. I am free to come and go as I please!"

Dawn's stern face, with the tightened lips and upraised chin, seemed to stare at him from the mirror. "You are tearing apart our marriage with your behavior. You cannot be married and still have all the privileges of a single man at the same time. You have a responsibility to make this marriage work!" She said with flashing eyes. "Stop being immature. Grow up! Be a man!"

The face in the mirror changed to his father's face. "Grow up! Stop being a child! It is time you were a man! Act like one! Be a man!"

Eric smashed his fist into the mirror. "No! You will not control me. I want my own identity!"

"Rabbi, Rabbi, are you all right? What happened? What broke?" Judy's voice sounded in alarm outside of the lavatory door. "Are you okay?"

"I….I…I'm okay, Judy, I, uh, I slipped and accidentally broke the mirror." Eric answered with a panting voice.

"Are you cut? Rabbi, please, open the door." Judy insisted. "Open the door."

"No, I'm really okay, Judy. I'll be right out."

"Well, I am waiting right here until I see for myself that you are all right," Judy adamantly replied.

"Damn women!" Eric muttered to himself. "Always bossing me around! "Can't do anything without women bossing me."

"What did you say?" Judy asked. "I didn't hear you."

Eric took a couple of paper towels and wrapped them around the cut on his hand. He ran water to wash away the blood that had run into the sink. Then he turned and flung open the door. "See, I'm still living! Sorry about the mirror. My mother always said I was a klutz!"

Judy looked at him suspiciously. She noticed he was holding one hand behind him. "Let me see that hand!" she demanded. Eric sheepishly held out the hand wrapped with paper towels.

"Uh huh!" she said, almost with satisfaction, her ponytail bobbing. "You are hurt! Let me see how bad!"

"Please, Judy, it's really nothing." Eric protested.

"I have four sons, Rabbi. I'll determine whether it is nothing or not. That's all I hear from my sons when they have been in trouble – 'it's nothing.'" She gently pulled off the paper towels and examined the cuts. "Could be worse," she stated with authority. "Come into m office, and I'll fix you up."

As Eric followed his secretary to her office, he thought to himself, "Why don't I mind when she bosses me around? Why does it infuriate me so when Dawn tries to do things for me or tell me what to do?" As Judy was fixing the cuts, Eric remarked, "With four sons, aren't you a little old to be wearing a pony-tail?" Judy shot a look at his face that had the innocent, earnest expression of a hound dog, then she deliberately put the tape of the bandage across the hairy part of his arm without saying a word.

The supper in Rachel's house was like old times. Eric was lighthearted and happy as if a tremendous weight had been lifted from him. How much he missed these weekly suppers at Rachel's house! How very much he missed Rachel and Paul! How good it was not to feel a constant state of tension! Eric kicked off his shoes, took off his tie, loosened the neck button on his shirt, and laid down on the couch. "It is good to be here," he said with a big sigh.

"It is good to have you back home again," Paul replied. Before anything further could be said, Rachel spoke, "I asked you over here for a special reason. I have something to tell you. I want you both to hear it."

Eric's heart fluttered. Paul had said it was good to have him back home again, and he was in Rachel's house. "Oh God, don't tell me that Rachel and Paul...." Eric held his breath.

"The mayor of Albany called me and said that the city wants to have a Holocaust Memorial event. They want a Remembrance Day which he would like me to chair..." Relief swept over Eric.

He released a chest full of air and took a deep breath. "Wow!"

"That is just the way I thought too," Rachel said. "Isn't it wonderful? If we can get the general population involved, then we can be sure the Holocaust will not be forgotten. If every year there can be a public memorial service or Remembrance Day, it will bring the Holocaust to the attention of the younger people. Then maybe its memory will be passed on from generation to generation as part

CHAPTER 22

of history. It will not die when the last survivor dies. So, my friends, this year, the first one of remembrance, must be exceptionally outstanding so that the city will institute it as a yearly observance and......" the phone interrupted her words. "Can both of you help me?" Rachel continued talking as she walked to the phone. "Hello."

An angry, tart voice said, "May I please speak to MY husband?"

Rachel turned to Eric. "I think this is for you, since you are the only 'husband' here." She held the receiver out to Eric.

Eric rose quickly and took the phone. "Hello."

"I don't think it is fair for you to leave me all alone while you run off to be with your whore!" Dawn spat out at him.

Eric's face turned red with restraint. "I will be home later, Dawn, I am busy now with important business."

"There isn't any business you have with her that you cannot have with me!" she replied. "You need me. You don't need her!"

"Dawn, this is not the time for discussion. I will talk to you when I get home."

"You will talk with me now!" Dawn demanded.

Rachel took Paul by his arm, "Come, Paul, help me get the dessert and coffee." They tactfully went to the kitchen.

"Dawn, you should not have called. I am busy and you are interrupting. I need a little freedom."

"From me?"

"Yes, from you."

"Am I so bad that you cannot stand to be with me? You would rather be with your whore?

"Now you're starting again. How many times must I tell you that you are wrong! I love you very much, but I need to work with other people. I need the independence to be with my friends occasionally, otherwise, I will lose my sanity."

Dawn's voice became soft and intimate, "But darling, don't you understand? Look at my side. You are away all day long with your counselling and your business, whatever you do, then you run to the hospitals at night. We rarely have much time together. I miss you. I want to be with you. I want to feel that you want me!"

Eric interrupted her. "You know as a rabbi; I can't keep set hours. At times, my work is 24 hours a day! You knew that when we got married, and you agreed. When people need me, I must be with them."

"I know that, love," Dawn was pleading, "and I don't mind you being with others; but when you have time off, I want you to rush home to be with me, not with another woman, not with someone else. I love you so much. I want you with me. Please come home NOW."

"I can't, Dawn. I'm in the middle of something very important. I understand and appreciate your feelings. We will discuss this later when I come home."

"When will you be home?" Dawn insisted on knowing.

Eric felt as if tight ropes were pulling across his chest, tighter and tighter. "I can't give you a definite time, but I will be home when I finish here," he answered.

"Okay, love heart, I'll be waiting with open arms. Don't be too long. I love you, Eric."

Paul and Rachel came back into the room carrying a tray of cakes, a coffee pot and cups.

"Me too, goodbye." Eric hung up the phone, rubbed his hands together, and said in a too bright voice, "Boy, oh boy, what do we have here? My favorite chocolate cakes!" "Everything okay, Eric?" Rachel asked.

"Yeah, sure," Eric replied nonchalantly. "Now what were you saying about the Holocaust Memorial Service?"

"I need your help. Can you both be main speakers?" Rachel replied.

"Paul, I still remember how you spoke a couple of years ago at the Holocaust Memorial Services in the synagogue. I liked it very much." Rachel commented.

Paul put his fingers to his mouth, "Aw gee, she likes me."

Rachel gave him a shove with a click of the tongue. "Can you come up with a topic?"

"I can speak as a humanitarian; that is, to speak on the human qualities that existed during the most inhuman time of our history."

"Excellent," Rachel smiled then turned to Eric. "What do you think your topic should be?"

"Well, my parents will probably be there, Rachel. I don't want to hurt them. I don't want to speak on private matters."

CHAPTER 22

"Okay, good point."

"I can talk about how the lives of Second-Generation children have been affected – positively and negatively, tell of my studies in the field. The idea is to let the people know that the Holocaust was not just a single horrible incident in history to be studied along with all other historical tragedies, but that it has affected generations of people and will continue to do so in the future." Eric was excited. He loved working together with Paul and Rachel. They made a good team.

"Oh yes, that is a most interesting topic," Rachel agreed. "One last thing. I would like to see both of your speeches before you give them."

Paul and Eric looked at each other. "She doesn't trust us."

"No, it is not that. I just want this whole program coordinated to perfection. I am asking to review ALL the speeches, not only yours." Rachel's face colored in embarrassment.

"Yes, Mommy," Eric teased.

"I want to do what Eric does," Paul joined in the joking.

"Naughty, naught," Rachel was not to be outdone. "Priests are not supposed to do things like that!" She shook her finger at Paul.

"Hey," Paul suddenly became serious. "Do you realize something?"

"What?" both Eric and Rachel asked together.

"This Holocaust service is our anniversary. Let's go out afterwards and celebrate." Paul excitedly suggested.

"Right on!" Eric lifted his coffee cup. "Here's to our friendship forever."

"Amen!" said Rachel and Paul together as they clicked their cups to Eric's in response.

"How about something better than coffee?" Rachael disappeared into the kitchen and came back with a bottle of wine.

"I'll drink to that," said Eric.

"Here's to friendship!" toasted Paul.

"I'll drink to that," chimed in Eric.

"Here's to a successful program!" added Rachel.

"I'll drink to that!" repeated Eric.

"Here's to Rachel, our hostess!" exclaimed Paul

"I'll drink to that!" laughed Eric.

With each toast, the laughter heightened, releasing all anxieties. Time stood still. Worries, tensions, and pains were forgotten as each basked in the others' friendship. They were again children without the difficulties of childhood.

Tears arose in Eric's eyes as he suddenly understood why he resented Dawn's displays of friendship. With Dawn, every action was a swap-off for something she wanted. He did not trust her sincerity of intention. He could hear her words, "After everything I have done for you! What about me? Why do I always have to sacrifice? Where are your sacrifices?" Never had he heard these words from Rachel or Paul. He felt their friendship was unconditional, understanding, with no ulterior motives. He did not feel that way with Dawn. Tears welled up in his eyes.

"I can't laugh anymore," Eric declared, wiping his eyes as if from laughter. "My stomach is aching." He knew Rachel was watching him, and he saw tears fill her eyes as well. He felt she knew what was in his heart.

"Me, too." Rachel said, "It's been a long time since I laughed so much!" She stood up. "Well, it is after eleven o'clock, tomorrow is another day. We'll get together again real soon. Okay, you two?"

Driving home, Eric felt guilty because he had had such a wonderful time. He thought of Dawn sitting at home by herself, and, momentarily forgetting their problems, he had great compassion for her. "She is intelligent, very personable, she will fit in with time," he tried to reassure himself. "She will be part of the group, and we will all have good times together."

When Eric came into the house, he found Dawn waiting for him, her face contorted with anger.

"Did you have a nice time?" she asked in an icy, mocking voice.

"Yes, VERY nice," Eric replied, emphasizing the word "very."

"Better than you have with me, I presume!" She began to shout.

"Why are you always comparing?" Eric asked. "I like you for what you are, and I like each of my friends for what they are. You all are different in your own way. It is not a matter of liking anyone better than anyone else."

"I had a wonderful evening planned for us! One which I am sure you would have enjoyed much more than 'very nice.'" Dawn argued.

CHAPTER 22

"I called the house. You were not home. I told Matilda I would not be home for supper." Eric's tone was conciliating.

"But you would not tell her where you were going!"

"Obviously you knew, didn't you? because you called me! Dawn, listen to me." He led her to the couch and sat facing her. "I do not mind sharing my day with you, but I resent your demanding attitude. You are not my boss. I don't have to report to you every move I make."

"Well, someone has to tell you what to do, especially when you display such irresponsible behavior!"

"Dawn, I am not a child. I don't want or need your reprimanding."

"I'll treat you like a child as long as you act like one!" she retaliated with eyes flashing.

Eric realized they were both shouting. "Oh, my God, Dawn, please keep your voice down. The neighbors will hear us! We will be disgraced. Let's talk quietly and discuss this situation like rational people"

"Let them hear!" Dawn raised her voice louder. "Let everyone hear how I have a husband who runs around with whores. I have a husband who leaves me alone at night to visit his whore!" She ran to the front door, threw it open and shouted as loudly as she could, "My husband, Rabbi Eric Froman, was with his whore tonight!"

Eric pulled her back and slammed the door. She responded by grabbing his shirt and ripping it off his body as she clawed at his face and chest. Pain seared his flesh as her long nails cut him.

The back of his hand whipped across her face. She fell to the floor, her head hitting the arm of the chair. She started to scream, "You have given me a concussion! Why are you beating me! Stop hitting me, please. Help! Help! Stop hitting me!"

Eric stood stunned at her rage. She got up and ran to the phone. She dialed 911 and called out her address and hung up before Eric could stop her. Within minutes the police were knocking at the door. "My husband is beating me," she told them, sobbing hysterically.

Eric stood aside as the police came in and then he closed the door. He felt humiliated and lost without any idea of what to do.

"Okay, lady. Quiet down and let's try to sort this out." The taller officer spoke to Dawn. "Are you the one who called the police?"

THE SECOND GENERATION

"Yes, I am. I had to do something to stop him from hitting me!"

The policeman turned to Eric. "Why were you beating her?"

"I was not beating her! I was defending myself. Look at me!" Eric asked. His torn shirt was hanging from him and blood still ran from the deep gashes her nails had carved.

"How did it start?" asked the older policeman.

"All I did was slap him," said Dawn, "and he began to beat me!"

"Lady, the law is whenever you attack someone, they have a right to defend themselves. It looks like you did a rather good job on him. I don't see any bruises on you."

"No, you are wrong!" insisted Dawn. He has no right to lay a finger on me even if I do slap him. He is much stronger than I am. He hit me in the head. I have a concussion, I know it. I feel it!"

The younger policeman began writing his report. "What is your name, Sir?"

"Eric Froman."

"RABBI Eric Froman," Dawn added with a twist of revenge in her voice.

"I'm sorry for the inconvenience caused you, officer," Eric said in an embarrassed voice. "Do you really have to put that in the report? We clergymen are human and have our difficulties like everyone else."

The policemen looked at Eric's pained face and then looked at each other. "It's okay, Rabbi, we don't have to designate a title in the report, just your name."

"Thank you," Eric said gratefully.

When the police left, Eric turned to Dawn. In a calm, sad voice he said, "Don't you realize what you have done? God knows who these policemen will tell about the rabbi and his wife fighting, hitting each other. Do you realize the harm that has been done against us -our people – the Jewish people? I married you, Dawn, because I had faith in you that you would be everything a rabbi's wife should be.

You and I, we are examples for all the Jews. We are role models. We are the Jewish leaders in the community and what has been done here? Only shame has been brought upon all of us."

CHAPTER 22

Dawn began to cry. "I'm so sorry, Eric. I don't know what happened. Why did we have such a terrible fight? We love each other. Where are we going wrong?" She walked over to him and put her arms around him. "My love, my darling, why do we do this to each other? Why do we torment each other so much?" She began leading Eric to the bedroom with tender words of affection, as she was undressing him.

The next day when Eric came home for lunch, he was greeted by his neighbor, Mrs. McLory. "Rabbi, please excuse me but I have to talk with you."

"Sure, Mrs. McLory, what is the matter?" Eric answered as he went to see what she wanted.

"I know you are a man of the cloth, Rabbi, but I just don't think it is right for a man of God to be so violent."

"I beg your pardon. I don't understand."

"I saw your wife this morning as shed was putting out the garbage, and I asked her what the police were doing at your house last night. I just wanted to know if anything was wrong and if I might be of any help….and she told me you beat her."

Eric felt a cold chill in his stomach. "Mrs. McLory, things are not always what they seem to be."

"Rabbi, she said you gave her a concussion. I saw the large bruise on her head."

"She fell and hit her head on the chair."

"Listen, Rabbi, I don't want to get involved in someone else's problems; however, I cannot sit by while a woman is being beaten, and not say anything."

"Mrs. McLory!" anger and shame filled Eric's heart.

"Remember, Rabbi, you are a man and considerably stronger than that slim, pretty wife of yours. You must hold your temper with her!"

Eric wanted to rip open his shirt and show Mrs. McLory the bruises and scratches on his neck and chest and to shout, "She has the strength of a bull and she is hard as a rock?" All he answered was, "Thank you, Mrs. McLory, for your concern," and walked to his house.

THE SECOND GENERATION

Mrs. McLory shouted after him, "I told Dawn to call the police the next time you lay a hand on her, and if she didn't, I would!"

When Eric went into the house, Dawn was waiting for him. Croissants, cheese, olives and salads were on the table with a bottle of wine. "Hi, sweetheart," she greeted him with a kiss. "I prepared a special lunch for you in reward for the great time we shared last night." She motioned to the table.

"Make sure you eat all the olives!" she laughed.

Eric tried to make his voice sound calm even though he was seething with anger. "Why did you tell Mrs. Mc Lory that I beat you last night?"

"I was taking out the garbage, and she saw the bruise on my head. You know I always tell the truth. I never lied. You know that!"

"I did not put that bruise on your head. You fell and hit your head on the chair!"

"But you knocked me down!"

"What you did to me doesn't count?" Eric was amazed at her words.

"All I did was give you a little slap. You have no right to hit me back!"

Eric opened his shirt and pointed to the scratches and bruises on his neck and chest. "And where did these come from?" he demanded.

Dawn began to chuckle. "Those are from our love-making last night. You were great, as usual!" She cocked her head to one side; her eyes were dancing. "Come on, sweetheart, lighten up. Let's always just remember the good times, forget the bad! Every marriage has good and bad. We have so much good in our marriage, let's concentrate on that, and the bad will eventually disappear. Come eat." I'll pour the wine. You know the old saying, 'Eat, drink, and be merry for later, we must make love!"

"That's not the way I heard it," said Eric.

"Well, that is the way it will always be with us," Dawn replied in a little girl's voice.

 # CHAPTER 23

IN RESPONSE TO his request, Paul came to his father's house for a Sunday dinner. When he arrived, his father was in an exceptionally good mood.

"Come on in, son," hie father happily greeted him at the door, shaking his hand. "How are you doing?"

"Okay."

His father put his arm on his shoulders and began to guide him toward the living room. "Come on, let's have a drink before dinner."

"No thank you." Paul sniffed the air. "Something smells delicious, I'm hungry. Let's eat."

"Hey, what is this, Paul? Did you come to see your old dad or just to eat?" He had a pretended hurt look on his face.

"Aw, come on Dad, you know I came to see you even though I must admit, the food isn't bad either." He laughed lightly.

"Then I insist we whet our appetites with a bit of the bubbly before we eat!"

"Champagne?! What is the occasion, Dad?"

"Come with me, son. I have a grand surprise for you." He motioned with his hand for Paul to follow him into the living room.

Paul never knew what to expect from his father's surprises. A nervous anxiousness gnawed at him. But he smiled, pretending to be excited. "What is it?"

As they walked into the living room, his two sisters, their husbands and five children greeted them with a shout of "Surprise!" followed by a round of "Happy Birthday." The children were clapping their hands and jumping with excitement.

"Well, this is certainly a wonderful surprise!" Paul happily hugged each of his sisters and shook hands with their spouses – the same thoughts running through his mind that he always had when he saw the men they married – how so very much they looked like the kind of man his father had always wanted him to be – muscular, athletic, and Aryan from the roots of their hair down to their toes. "It is true, daughters do marry their fathers," he mused.

His three nephews, who were in their early teens, also shook his hand, following their fathers in looks and mannerism. His two little nieces, five and seven, however, flung themselves into his arms for warm hugs and kisses. He lifted them up, one on each arm, and snuggled his nose against their necks as they giggled with delight.

While all the greetings, hugs and kisses were going on, Curt Steiger opened a bottle of champagne and poured it into champagne glasses.

"All right, everyone," he announced, "a toast to Paul on his 35th birthday. May we all celebrate only happy occasions together for many years to come!"

With a chorus of approving comments, all drank their champagne with laughter as the five-year-old sneezed when the bubbles tickled her nose.

Everyone looked to Paul for acknowledgement of the toast. For a second, there was an awkward silence as Paul groped for words. His eyes swept over his family; he felt no kinship to them. He felt no happiness or any joy. "Yes, yes," he stammered; may we all celebrate only happy occasions together for many years to come!"

"First damn time I ever saw a clergyman at a loss for words!" his brother-in-law, Jordan, commented.

"Oh, come now," his father came to his defense. "He is just overcome with emotion. You know Paul was always the 'sensitive' one!" Curt accented the word 'sensitive' as if it had a negative connotation.

In defense, Paul again sniffed he air. "As I said before, something smells delicious.....shall we eat? I'm starved!"

Obviously, everyone agreed. "Now that's a decent comment!" Joran slapped Paul on the back.

Anger ignited in Paul. "Why do I have to always be defensive?" he quested himself.

"Sure, dinner is served, ladies and gentlemen." Mr. Steiger motioned with his arm for everyone to follow him.

CHAPTER 23

Paul knew his father was disappointed that he had not made mention of him in his toast, that he had not paid homage to him as patriarch of the family. The same as when his was a child, he felt guilty that he had disappointed his father again. He felt inept at his ability to please him, to never live up to his expectations.

As they walked into the dining room, guilt overwhelmed Paul when he saw the elaborate arrangements of red roses and sprigs of white baby's breath flowers. The red napkins formed bouquets out of the wine glasses complimenting the red roses. Dishes with gold trim matched the gold table settings. The table was indeed worthy of a picture in a fashion magazine.

"Wow, Dad, this is magnificent!" Paul spoke with true honesty. "All this just for my birthday?"

"Well, it is the first time we have all been together in a long time. I wanted your 35th birthday to be special. I'm not getting any younger, you know, and I want special evenings to remember with the children I love. If only Christina were here now, and my beloved Bertha, my life would be perfect." As he spoke, his voice softened with remembrance.

"Ah, Dad, that is SO sweet." Paul's younger sister rushed to her father and gave him a big hug and kiss. "You will be with us for many years to come, and we'll have many memorable times together. You are still a young man and always will be in our eyes. Won't he?" shaking her head positively, she looked at the others for support.

Her husband agreed. "Of course, just look at your body. Like a young man, certainly better than Paul's on his 35th birthday!"

"Yeah, is that why you decided to a priest, Paul," chimed in Jordan, "to cover up your body under your frock?" He teased Paul, slapping him on the back again.

"Hey," his other sister laughingly jumped in, taking Paul's arm. "Don't you pick on my little brother!"

Trying to conceal the anger flaming in his chest, Paul ignored the comments. "Come on, let's sit down. Any special place you want us to sit, Dad?"

"You sit here on my right, Paul. Jordan, you and your family sit next to Paul. Frank, you and your family sit here on my left." He had completely ignored his daughters, addressing only the men.

"You slap me with one hand and pet me with the other." Paul thought as he sat down. "You want me to sit at your right hand, but you laugh at Jordan's cruel comment." He was also aware that his other sister had joined in the laughter. "I wonder what Christina would have said, had she been here?"

"Paul, are you with us or are you in another world?" Frank was speaking to him.

"Oh, I'm sorry. I was thinking of something. What did you say?"

"Is it true that you were told by your monsignor that you are allowed to speak with nuns, but you're are not to get into their 'habits'?"

Everyone roared with laughter, especially his father who responded with, "I don't think that would be one of Paul's problems!"

Paul's anger turned his face red as his mind desperately raced to find an appropriate reply.

"What kind of habits do nuns have that Paul is not supposed to pick up?" asked his seven-year-old niece, Bertha. The quizzical and confused look on her small face as to why everyone was laughing added to the gaiety. Paul was thankful the focus of attention was taken from him.

The meal matched the table decorations, expertly prepared and a delight to the eyes, as well as to the palate. After the main meal, before dessert, Curt Steiger arose and announced: "Now, I have a special gift for Paul. Please sit still until I return." His words were more of a command than a request. Paul watched his father walk away from the table into the next room. His father walked with sure, deliberate steps, head held high, shoulders back. He strode like a soldier proudly marching. Paul hated that walk. His father had tried to make him walk like that when he was a child, but he just could not reach the perfection his father wanted, regardless of how hard he tried. He again recalled the heavy backpack cutting into his shoulders when he was a little boy, as he tried to march through the woods, his father behind him calling out instructions.

"Hold that head up! Stand tall and walk straight! Chest out! Put those feet down with strength, deliberately. Eyes forward!"

"But suppose there is some little creature, maybe a baby bird that fell out of the nest. I'll crush it if I don't watch where I step!"

CHAPTER 23

"You are the master!" his father commanded. "Crush whatever gets in your way. You are greater than anyone else. There is no place in this world for weaklings! March! March!" The words roared louder and louder in Paul's head.

"This is for you, son." Paul was jerked back to reality. His father handed him a box wrapped in gold paper with a large golden bow. The box was a little larger than his hand.

"Thanks," Paul mumbled. Without enthusiasm he began to slowly open the package. His nieces gathered around him eager to see the present. Inside the box, enveloped in tissue paper, was an unusual cross. It was made of highly polished metal with each of its four ends tapered to fine points. In the center, however, where the figure of Jesus should be as part of the crucifixion, was an eagle, its wings outspread horizontally, head held proudly upward and its legs forming the bottom part. Each feather was delicately cut into the metal and in the place of the eyes, were small rubies. Paul took the cross and held it in his hand. Though it was as large as his hand, it was surprisingly light.

"It is the finest tempered steel, Paul. Do you like it?" his father anxiously looked at him. "Do you like it?" he repeated. "I designed it and had it made especially for you."

"I have never seen anything like this in my life. It is magnificent!" Paul slowly petted the eagle on the cross. "But why is there an eagle on the cross?"

"It is bootiful," declared his smallest niece, Irene. "Now open my present, Uncle Paul!" She shoved a rather large box into his lap.

To tease the children, Paul opened the box very slowly. Impatiently, they tried to help him rip off the paper as they squealed with delight. A large afghan was in the big box. "What does one get a priest?" asked his sister with shrugged shoulders.

"This is wonderful. When I relax in my special chair, it will make a perfect cover." He took it out of the box, held it up and then rubbed it against his cheek. "How soft it is!"

"It is combed cotton and alpaca wool. Do you really like it?" His sister was insisting on more emotion.

"Oh yes, I really do! Very much so! I love the mixture of colors." He stroked the light tan and dark blue squares with lines of yellow. "It truly is lovely."

The next box was rather large with five boxes each inside the other. Every time Paul opened a box to find another box, the children roared with laughter. Finally, the last box contained a gift certificate for $50.00 to a local bookstore.

"This is really a great present!" Paul exclaimed in sincere delight. "I love this bookstore! Well, this has certainly been my day. I thank you all very much. I shall never forget my 35th birthday, that is. for sure!" He turned to his father. "And a special thanks to you, Dad, for arranging such a wonderful party for me. You are truly a good father! The best any son could have!" Paul hated himself for saying words he knew his father wanted to hear. Instead of relief in pleasing his father, anger churned in his guts as fire-hot tears burned in his eyes.

Steiger's apparently pleased acknowledgement of Paul's praise infuriated Paul even more. Paul put his hands under the table and dug his nails into his palms to help him control himself from lashing out at his father and his brothers-in-law. He hated them all. He prayed no one would notice his quivering lips as he repeatedly licked him. He looked around. The walls again were moving toward him, making his breathing difficult. Paul \jumped up abruptly.

"Where are you going?" his father asked.

Paul looked at his watch. "It's getting late. I have an early Mass tomorrow. I had better be going."

"No, you can't go yet," his father protested. "I have something very special planned."

"Come on, Paul, it is only 9:00 o'clock. You'll still have plenty of time t get your beauty rest!" Jordan's voice was insolent.

"What about the birthday cake?" seven-year-old Stephanie was concerned. "Who will blow out the candles?"

"Okay, sweetheart," Paul gave her a wide grin. "I'll blow out those candles if you promise to help me."

"Okay!" her face brightened with a large grin. "I'll even help you make a wish!"

CHAPTER 23

"It's a deal! I'll be right back." Paul went to the bathroom and threw cold water on his face and then investigated the face in the mirror above the sink. A pale, tormented face looked back at him. "No wonder they are picking on you. You look like something the cats drugged in and then threw away. Stop looking so pathetic, and act like man, not a baby!" he chided himself. He took a comb from the shelf nearby and combed his blond hair, straightened his jacket and tie, took a deep breath and went back to the table.

His father had opened a bottle of red wine and poured a glass full for everyone at the table. He was waiting for Paul to return. When Paul sat down in his seat, Curt Steiger arose and lifted his wine glass.

"Today, loved ones, we toast to a great occasion in the history of the world. We toast the breaking down of the Berlin Wall…. the day when Germany becomes one nation again. This time, my children, we toast the united Germany with rich red wine which is significant of the blood of our Germany. With pride we can call her our country!"

"Ach!" respond Jordan, "now THAT is a toast to which I gladly raise my glass!"

Gall choked in Paul's throat. He knew that the celebration of his birthday was only a cover-up for the real reason of today's party. His father continued. "May we all live to see the day when Germany will again rise to be the leading nation of the world, pure of blood, when Germany will take its rightful place in world history as a leader of nations in strength and intellect."

Paul did not remember ever hearing such joy in his father's voice or on his face. Anger pounded in Paul's soul, and before anyone could respond to his father's toast, Paul spoke: "But this time, may Germany not become a killer nation, without compassion or mercy!"

Stunned silence pervaded the room as all eyes incredulously searched Paul's face for an explanation of his words. Exaltation at their shock gave power to Paul's defiance. "Yes, Germany was without pity. Its big brave soldiers killed babies, pregnant women, and old people. It enslaved and tortured scholars, teachers, and plain everyday people."

"But we were at war. Terrible things happen in a war." Jordan sound almost apologetic.

"A war that Germany started, which ended by taking over 50 million lives in the world," Paul continued, still feeling in control. "And what about the millions of destroyed lives? Families torn apart, tortured, experimented on. You speak of the greatness of Germany? All its intellectual accomplishments have been dimmed by its grotesque inhumanity to mankind. History will forever sing of its evil deeds, not of its grandeur!"

"How dare you speak like this in my house!" As usual, whenever he was excited, Steiger banged his fist on the table, again causing the wine glasses to turn over, spilling their contents across the white tablecloth. A sarcastic laugh tore out of Paul's throat as he watched the red wine soaking like blood through the white tablecloth.

Paul arose and pointed to the spilled wine. "You have given your symbolism of Nazi Germany," Paul sneered. "Wherever the Nazis went, blood of the innocent and pure soaked the earth!"

Curt lifted his hand to slap Paul's face, but instead, pushed him back into his chair with force. This time there were no tears in Paul's eyes, only intense hatred. He spoke between clenched teeth with a tremendous satisfaction. "Do you want to beat me into submission as the Germans beat their slave laborers?" He shot out his arm, pulled up his sleeve, exposing his arm. "Here, why don't you tattoo a number on my arm as well?"

"What have I done to deserve a son like you?" Curt clenched his hands in front of him. "You are my only son. You were supposed to carry my name on, but what did you do? You became a priest so you would not have to bother with women. You come from good stock. What made you like this?" Curt was to the point of pleading, his voice shaking. The rest of the family at the table were silent, watching the exchange between father and son.

It was the first time in his life that Paul had ever seen weakness in his father, and it frightened him. Paul softened. "Father, I do not deny that from Germany have come some of the finest minds in the world. I do not deny that it was once the leading nation of the world intellectually and culturally, but we cannot ignore the truth. Germany committed terrible crimes, Father. We must never let it

CHAPTER 23

happen again. But, first, we must admit to those crimes, or we will never be free of them."

Curt shook his head unbelievingly. "Who is putting all this nonsense in your head?"

"It is not nonsense, Father, I have seen results of the Holocaust!"

The old Curt returned with raised fists. "I told you there was no such thing as a Holocaust!" he angrily insisted. "It is a bunch of lies made up by Jews so that they could get sympathy from the world when they took Palestine away from the Arabs. I thought we already went over this once before."

"No, Father, it is true. I saw with my own eyes the numbers cut in the flesh of the survivors!" Paul motioned to his arm as he spoke.

"Survivors?" Mr. Steiger's face was red with anger. "Where, may I ask, have you met survivors?"

"I have met survivors of the Holocaust!" Paul raised his voice. It does not matter when or where. I'm telling you I have met survivors with numbers burned in their arms!"

"How dare you raise your voice to me!" Paul instinctively ducked as Curt lifted his hand, but he only pointed his finger at Paul.

"I'm sorry, Father. I apologize for raising y voice to you, but the University library has a complete section on the Holocaust with many books written by gentiles as well as Jews. There are authentic records. Furthermore, even the Catholic Church acknowledges it and has records of taking in some Jewish children for protection."

Frank spoke. "it is true. Some Germans did commit atrocities, but they were only following orders. There were a few who may not have done the right thing, but you cannot blame all Germans.

Orders must be followed or there would be no discipline whatsoever in the army and you know as well as anyone, no discipline, no army."

"That's bull, Frank, and you know it! It is a week excuse that everyone uses. One must have his own conscience and his own convictions as a human being. One does not do terrible things just because someone tells him to!"

"Wait a minute," Jordan pushed in. "What kind of world would this be if everyone did what he thought was right, without leadership, without anyone guiding them and leading them?"

THE SECOND GENERATION

"A much better one than we have now." Paul shot back at him. "If we would teach every child compassion, mercy and respect for his fellow person, then there would be no need for leaders telling us what to do."

"That's communism!" Jordan proclaimed.

"No, I did not say that the government should be in control of everything. I said that each person should be taught to be responsible for his own actions, especially if they hurt anyone else."

"Why are you so interested in the Holocaust, Paul? His father asked. "How come you know about the Holocaust section in the library?" Paul noticed with satisfaction that his father's temples were palpitating beneath the greying sideburns.

"I am again one of the featured speakers at the Holocaust Memorial at the University on June 6." Paul ignored the shocked looks from the people around the table.

His father spoke very quietly: "The Jews are using you, Paul, using you to accuse Germany. They tried to destroy the greatest nation on earth and now they are using you to cover up their sins with exaggerated emotional lies." Steiger's steel-blue eyes were flashing with contempt. "They are dirty, and they are diseased! They are the ones without feeling or sensitivity."

"Feeling or sensitivity," rang in Paul's ears. He again recalled his father's words on that camping trip when he was a little boy. "You threw way your food and sleeping bag? Then sleep on the wet ground and go hungry!" His father had told him as he ate his own supper in front of his little child and then crawled into his warm sleeping bag.

His father's rising voice brought him back to the dinner table. "Tell me, Paul, why do you want to even go, much less speak at that farce!" he demanded.

"I must, I have given my word." Paul softly replied. "If you don't believe me, why don't you come and see for yourself." He turned to everyone at the table. "Why don't you all come and see for yourselves?" There was silence, except from Jordan.

"Listen, Paul, just because you have become a Jew lover, it doesn't mean the rest of us have to follow suit." He pretended to shudder. "Why do I have to associate with vermin when I can soar with

CHAPTER 23

eagles. I guess that is one of the negatives about being a priest. You have to associate with everyone, scum and all!"

I don't have to associate with Jews or anyone else. To me a person is a human being created in the image of G-d. It does not concern me who he is or where he came from. Besides, Jews will not be the only ones there. There will be many gentiles as well – the mayor, the senators, the congressmen as well as leaders of several religious denominations. Why don't you come too, Father?

Paul saw his father set his jaw in defiance. He picked up the cross his father had given to him and quickly before his father could say 'no' added "Wouldn't it give you satisfaction to see me wear this cross as I speak before all the people. Don't you feel proud that I shall be speaking before a multitude of people, non-Jews as well as Jews. They will all be listening to me. I shall be the master of my heritage as I proudly wear this special cross before the masses!" Paul was knowingly manipulative because he desperately wanted his father to be at the Holocaust Memorial. "When he sees the survivors and hears their stories, he will have to believe there was a Holocaust," Paul thought to himself. He continued, "Most of all, I want you to be there, Father. I know I have not lived up to be the man you so desperately craved for a son, but perhaps my intellectual accomplishments, my leadership in the name of God will some way compensate for your disappointment. I want you there, Dad. Do come to see me speak."

Steiger was flattered. "Okay, if you really want me, then I shall be there!"

"Yes, I really do! Thank you, Father." Even though Paul felt a small victory over his father, his disgust for him did not lessen.

"When are we going to have the birthday cake?" piped in the youngest niece. "All this talking is giving me a headache!"

The older niece was not to be left out. "Can I help blow out the candles now, Uncle Paul?"

"Sure can, sweethearts, come over here and sit on my lap, both of you, come on." Paul motioned with his arm for them to come to him. He didn't have to ask them twice.

After the cutting of the cake, Paul insisted on leaving. With relief he gasped for the cool night air as he walked out of the house. He felt no connection with those people. Through the open window he heard them sing, "Deutschland, Deutschland Ubber Allas" – Germany, Germany over Everything – the national anthem of Germany. Complete revulsion and anger consumed him. He deplored their attitude of superiority and self-righteousness.

This was his family, but they were strangers to him. After Christina died, his sisters made few attempts to comfort him. He felt alone and empty now. He ached for warmth and closeness with people whom he could share his feelings without tension and anger. The singing from the house grated on his nerves. He hurried to his car, quickly got into it and slammed the door. He made sure each window as tightly closed to block out the sound of the voices. He sat for a few moments, breathing deeply before turning the key in the ignition. Perspiration covered his body and ran down his back, his legs, and his arms; yet he felt chills.

He reached in his pocket and took out the cross with the eagle, examining it closely. He saw blood dropping from the eagle's ruby eyes. Paul started to shake uncontrollably as he dropped the cross to the car floor. He reached down to pick it up and as he lifted it, the foot of the cross scratched his thigh. How comforting the physical pain was! It was real. He pulled up his pant leg and slipped his hand over the scratch. When he lifted his hand, there was blood on his fingers. The blood from the scratch was real. "Thank you, Oh Lord, thank you!" he cried out in relief as he put the car in gear and drove off.

CHAPTER 24

THE UNIVERSITY AUDITORIUM had been granted for the Holocaust Memorial. The large stage was filled with dignitaries. Every seat was filled in the audience, and people were standing in the back and along the sides of the room. Ushers were bringing in folding chairs. Paul's eyes searched the room for his father, but with the dimmed lights and multitude of people, he could not find him. Paul thought he caught a glimpse of him standing in the back, but a group of people walked by, and he was no longer there after they passed. He fingered the cross he had in his pocket, debating with himself whether he should wear it, as he had promised his father. He finally made an agreement with himself – should he see his father; he would put it on. If he did not see his father, he would leave it in his pocket. His eyes searched and searched as he fingered the cross until the program began.

A welcome was given by Rachel, who was the chairperson. With a soft, crisp voice, she introduced the guests on the stage and the program.

First on the program was a forty-five-minute film depicting the history of the Holocaust. It covered from the beginning of Hitler's rise to power, with the night parades, Hitler's Youth marching proudly, followed by the rounding up of Jews, the shooting and burning of them alive in the streets, and ended with the gas chambers, the ovens and heaps of corpses. The walking dead were shown, as were interviews with survivors in the Displaced Persons Camps.

Never had Paul seen anything like this. The books he had read were like stories, science fiction, but seeing it on film, with shots of actual footage taken from the German archives, Paul knew his father was wrong. This was not propaganda. This was too appalling, to horrifying to be a figment of even the most twisted mind. He prayed his father was there watching the film. This would surely prove to him that there was truly a Holocaust. He would not be able to deny it any longer.

"In Jerusalem, the path leading to Yad V'Shem – the eternal memorial of the Holocaust, the path is lined with names of righteous gentiles who tried to help the Jewish people in their time of suffering," Rachel was speaking. "Their names are preserved for all eternity along with the names of the martyrs who perished because they resisted evil and faced death rather then succumb t be a part of the madness sweeping Europe. In our Passover Haggadah, it is written, 'And they shall rise in every generation to annihilate us....' And also in every generation there arises the righteous gentile who sides with God against the evil that arises in His beautiful world. I am very pleased to introduce to you a righteous gentile from our generation – Father Paul Steiger."

It was obvious that Paul was caught by surprise. He had not taken time to glance at the program because he was concentrating on finding his father in the audience. Furthermore, he had not thought he would be so early to speak. The audience, however, interpreted his surprise as modesty, which appealed to them. Paul rose to speak; his voice was soft, and his words emanated from his soul.

"This is the second Holocaust memorial I have attended, but I am no loss horrified at the evil which was perpetrated by one people against another. In fact, the magnitude of the wicked sins committed in our so-called civilized world is strong enough to shake the very foundations on which our planet rests. What is appalling to man's soul is that the people in the countries where the crimes took place did not stand up and fight the devastation of life and put an end to the inhumanity being committed in their own back yard. I must also add that the Church with its organized network over Europe could have saved more lives. Its silence was not golden but was a death penalty for thousands of Jews and many other peoples. It is a lesson to mankind that one cannot remain silent. One must take on the responsibility of a human being towards another human being regardless of who he is. We are our 'brother's keeper' because we are each a creation of God, and as such, regardless of our customs, our beliefs, our origins or our religions, we are, each

CHAPTER 24

one, God's children. Not one of us has the right to deny another one his place on this earth. No one has the right to say, 'I am better than another person.'"

Paul's eyes searched the audience for his father as he spoke. He noted with satisfaction how everyone was listening to him, many nodding their heads in agreement. Paul felt pride in being alive. Words were flowing from his mouth with ease. "I am speaking here today to give you my solemn oath before God that I shall use whatever powers or influence I hold to be a pathway to justice. I may be only a grain of sand, but a grain of sand in the eye can be quite irritating. I know I shall be joined by other grains of sand and as the shore holds back the mighty ocean, so shall we strive to push back the inhumanity of the world."

When Paul finished speaking, there was a brief silence followed by a great wave of applause as the audience gave him a standing ovation. For the very first time in his life, Paul experience an immense inner jubilance. "Thank you, God, thank you," his lips moved silently.

The next speaker was Eric. "I am a second-generation survivor and I am proud to stand here today because I am proud that my parents survived despite all that was done to them. I am proud to be the son of a people, who though persecuted and slaughtered, have the will to live and to see the fall of their persecutors, proud to bear witness to the world of what has been done to my people. I am proud to be the son of a people who not only had the will to survive, but still have faith in tomorrow. I am proud to be the son of a people who want to marry, to rear children, and to teach those children that this is a bountiful, beautiful world full of G-d's precious gifts to mankind, to want to prepare those children for a better tomorrow where hatred of another human being will be eradicated.

It is my belief that those who survived the horrors of the Holocaust and still have faith in G-d are people who reflect the image of God, people who though tried and tested through the hottest flame, emerged as the finest steel – not broken, not defeated, but with courage to turn their faces heavenward and proclaim: 'Blessed are Thou, O Lord, our God, King of the Universe, who has kept us, sustained us and brought us to this time."

THE SECOND GENERATION

Eric's mother and father suddenly stood up with arms held high, bearing the numbers engraved on their arms, tears streaming down their faces. Others followed and there were many arms, held high, exposing their tattooed numbers with pride. A wave of euphoria swept across the audience as someone began singing, "Ani MaAmin – I believe with perfect faith in the coming of the Messiah, and though he may tarry, I believe!"

Eric picked up on the theme of the song when the singing had subsided. "And so shall always be the cry of our people, and of all peoples of good hearts, believers in justice – the song of the Warsaw Ghetto fighters that not in spite of, but precisely because of what happens to us, whatever is perpetuated against us, we shall always believe in God and His goodness. No one, no power, will ever turn us from our faith, nor from our mission on this earth to be the proof that there is an Eternal Father whom we represent, whose Will we must live on this earth.

Part of our mission on this earth is never to let humanity forget what has happened in the past in order to prevent a recurrence in the future. There can be no 'forgetting and forgiving' because forgiveness can only come from those against whom the crimes were committed. Their stories must be told and retold for it is their blood that cries out from the ground –'Azchor!' remember! Yes, there is no doubt that we are our brother's keeper. By remembering, we keep their memories alive." Eric turned and with his hand motioned to the dignitaries sitting on the stage. "All these good people here tonight who represent all peoples of our community, are the beacons of light to guide mankind out of darkness to light, to the light of hope that someday……'nation shall no longer raise sword against nation, nor shall they know war any more. Thank you."

With shouts of "Amen" and "Yeshor Koach -May you have strength to continue your good work," the audience also gave Eric a standing ovation.

Paul came forward to shake Eric's hand but instead, grabbed him in a warm hug to the delight of the audience. "You were great!" Paul declared with admiration.

Etic pulled back, "So were you, Paul!"

CHAPTER 24

After the listed speakers, the traditional candle-lighting ceremony followed, and then the program was summed up by the chairperson, Rachel.

As soon as the last word was spoken, Paul said to Eric, "Where is the Men's Room? All this excitement has wrought havoc on my poor kidneys!"

Eric laughed. "Come on, I need to go too. Let's go quickly before the rush."

As they walked down the hall towards the men's room, Paul was talking excitedly. "I was overwhelmed with the first Holocaust memorial at your synagogue, but this one – I have never experienced anything like this in my entire life, such an outpour of emotion. Man, when all those arms went up spontaneously, those numbers seemed to shine with an iridescent glow. It was almost…"

Paul did not finish his sentence for as the two entered the men's room both stopped, stunned.

A man was crouching between two urinals like a cornered animal ready to spring. His open hands before him were poised to grasp an invisible object. His two black eyes resembled pieces of coal sunken into his head, his mouth was set in a determined grimace. Standing over the crouched figure was a tall muscular man, legs apart, fists resting on his hips. Their concentration was so total that they neither recognized nor acknowledged the entrance of their sons into the room.

"Steigerhaus, at last I am going to kill you!" the man between the urinals declared between clinched teeth. On his extended hands, he formed claws to strangle his old antagonist. "I'm going to get what I have prayed for! I am going to chew out your throat and feel your cold blood pouring over my body. I'm going to tear out your eyes and pull out your guts!"

"You dirty stinking Jew dog! I am finally going to break you, except this time, I'll break your neck as well! I want to hear your bones crunch, one by one! Come on, you bastard Jew, come on!" He took his hands off his hips and forming a fist with his left hand, motioned with his right hand for Froman to come to him.

Froman tried to attack, but his feet refused to move. He was frozen, paralyzed by an ancient fear as a bird is hypnotized by the snake that is going to devour him. Steigerhaus still had power over him. How many times had he dreamt of this moment, of meeting his tormentor and getting his revenge, and now he couldn't move!

More men entered the room, but all stood mesmerized by the scene. "What's happening?" "Who are they?" They whispered to each other. But the two men, locked in mortal combat, were oblivious to the world around them.

Steigerhaus sneered. "Still a coward dog?"" His fist flew forward, and Froman's nose began to bleed as he fell back against the wall.

"Papa!" Eric shouted and ran to his father. He squatted down in front of his father.

Paul shouted, "Father!" but could not move. Without turning or taking his eyes off his victim, Steigerhaus motioned for his son to come to him. Steigerhaus' face was triumph with a sure victory.

"Come here, son. Come and see how we squash these insects, these roaches! This stubborn Jew bastard held onto life in the camp, and here he is now with all his scummy friends, trying to take my son away from me! Poisoning his mind with his lies! These vermin have crawled out of their cesspools and stinking holes to pollute our world again. Come, son," he again motioned with his arm, "Let me give you a lesson in exterminating vermin. We'll crush them, one by one." Paul tried but he could not move his feet.

Froman slipped down the wall to a sitting position on the floor. He held his hands up in front of him, examining them. His mind slipped back in time to the scene at the frozen camp. "My hands, my hands," he cried in a shrill voice. "The skin is gone from my hands!" He looked up at Steogerhaus."Why did you do this to me, Steigerhaus, why?"

"Scum!" shouted Steiger. Again, he motioned to Paul. "Come son, be a man, nota weakling, a baby...show you ae a man! Let's crush their heads!" Steiger lifted his foot to stomp Froman. Eric threw himself in front of his father, pushing him to the side, so that the heavy boot came down on the side if Isaac Froman's face, rather than his head.

"You slippery bastard! I'll make your head explode into a thousand pieces!" Steiger's arms swung to gain power for his lifted foot.

CHAPTER 24

The squirrel's head exploded in Paul's brain. He reached into his pocket and pulled out the cross his father had given to him. Holding it by the top cross-section, Paul jumped forward and sunk the cross's sharp bottom edge into the side of his father's neck, penetrating the jugular vein. As if in slow motion, blood shot up into the air, splattering on Eric and his father, as Steigerhaus fell backwards, his raised boot grasping for a hold.

The excitement was gone, the pounding in Paul's head stopped abruptly and a serene peace enveloped his body. Without looking at his father lying on the floor, Paul bent over and wiped the blood from Eric's cheek with is hand, looking into his eyes, smiled and softly said: "It is over at long last. I'm at peace now, Eric, my friend." He arose, silently walked out of the men's room, not cognizant of the men moving out of his way. He sat down on a bench outside of the door and began to stare blankly straight ahead of him.

The auditorium was filled with hysterical people, trying to grasp what had happened. Rumors flew like feathers in the wind. "The priest just killed someone with a cross!" "A Nazi was killing a Jew!" "A Jew was killing a Nazi!" "Who was it?" "A Nazi war criminal has been killed!" "Justice!" "See, there is a God!" 'A Nazi war criminal killed at a Holocaust memorial! It is a sign! I'm telling you, it is a sign!" Electrical currents could have not travelled faster and with more effect.

Eric tried to help his father stand, but Mr. Froman shrugged him away. He struggled up by himself, brushed and straightened his clothes, mindless of all the people watching him. He looked at the gashed and bloody neck of the dead man. His eyes did not see the cross lying on the floor in a pool of blood. "I did it! He declared. "You son of a bitch! I ripped out your neck just like I dreamed all these years, with these hands!" Then he looked at his hands, studied them for a few seconds and asked with innocence. "Why isn't there blood on my hands?" He hesitated, looked at his hands again and again, and then demanded to know. "Why is there no blood on my hands?!"

Eric's mother, Miriam Froman, pushed into the room screaming, "Isaac! Isaac! Are you all right? Are you hurt? What happened?"

Isaac held out his arms to her, "Come, Ruthie, come. It is all right now. They are coming to get us, but we'll go together. We'll never be apart again."

"Your face, Isaac, look at your face!" The left side of Isaac's face was turning blue and swollen where the boat had grazed it.

"It's okay, Ruthie. See, your face is not hurt." He touched her check. "The rifle hit me instead. See, I took your hurt. You won't have to worry about any more pain. No more pain." He gathered her into his arms, holding her tightly as he placed his head against hers.

Miriam Froman looked helplessly at Eric. "Eric?" she weakly cried in desperation.

"Sh-h-h, Mama, Sh-h-h. We'll get him to a doctor. He'll be all right." Eric, Miriam and Isaac were all taken to Memorial Hospital. Paul, rigid and unresponsive, was placed for observation in the psychiatric ward, where they also wanted to hold Isaac, but Miriam refused to let her husband remain in the hospital. She insisted on taking him home with her. "He'll be all right," she reassured the doctors. "I know him better than any of you. You don't know how to treat a man with what he has been through! I do!"

The next few days, the news was sensationalized. "Nazi War Criminal killed at Holocaust Memorial Service." "Priest slays own father," screamed the media. Editorials and letters to the editors swamped the newspapers. There was some talk of a Church coverup, while others declared that as a priest, Paul was commissioned by God to root out evil. Still others argued that Paul be prosecuted as a murderer because Nazi criminal or not, Curt Steigerhaus did not deserve to die but should have been entitled to a fair trial in America because after all, isn't that what Americas stands for – justice, even for the alleged criminal?

Reporters from television stations, newspapers, and tabloids made their rounds from the parish rectory, to the synagogue, to the home of the Fromans, and to Eric and Dawn's house. The story was "top of the news," front-page material for several days, as the media probed every aspect to stretch the unusual event as far as it could.

The public waited, but there was no funeral. Curt Steigerhaus was cremated, his ashes given to his daughters who held a private ceremony for family and close friends at an undisclosed time and

CHAPTER 24

location. The news gatherers waited outside of the hospital for a few days, hoping that Paul would be taken out for the funeral. However, Paul passed the day of his father's funeral sitting passively on the side of his narrow bed, gazing calmly at the beige wall. He quietly obeyed any instruction he was given – to eat, to sit down, go to the bathroom, walk, dress, undress. Attempts to induce verbal responses from him failed. He did not acknowledge anyone who came into his room but only sat with a steady, unblinking gaze. Paul had deeply withdrawn, giving no clue as to what was occurring inside his being.

The prosecutor's office was inundated with mail. There were even letters from Holocaust survivors living in Israel asking that they be allowed to come to the trial of Father Paul Steiger to testify on his behalf, to reveal who his father was and the crimes he had committed against them. Petitions were circulated and signed, demanding that a direct verdict of "not guilty" be handed down without a trial.

The defense for Paul advised the State that they were entering a plea of "not guilty by reason of insanity" and in return, the state psychiatrist was sent to Memorial Hospital to examine Paul. After the examination, Paul was declared to be mentally incompetent, not legally sane to stand trial. On the orders of the court, Paul was transferred to a mental institution where he was to stay until the doctors felt he had improved sufficiently to be out in society, is such improvement ever occurred.

"If you intend to visit Paul Steiger frequently," the psychiatrist told Eric and Rachel, "it must be at a regular time. Routine has to be established in his life if he is going to be brought back to reality."

"Will he ever be brought back to reality?" Rachel inquired.

"I don't know. He is suffering from post-traumatic stress syndrome. There is a possibility that he may recover; but on the other hand, there is the chance that Paul will remain in this catatonic state the rest of his life. The mind, in self-defense, sometimes blocks out events that are too painful to face. You realize that there must have been other events in his life that led to the killing of his father. We would expect normal behavior to be a simple attempt to stop his father's action, not to kill him."

"What do you think those other events were, Doctor?" Eric asked.

"Well, I think Paul did not kill his father to just save your father, Rabbi. I think he acted out of a long-time fantasy that he has suppressed for many years, probably from childhood. The interaction between your fathers just triggered Paul.

"The idea then is to try to find out what those long-time reasons are and to get them out of Paul?" Eric half asked and half stated.

"Precisely," responded the doctor. "Whatever they were, he has to pull them up out of his memory and fac them. As his friends, has he ever confided anything of his past to you?"

Eric and Rachel looked at each other. Both shook their heads. "No," Eric spoke. "We just accepted each other the way we are. None of us really have spoken of our pasts."

Rachel nodded in agreement. "Paul is a sensitive person. Kind and gentle. I would never believe he could kill anything, much less his own father."

"A rubber band stretches and stretches until it reaches a breaking point. The human psyche is similar. As the old saying goes, 'everyone has his breaking point,' even the strongest. The survivors and victims of the war have taught us that lesson repeatedly."

"What about his sisters? Can't you get any information from them?" Rachel suggested.

"We tried, but they will not even speak to us on the phone. Do you know them well enough to speak with them?" The doctor directed his question to the Rabbi.

"I didn't even know he had sisters until I read it in the paper, but I will certainly try to contact them." Eric answered.

"I would suggest that you try to speak with them when their husbands are not present. They were quite abusive to me on the phone and very empathic that their wives wanted nothing to do with Paul." Dr. Siegelman added. "Be careful of them, Rabbi, I didn't like their words to me as a Jewish doctor."

"Neo-Nazis?" Rachel spit out.

"Could be. They commented that the traitor, Paul, deserved to be with his Jew-loving friends!"

"I've lived with the effects of Nazism all my life, Dr. Siegelman, they can't scare me." Eric said matter-of-factly.

CHAPTER 24

"Paul will come back to us. I know he will. I just know he will!" Rachel was emphatic.

Eric responded before the doctor could. "With the good doctor's help, I'm sure he will." Eric stretched out his hand to the doctor. "Thanks, Doc." Eric felt a lump forming in his throat as they shook hands.

In his cell-like room, Paul sat mute, eye staring at nothing in his surrounding world, but seeing inwardly the images of his childhood fears and torments and his father lying in his own blood.

Paul was finally free of his father's tyranny but was held prisoner by his own demons.

CHAPTER 25

ISAAC FROMAN SAT on the front porch of his house, rocking back and forth in the rocking chair. Everyone who came to see him heard the story of how he had at long last killed the famous Curt Steigerhaus. No one had the courage to contradict him or try to tell him the truth. They politely listened, nodding their head in agreement, patting him on the back and wishing him well.

Eric sadly looked at the swollen face of his father, his gnarled, scarred hands and grey hair. The scar on the swollen cheek was an ugly red, accented by the sunken right cheek. Eric realized the humiliation his father must have felt when he could not move against his tormentor but had to let himself again be beaten by him.

Eric took his father's right and held it between his two hands. "Papa?" No response. "Papa. I am your eldest son, Eric. I love you, Papa." Tears filled Eric's eyes. "I am so proud of you. I am so proud of you, Papa."

Isaac turned slowly to his son, with a gleam of light in his eyes, he said,"because I killed Steigerhaus?"

"Papa, you did not kill Steigerhaus in that men's room." Isaac's face fell. "I am proud of you, Papa, because every day that you survived in the slave labor camp, you killed a bit of him. You would not allow his total control; you did not give in to him. You did not have to kill him in that toilet. He was already dead. I saw, Papa, I saw death in his fury that he could not break you. No, Papa, you could not physically kill him because you are not a murderer like he was. You are a brave, strong man. Steigerhaus' punishment was greater than any you could have given to him. The doctor told me, Papa, Paul did not kill his father to save us. He killed his father because he hated him."

Isaac was searching Eric's face for the truth. Eric continued. "Papa, we all may not have always gotten along in our family. We fought. We argued, but despite everything, we had love for each other. If any of us were in trouble, the rest of the family would have been there to help. No matter what, we helped each other."

Eric was silent, waiting to see what effect his words would have on his father. Slowly he lifted his large head, withdrew his hand out of Eric's hands and put them around Eric's body. "I know, my son, I know. I know you threw yourself in front of ne to keep Steigerhaus from kicking me. I love you, son, my *behor* -my oldest son."

It was the first time in his life that Eric had heard his father say 'I love you' to him. "*HaMashiach yavo machar,*" he mumbled to himself. "The Messiah will come tomorrow!" He hugged his father back.

Inside the house, on the other side of the curtain where Eric, as a child, had once tried to listen to the conversation on the porch, Miriam Froman listened to the exchange between her eldest son and her husband. Her happiness was entwined with a twinge of jealousy.

CHAPTER 26

ERIC PULLED A chair next to Paul's bed and sat down facing him. He searched Paul's face for some sign of recognition, but Paul's steel-blue eyes gazed straight ahead, engrossed in an event in a far-off time, in a far-off place. Little beads of perspiration matted down the hair around his forehead and temples. Blue pajamas hung on his frail body.

Eric gently took the bony hand in both of his. "Paul," he pleaded softly, "It's Eric. Look at me, Paul, please look at me." There was not a sign of movement on Paul's faced. His eyes continued their search into some mysterious vision. Eric felt the same helplessness he always had when he visited Paul. For six weeks, his feelings of frustration had been building.

"I've had enough of this!" Eric jumped up suddenly, knocking over the chair. He reached over and grabbed Paul under the arms and lifted him up against the backboard of the bed, propping pillows behind him. He grabbed a handful of paper tissues, dipped them in the water pitcher and wiped Paul's face. He took a comb out of his breast pocket and combed Paul's hair back from his face.

Eric then sat on the side of the bed, took Paul's face in both of his hands and turned his head towards hm. "Paul, I am not going to let you sit here like a zombie. I've been here time after time, and you won't even look at me! You must come alive again! Come on, my friend, you have a life to live!"

As Eric spoke, he lightly shook Paul's head. He noticed a glimmer of response. Paul blinked his eye several times. Eric let go of Paul's face, and with both hands grabbed his shoulders, shaking them.

"What gives you the right to hide from life?" he demanded. "What gives you the right to wall yourself up from the pain of living?" He gently shook him again. "Who gives you permission to release

THE SECOND GENERATION

yourself from reality to live in your own little world? How dare you not to live up to your vows to serve your people!"

To Eric's utter surprise, Paul responded with an outburst of shouting. He cupped his hands over his ears and yelled, "You have to be strong! You must be strong! You have to be strong!" He shouted repeatedly, squeezing his hands over his ears. "I am a human being, not an animal or a machine! No! I do not have to be strong all the time. I have feelings! I have emotions! I hurt, and if I want to cry, I'll cry!" He could not stop shouting.

"If I am supposed to be strong and never cry, why did God give me tears? Why did God give me a heart? Show me where it is written that I am supposed to be strong all the time!!" Perspiration flooded his face. His fists beat the air, the bed; his head thrashed as tears ran from his eyes.

Nurses and attendants filled the room. One nurse was holding a hypodermic syringe.

"No!" shouted Eric. "Leave him alone! Don't stop him!"

"He's hysterical! He must be calmed down."

"No! Let him shout! Let him get it all out!" Eric begged. But the needle acted fast, and soon Paul was sleeping quietly.

Eric rushed to Dr. Siegelman's office and informed him what had happened. Dr. Siegelman was visibly irritated that he had not been called immediately when Paul began to talk, and that the nurse had made the decision on her own, to give Paul a sedative. "I will take care of everything. I guarantee you it will not happen again," he assured Eric.

"Thank you, Dr. Siegelman. I really appreciate your concern for Paul." Eric shook his hand with a strong grip and a wide smile.

"Rabbi, do you mind if I ask you a question…..uh, a personal question?"

"No, of course not. What is it?"

"How come you, an orthodox rabbi….I presume you are orthodox?"

Eric motioned affirmative with his head.

"How did you become such good friends with a priest, a Roman Catholic one at that?"

Eric was amused. "Why does it seem strange for a rabbi and a priest to be friends?"

CHAPTER 26

The doctor took a pipe from his side coat pocket, a bag of tobacco from another pocket, filled his pipe and put it in his mouth.

"It is not strange for leaders of different religions to be friends. No, that is not what I mean."

He hesitated as he lit the pipe and took a puff. "There is a closeness between you two like brothers. I notice you are here every day except Shabbos. The way you speak with Paul, plead with him and try to reach him. It is not a usual occurrence."

"Why, Dr. Siegelman, you have been spying on me!" Eric teased. He liked this big, gawky man, whose shirt sleeves were too short for his arms and his shoulders bent a if he were carrying the weight of the world on them. A heavy shock of unruly light brown hair covered his head.

"Of course, I have," he answered matter-of-factly. "It's my job to learn all I can about my patients, their families and friends." He puffed again on his pipe. "Don't you have irreconcilable theological differences that get in the way of friendship?"

Eric half-sat, half-leaned on the corner of the desk. "Doc, I may be a rabbi, but I am also a human being. Paul may be a priest, but he is also a human being. Sometimes, the soul of one human being calls out to the soul of another human being. I don't know why we became such good friends. I know absolutely nothing about his past, and he knows nothing about mine. Being a good friend doesn't always mean spilling your guts, but to share the joys of life together. We share mutual experiences. Yes, we have had plenty of theological discussions, heated ones at that, but for some reason or another, it was always like two friends arguing. We never took anything personally. I don't know," Eric shrugged his shoulders. "I guess I respect his beliefs even though I may not agree with them, and he respects my beliefs even though he does not follow them."

"When did you first meet?"

"We first met in the hospital in the middle of the night when we both lost someone special. Then fate brought us together again at the funeral of a woman from a mixed marriage."

"But how did you get to be such good friends?" The doctor crossed one arm over his stomach, and propping the other elbow on it, he held the pipe in his mouth.

"I don't know. I had invited him to speak at a Holocaust Memorial in my synagogue. I was impressed with his sincerity, his compassion, and above all, with his sensitivity. He will not even kill an ant in his house but catches it and puts it outside! He does not believe in taking any kind of life. If he sees a dead animal run over on the road, he comes near to crying. You know, Doctor, when I see him sitting in that bed with his face full of anguish, it tears my heart out." Eric looked at the doctor. "What terrible things is he remembering?"

Dr. Siegelman took the pipe from his mouth and tapped it out into the ashtray on the desk. "I don't know, but we have to get them out of him, or he will never recover."

Eric stood up. "Do you think you will be able to make him tell you what has happened to him during his lifetime?"

"Well," he put the pipe back into his pocket. "It seems that you have opened the first door. Now we have to try to find the locks to the other doors."

"Then, if need be, we'll give him a shot of sodium amytal to obtain some sort of working history. Do you still intend to get in touch with his sisters?"

"Yes, I do."

Dr. Siegelman shook his head and extended his hand. "Good luck, Rabbi. Let me know how you make out."

"Sure thing. Thank you!"

The doctor had walked Eric to the door. "Thanks again, Rabbi, for coming to see me. I enjoyed our talk."

"Likewise! So long, Doc."

Eric left the psychiatric ward with a feeling of satisfaction. He had accidently found the key words, "You have to be strong!" Why did they affect Paul so dramatically? He was anxious for his next visit with Paul.

Eric decided to stop off at Rachel's to share the good news with her. He knew how depressed she was about Paul. Besides, Eric felt a little guilty that Rachel was alone now. He was rarely able to see her, and with Paul gone, he worried that she might be lonely.

CHAPTER 27

RACHEL'S FACE LIT up when she opened the door. "HEY, Eric, long time, no see. Come on in!" She motioned for him to come in with a little bow of her head and sweep of her arm. She was adorable in her blue sweatpants and shirt with sloppy socks of bright green.

He realized that he was not here because he thought Rachel might be lonely, but because he missed her. He missed the comfortableness he felt in her presence, the lack of tension, of pressure. Yes, he was extremely glad to see her! He grabbed her hand and pulled her to him, encircling her with a big hug. She did not resist. "Great to see you!"

"Yep, same here!"

"I got a reaction out of Paul today!"

"Really! Tell me what happened." She pulled out of his arms. "How did you do it? What happened? Come on, sit down and tell me all about it." She gestured to the chair and perched herself on the couch.

"I don't really know, but when I said, 'You have to be strong,' he went crazy, slinging his arms, shaking his fists, and shouting!"

"What did he say?"

"He repeated my words, 'You have to be strong; you have to be strong' over and over again."

"Well, obviously, you hit a raw nerve. Who do you think said that to him, and why would it affect him so? Do you think it was his father?" Excitement was in her voice.

Before Eric could answer, the phone rang. Rachel pick up the receiver. "Hello… oh hello, Dawn. Yes, Eric is here. Hold on."

Rachel covered the mouthpiece with her hand. "It's Dawn. She called here a few times before." She handed the phone to Eric and started to walk out of the room. "I'll make us some coffee."

Rachel could hear Eric's voice from the living room a she worked in the kitchen. "I'll be home shortly. I just stopped by for a few minutes to tell Rachel about Paul. I got a reaction out of him today for the first time! Dawn, this not the time for discussion. We will talk when I get home. Stop crowding me, Dawn! I have a right to have outside friends – male and female. I do not have to ask your permission. Dawn! I am NOT here all the time! I have not seen Rachel in a long time. Goodbye, Dawn. I'll be home in a little while!"

"Rachel?" Eric called as he slammed down the phone.

"I'm in the kitchen. Coffee's almost ready. Come on in."

"Ah! Smells good," Eric strove for nonchalance; however, his seething anger was obvious.

"I baked some fresh muffins today. How about one of these?" She put a large cookie jar full of blueberry muffins on the table.

"Hell, yes!" Eric kidded.

"Do you think you'll be able to talk to Paul now, since you got him to acknowledge you?"

"Well, he didn't actually acknowledge me. But now, since he did begin to talk, maybe I'll be able to get him in a conversation." He picked up a muffin and bit into it. "Um-m-m-m, good!" He shook his head in emphasis, "But I'll have to go slowly with Paul. I don't want to lose him again."

Again, the phone rang. Rachel picked up the kitchen wall-phone.

"You despicable whore! Have you still got my husband there?" the angry voice demanded at the other end of the line, loud enough to be heard by Eric. Rachel handed him the phone without answering.

Eric's face was dark with anger. He spoke between clenched teeth. "I'll be home soon. Do NOT call me again!" He rose and slammed the phone onto the hook.

"I think you had better go home now, Eric." Rachel said calmly, though her hands were shaking.

"But I want to talk with you! I miss you!"

"Yes, I would like to talk with you, too, and I also miss you. But I still think you had better go home now."

CHAPTER 27

"I guess you're right," Eric replied with a deep sigh. "But I promise you, I'll come again, soon."

"That would be nice, that you."

Eric gave Rachel another bear-hug at the door. "I really do miss you, Rachel."

"Yeah, I really do miss you, too, Eric. Hang in there, things will work out – I hope." Closing the door, Rachel leaned against it and cried.

As Eric left the house, he felt a tightening in his chest. "Just nerves," he told himself. He slammed the car door and started the motor in a rage.

Eric was met with a slap across the face when he walked through his front door. Dawn grabbed the front of his shirt and ripped it from the neck to the hem. He was, as always, surprised at her great strength when she was angry.

"Don't hit me again," he warned her. He could feel the pulses in his temples pounding.

"I'll teach you to go to that piece of trash, that slut!" she shouted as her long nails tore into his face and neck.

Blind with fury, Eric struck back at her, throwing her against the wall.

"How dare you hit me!" she screamed at the top of her lungs.

"You have no right hitting me!" he shouted back. "I told you not to hit me!"

"You're a liar!" she yelled.

"I am not a liar! What do you want from me?"

"I want you to stop going to that whore! I am the one who is your wife, not her!"

"She is not a whore. She is my friend, and I will not allow you to call her names. Dawn, so help me, I'm going to leave you!"

"Leave me?" Dawn seemed surprised. Her whole manner changed instantly from hysterical anger to serene sweetness. She'd answered him in a matter-of-fact voice with a small laugh. "Why would you want to leave me? Just because we had a little argument. That's ludicrous! Come, sweetheart, I have prepared a wonderful meal for you."

THE SECOND GENERATION

Eric's heart was racing. Her calmness, as if nothing had happened, infuriated him as much as her anger.

"Look at me!" he held out his hands and pointed to his neck, chest and face, where blood was running from the deep scratches onto his torn shirt.

"You deserved it." Dawn calmly replied. "Now be a good boy and sit down and eat."

In frustrated fury, Eric picked up the dish of food, slung it against the wall with all his might, and started towards Dawn. Dawn grabbed a glass vase from the table and smashed it over Eric's head. He dropped unconscious to the floor.

When Eric awoke, the house was dark, and he was lying in sticky blood on the floor. He got up painfully, turned on the lights, and found himself alone. Dawn was gone. He stumbled to the bathroom, and leaning over the sink, splashed cold water on his face and neck. Looking into the mirror, he began to sob uncontrollably. "My God, my God! What am I going to do? I can't go to a doctor! What would I tell him? I'll be disgraced in the community! It would probably make the papers." He went to the phone and called Rachel.

"Eric, what is the matter?" Rachel asked in alarm.

"Come and get me! Please, Rachel, Please!"

"Where is Dawn?"

"I don't know. She is gone. She is not here. I am hurt! I'm bleeding!"

"I'll be right there." Rachel hung up the phone.

Rachel slipped on a pair of jeans, her sneakers, and a heavy sweater. Her heart was pounding with fear. What could have happened? Eric was hurt! Bleeding!

When Rachel arrived at Eric's house, she found him sitting in a daze, dried blood still evident on his head, his face, and his ripped shirt.

"Come on, I'll take you to the hospital. You may need some stitches."

"No, I can't go to any hospital! There will be a scandal if anyone finds out about this!"

"Where do you want to go?"

"take me to your house."

CHAPTER 27

"Isn't it dangerous? Dawn will come over and make a scene."

"No, she won't. I know her. She will not do that. Please, Rachel, take me to your place. I have nowhere else to go. Please help me."

"How about your parent's house?"

"No, my father is still not well. If he sees me like this, I do not know what kind of reaction he will have. Please, Rachel, you are all I have. Please help me." Eric's dark eyes pleaded with pain.

"Okay, come on!" Rachel started to help him up, when the front door flew open and Dawn burst in with two policemen, both familiar to Eric.

"I won't stand you beating me anymore, Eric! I am going to the Women's Shelter, away from you, until we can get this worked out."

"The Women's Shelter?" Eric could not believe what he was hearing.

"Yes, the shelter for battered women. These policemen will protect me while I get what I need, so don't try anything." She turned to the officers. "This is my husband, RABBI Eric Froman," she said, "Please don't let him hit me when I turn my back to get some of my things."

Humiliation filled Eric's soul. He did not know what to say or what to do.

One policeman answered, "But, lady, he looks in worse shape than you do! I'm not sure who battered who! He's all bloody and you aren't even marked!"

"You don't know," she said, lifting her blouse and showing bruises on her shoulder and back. "See where he beat me? And here he is with his whore in our home!"

Eric didn't remember hitting her. Maybe he had, he thought. He didn't remember.

Rachel stood humiliated and degraded. She did not want to be in this mess between husband and wife, but Eric was her friend, and he had called her for help. She remained with Eric, quietly standing next to him until Dawn left with the policemen. Then, letting him lean on her, she gently guided him to her car.

At home, Rachel washed away the dried blood and pulled out some slivers of glass. A couple of the cuts were quite deep, deep enough for stitches she was sure, but Eric again firmly refused to call a doctor or to go to the hospital. Rachel pulled the skin together as best as she could with butterfly band-aides. Thank God he wears a yarmulke all the time, she thought to herself. It will cover the scars! She put him in her bed and made up a bed for herself on the couch. Exhausted Eric fell into a restless sleep. At three o'clock in the morning, the phone range. It was Dawn. Rachel woke Eric and gave him the phone.

"What happened, love heart?" she purred. "Why are we sleeping in two different places?"

"What do you mean, 'what happened?' We almost killed each other!" Eric struggled to cope with her astonishing about-face.

"Nonsense, Eric, my love, we are LIVING – it's exciting! Life is so exciting for us! Sure, we fight, but remember how we make love, especially after we fight! What has one thing got to do with the other?"

"You hurt me, Dawn, and I hurt you! We hurt each other, emotionally as well as physically."

"No, my love, I love you. Didn't you hear what I said? I love you so much! It doesn't matter that we fight. It's good, we let out all our feelings. Our life is not boring like other couples. We lead an exciting life together! We love each other! How can two people who can't bear getting out of bed, not love each other? Come on home, now. I want you to hold me in your arms."

"But you said you were staying at the Women's Shelter!" Eric groped for understanding of what he was hearing. Wasn't she angry? Hadn't they fought each other? The policemen were real, weren't they? Was he going crazy?

"No, my love, I am in our bed waiting for you. Come to me lover. I long to feel your wonderful body next to mine."

"No, Dawn, I'm tired and I hurt. Tomorrow I will come home, and we will try to talk."

"Think of my body next to yours, my sweet love. Think of me kissing you all over. Think of my lips on your body, lover. Don't you want me as much as I want you, my darling?"

"Dawn, I can't stand this roller-coaster of love and abuse! How can you say you love me, after nearly killing me? I just want to sleep and rest. Goodnight, Dawn, I'll come home tomorrow."

CHAPTER 27

At four o'clock, Rachel's doorbell rang, then every other doorbell in the apartment house was rung, as buttons were punched frantically. Awakened out of deep sleep, Eric did not know where he was, and could not distinguish whether the doorbell or the phone was ringing. Rachel jumped up from the couch, her heart pounding as blows fell repeatedly on the door. Someone in the complex had released the front door entrance, and someone was outside her apartment, beating on the door!

"Who is it? Who's there?" Rachel called.

"Open up at once! It's Dawn."

"What's the matter?" Rachel asked in alarm as she opened the door.

Dawn pushed into the house, grabbing Rachel's breast and twisting it with force. "Where's my husband, slut?" she demanded loudly.

When Eric heard her voice, he began to shake. He wanted to run from her, to hide. He wanted to get away from her. He jumped out of bed and disappeared into the closet.

"Stop it, you're hurting me!" he heard Rachel cry out.

Dawn stormed into the bedroom, and not seeing Eric anywhere, she began to push and shove Rachel, shouting, "Where is he? Whore! Slut! He belongs to me!"

"Obviously, he isn't here," Rachel answered, protecting Eric. "Get out of my apartment! Get out right now!"

"Where did he go?" Dawn ran from room to room. Then she ran to the front door, opened it and shouted into the hallway. "My husband, RABBI Eric Froman, is sleeping with this despicable whore!" Since Dawn had already awakened everyone by punching all the doorbells, heads popped out of all the apartments, voices said, "Be quiet, we're trying to sleep!" and "What is it? What's the matter?"

In desperation, Rachel tried to pull Dawn back into the apartment. Dawn responded with, "Hit me! Hit me! I dare you to hit me!" Then she turned and ran back into the bedroom, shouting, "Where is he? I KNOW he is here!" She stopped compulsively before the dresser mirror to admire herself, fixing her hair and straightening her clothing, enjoying her high color and the flash of her eyes. Then she returned to her search. Her eyes rested on the closet. She gleefully opened the closet, pushing clothes left and right until she found Eric sitting on a box in back corner.

"Come, my darling," she said seductively, taking him by the hand, "Come with me. Let's talk."

"I don't want to talk with you! I don't want to be with you now, Dawn, please leave me alone!"

"Oh, yes, you do, my precious love." Tears began to flow from her eyes. "I love you. I want to talk with you and get our problems straightened out. Please, please come with me," she said in her little-girl voice.

Rachel also began to plead with Eric. "Please, Eric, come out and take this wild animal out of my house! I am disgraced and mortified! Please just get her out of here NOW, Eric!"

Eric reluctantly and with pain slowly emerged from the closet. "Leave now, Dawn. I am coming with you." He put on his cot and as they walked to the door, Dawn, hanging onto his arm and giggling with delight, paused to say to Rachel, "We really do love each other, very, very much. We just have some minor problems to work out. But we love each other and that's all that matters. I'm sorry if you were caught up in the middle." Again, she giggled, like a little girl playing a game.

"Get out of my house and never come back!" Rachel replied firmly as she closed the door behind them.

In the morning, the building superintendent called Rachel. "I don't care what your private life is, but please don't let it disturb the whole complex. If there is another disturbance like last night, I will have to ask you to move."

The following day, Rachel began looking for another place to live.

After driving home in Dawn's car in silence, Eric went immediately to their bedroom, wanting only now to escape from Dawn. But Dawn followed him, and as he turned from hanging his coat in the closet, they stood face to face. Both searched for some signs that would communicate the direction their relationship would now take. As Eric stood looking at Dawn, her fingers began to unfasten her clothing. She allowed each piece to drop to the floor, balancing on each foot to strip off shoes and stockings. Naked, she stretched in front of Eric on tiptoe, arching her body and cupping her breasts

CHAPTER 27

sensuously, holding Eric with her measuring, Taunting stare. His eyes dropped to the length of her legs, then rose to her flat stomach, continuing to the pink-tipped breasts she held pointing tantalizing. Eric said nothing, but turned and walked to the bed, lying down on his back fully clothed. He did not move as Dawn lay down beside him, turning on her side to place her arms around him. She snuggled as close as she could. Eric made no move away from her.

"I'm lost," he thought to himself. "My career cannot withstand another divorce. My reputation will suffer. I must work out our problems. I must save our marriage. I have counseled other troubled marriages and made them work." In his heart, Eric also knew that even after all she had done, he still loved her. He still desired her! As he turned and encircled her in his protective arms like a baby, he did not see her triumphant smile, as he had not seen it many times in the past.

CHAPTER 28

THE NEXT MORNING, Eric phoned Rachel from his office. "I'm sorry, Rachel, for what happened last night."

"I'm humiliated, Eric. Everyone here is ignoring me, and I got a warning from the landlord to quiet down or move out. He told me that they didn't care about my personal life, but I am not to disturb the other tenants again. Eric, I am sure they all think I'm having an affair with you!" She began to cry.

"Rachel, please don't cry! I promise you it won't happen again!"

There was a buzz from the intercom system. "Rabbi," Judy, said "you have an important call on the other line."

"Who is it?" Eric asked impatiently.

"It's long distance from Philadelphia. A Mr. Blackman. He said it was especially important."

"Okay, hold him for one minute." Eric pushed the extension on Rachel's call.

"Rachel, can you meet me at three today at the Institution? I want you to go with me to see Paul; then afterwards we'll talk."

There was a sigh, and silence at the other end of the line.

"Please, Rachel, please come with me to see Paul."

"Okay," she gave an even deeper sigh. "I'll be there. Goodbye." There was a click on the line.

Eric took the other call. "I know why you are calling, Mr. Blackman. I haven't sent in the marriage license from your daughter's wedding. I'm very sorry. I'll send it in today. Thank you for calling!"

After Eric hung up the phone, he leaned back in the chair and ran his hands through his hair. "I can't take this tension! It's affecting my work, my life. It's killing me!" he said aloud to himself.

Rachel was waiting for Paul on a bench in front of the Institution. She stood to meet him, and he put his arms around her, holding her head against his chest. "Thank you for coming."

"Eric, I have to talk with you."

"Later. Let's see Paul now."

When they came into the room, Paul was sleeping. He looked so frail and helpless! His sunken eye sockets were surrounded by grayness, and his eyes visibly flickered under their lids, as soft moans and groans gurgled in his throat.

Rachel bent over and gently kissed him on the cheek. Paul's eyes flew open and his arms clutched her, pulling her down to him so that her head was facing his on the pillow, her body crouched awkwardly by the side of the bed.

"Christina! You have come to me! I knew you would come!" His hollow eyes were alighting with happiness.

"Paul..." Before Rachel could speak, Eric placed his hand on her shoulder.

"Sh-h-h. Just keep him talking," he whispered, and hurried out of the room. Within minutes, Eric returned with Dr. Siegelman. Rachel looked at the doctor and raised her eyebrows, indicating she did not know what to do.

The doctor pulled a chair around to face Paul and Rachel and sat down. He spoke nonchalantly, "Hey Paul, introduce me to this beautiful lady who came to see you!"

Paul ignored the question and directed his attention only to Rachel. "I have missed you so, Christina! I'm so happy to see you again! Hold me like you used to, please?" He released Rachel and sat up in the bed, holding out his arms to her. "Hold me?"

Rachel looked at the doctor. He motioned her to comply. She sat down beside Paul and took him in her arms. He laid his head on her breast. They were both in an awkward position, but Paul did not seem to mind. The tears streamed down his face. "You have grown quite a bit, Paul. You don't exactly fit in my lap anymore." Rachel tried to pet his head.

"You had no right leaving me, Christina! Why did you leave me? You know I needed you!" Paul demanded.

CHAPTER 28

Rachel looked at the doctor, who mouth the words for Rachel to say: "Why do you think I left you, Paul?"

Apparently, the awkward position was too much for Paul. He pulled back, wiping the tears with his sleeve. "You didn't want to leave me, did you? You loved me, didn't you, Christina? You did love me!"

Rachel, fearful of saying something wrong, kept looking to the doctor for prompting. He shook his head affirmatively. "Yes, of course I love you, very, very much! Why would you ever doubt that I love you, Paul?"

Paul burst out into loud wailing. "I didn't mean to kill you, Christina! I love you! I have always loved you!"

Shocked, Rachel instinctively moved back from Paul. Eric, standing beside Dr. Siegelman, opened his mouth. Siegelman reached to his side and grabbed Eric's hand as a signal to be quiet. "He did not even look at me," Eric though, "how could he know I was about to say something?"

With his other hand, he motioned to Rachel to move back to Paul, and to ask him how and why he had killed her. Rachel complied, taking Paul's hand, she patted it a few times, then innocently asked, "How did you kill me, Paul?"

"I wished you were dead, and you died!"

Rachel breathed a sigh of relief. "Why did you wish I was dead?"

"Because you didn't come to me that night when I really needed you. You went out with your

Boyfriend instead! Your boyfriend meant more to you than I did!" Paul turned his head aside and looked at Rachel. With his lower lip extended in a pout, he declared, "I'm mad at you, Christina!"

Rachel's heart melted. She did not wait for any instructions from Dr. Siegelman, but leaned over and took Paul in her arms, rocking back and forth with him. "Aw, you poor little boy. My death wasn't your fault. It just happened. I love you very much, Paul. Everything will be all right. You just wait and see. Everything will be all right."

Suddenly, Paul let Rachel go. "I'm very tired now. I would like to sleep. Thank you for coming to me, Christina. I love you so much!

Goodnight!" He lay down on his side, pulled the sheet over his shoulder and fell at once into a peaceful, deep sleep.

Rachel turned to Dr. Siegelman. "I'm sorry, but he just looked so pathetic."

"It's okay," the doctor answered her. "I don't think we could have gotten any more out of him today, anyway."

"I'm drained," Eric pushed back his hair from his brow. "The doctor and I did all the work, and you're tired!" Rachel asked sarcastically.

Eric ignored her. "Come on, Doc. Let me treat you to a cup of coffee. You were really great!"

"Thanks, but I can't leave now. I'm on duty."

"Don't you have a cafeteria here?" Eric asked.

"Sure, but they don't exactly serve kosher ham! Will you eat in it?"

"Do they have tea bags?"

"Of course!"

"And do they have paper cups?"

"I get the picture! Sure, I'll share a drink with you!" The doctor grinned at Eric.

"What about me? What am I, chopped liver?" Rachel demanded.

"Of course not." The doctor held out a bent arm. "My most able assistant, could I please offer you a cup of tea.... in a paper cup?"

"Delighted, of course, Sir. I would be most delighted." Rachel took his arm, and the three of them headed toward the elevator.

"Didn't Paul once tell us that his sister, Christina, was killed when he fell off a horse?" Rachel asked as they were riding in the elevator.

"Yes, now since you mentioned it, I think he did, but no other details." Eric responded.

The doctor added, "Well, whoever she was, I think she was older than Paul."

"How do you know that?" Eric asked.

"Well, the way Paul tried to snuggle up in Rachel's arms, he must have been a small boy. I don't think he would have related like that to someone younger than he."

"Hey, you're right!" Eric interjected excitedly. "Remember, Paul said that Christina preferred her boyfriend over him, and he had

CHAPTER 28

wished her to be dead? Through the process of elimination, we can figure it out. He thanked you, Rachel, for coming to him like he knew you would. It was not his mother because he would not call his mother Christina. I don't think it would be an aunt. It would have to be either a friend or a sister. What do you think, Doctor Siegelman?"

"Could be. What you say sounds logical. Did you try to contact Paul's sisters?"

"I've been thinking about that. I have a plan. Come on, let's pick up our tea, and I'll pass it by you to see what you think." They had exited the elevator and were walking up the hall to the café.

On the counter was a bowel of raisin cooks, individually wrapped. Dr. Siegelman picked one up and examined it. "Hey, how about a cookie. They are kosher."

"Okay," Eric replied as he got the tea.

When they sat at the table, the doctor asked, "Now, what is your plan?"

"What plan?" Eric asked.

"The plan about Paul's sisters. Gee, I don't need any more patients with slipped minds, Rabbi!"

"Oh. Well, this is what I was thinking." He put two teaspoons of sugar in his tea. "You said that the sisters would not speak with you, and you are a doctor trying to help their brother."

"I said their husbands would not let me speak to them."

"Which means that their husbands probably have complete control over them or that they agree with their husbands. I tell you right now, if it were my brother, I would not listen to my wife not to help him!" Eric passionately stated.

Rachel cleared her throat but kept her eyes on her cookie packet, intently reading the ingredients. She did not see the glance that Eric shot at her.

"So, what is your plan?" the doctor repeated.

"I think Rachel should visit the sisters under the guise of being an old friend of Christina's. She just heard the news of what happened to Paul and his father and came to express her sympathy."

"Oh great, I'm sure they will just welcome Rachel Winograd with open arms, especially after complaining to the doctor about Paul's Jewish friends!" Rachel looked at Eric as if he were nuts.

"You won't be Rachel Winograd. You will be Jennifer Schmidt. Listen, Paul thought you were Christina. It wasn't that you were a woman. It was because you resemble Christina. Blond hair, blue eyes, fair skin. You even have a small delicate nose." Eric was excited.

"I don't even know who Christina was! Besides, it was plastered all over the news. How could I have just found out about it?"

"You have been in the islands with your husband on business. Okay, you heard about it, but you just got back and even though you have been out of touch with the family for many years, you did remember Christina and the tragedy of her death, and so on and so on. You can do it, Rachel!" Eric was excited about possibly finding a way to help Paul.

Rachel looked at the doctor. "What do you think?"

"I don't know what to tell you. It may work. Who knows? They may be nice ladies, but then again, if they are neo-Nazis, there could be some danger involved."

"No, that is not what I am scared of," Rachel answered. "I just feel bad about pushing in on someone's privacy and lying about it."

"Rachel, I am not suggesting you lie for no reason. If we are going to help Paul, we must know something about his past! Isn't that right, Doc?"

"Yes, that is true, but I can give Paul a shot of sodium amytal to try to obtain some sort of working history."

"But if you already knew something of his past, when you give him the shot, wouldn't it be easier to get him to talk because you would have targeted questions to ask him?"

"Yes, that is true. Any pre-information I have about the relationship between him and his father would be invaluable."

Rachel gave a deep sigh. She spread her hands on the table in front of her and studied them for a few seconds. "I'll do it!"

Doctor Siegelman looked at her with concern.

"I'll call one of them and ask if I can come to visit. Would it be helpful if I carried a small tape recorder in my pocket to record our conversation? Would that be of help to you, Doctor?"

CHAPTER 28

"Firsthand rather than secondary information is always better," Dr. Siegelman replied, "But I am worried about your safety."

"I don't want you in their house; instead, invite her out to an exclusive little coffee house like the Mozart Café and talk there," Eric suggested.

Doctor Siegelman was paged on the PR system to go to Room 582 immediately.

"Got to go, folks," he stood up. "Thanks for the tea and good company." He gave them a big smile as he hurried toward the elevator.

After a few minutes of silence, Rachel started to get up. "Well, I better be getting along too."

Eric reached over and took her hand. "No, sit here and let's talk."

Rachel sat down and look at Eric as she took back her hand.

"Rachel, I just want to tell you how thankful I am that you are still my friend and will still talk with me in spite of that last incident with Dawn."

"First of all, Eric, it was more than an incident. I can't even face any of the people living in my complex. I'm looking for a new apartment." Eric started to speak, but Rachel continued. "And secondly, you are my friend. You, yourself, haven't done anything to me, except of course, to bring that devasting character into my life. I won't let her ruin a good friendship, at least from my side of the friendship."

"Oh no, Rachel, I will never let anyone interfere with our friendship! But please, you must try to be objective. Put yourself in her place. After all, she did find her husband in your house, even in your bed! Her outburst could be defined as a crime of passion. People have been cleared by the courts as not guilty for so called 'crimes of passion.'"

"Hold it a minute!" Rachel's nostrils flared in anger. "She has no case! She knew you had come to my house after she attacked you."

Eric ignored her argument and tried to rationalize Dawn's behavior. "I hit her, too!"

"I know you! You would never have hit her if she had not struck you or done something to you first to provoke you. Have you ever hit anyone before in your whole life?"

"No, never!"

"Then why did you hit Dawn? Why, Eric?"

"When she slapped me across the face, screaming at me, I went crazy. But I should not have hit her! I should learn to control my temper!" Eric was shaking his head furiously back and forth. "I suddenly saw my father hitting my mother and I just struck out! I shouldn't have done it!"

"That's true. You should not have hit her, regardless, but for some reason or other, she seems to bring out the worst in you." Eric opened his mouth to reply, but Rachel held up her hand for him to be silent. "I'm not finished. Even if she did find you in my apartment, and even if she felt she was right, her behavior was unwarranted. All right, so she yelled at me and shove me around. I might be able to understand that, and even call it a 'crime of passion,' but if she is supposed to be so desperately in love with you, why did she try to destroy you? Disgrace you? How can she treat you with so little respect? Is that love? Is it?"

"She lost herself. She promised me that she would never do such a thing again."

"I don't believe her! She doesn't give a damn about reputation – hers or yours. Just so she gets what she wants and that is to control you. To totally control you!"

"Rachel, I know Dawn and we have our problems, but I still love her. She is my wife. Please, Rachel, I don't want to lose you as a friend either. I need you. I know Dawn's intentions are to destroy our bond, our friendship. But please, please, Rachel, hang in there until I can get this thing settled."

"I refuse to be a pawn, Eric. If you want to live with that wild animal, that is your business, but I do not have to tolerate her in my house and in my life."

"You are right, Rachel, but please give her another chance.... For my sake."

"What do you mean? What do you want me to do? I told you, I cannot be friends with her."

"Just try to understand that I am talking with her. Maybe I can get her to be secure, then she won't react so violently when she thinks her position is being challenged. I don't ask you to be friends with her. All I am asking is that if we happen to be together in public, try to be nice to her, please?"

CHAPTER 28

Tears of frustration welled up in Rachel's eyes. "She rings every one's doorbell in the middle of the night and shouts in the hallway, 'MY husband, RABBI Eric Froman is sleeping with this despicable whore,' and you want ME to be nice to her in public?!! Did you ever ask her to be nice to ME in public?" Tears were pouring down Rachel's cheeks.

Eric reached across the table, took Rachel's napkin, and patted the tears from her face. "You're right. You're right, but I am married to her. We have a lot of troubles, but I think we can work the out with tie. I must work on this marriage, Rachel. It is my second, and I don't want to be a two-time loser. I am a rabbi; I need to set an example of matrimonial compatibility for my professional survival."

"You are not a failure, Eric. I told you before you married her that she would destroy you. There is more to her than you know."

"Like what?" Eric was visibly irritated.

"I should have told you this before you married her."

"Don't play games with me, Rachel, what is it?" Eric spoke between clenched teeth.

"Dawn was not born Jewish. The Fieldstones adopted her when she was a little girl. They had difficulty having children and they adopted her. Afterwards, her brother was born."

"I know that. Dawn told me. In fact, that is one of the things about her that fascinated me, why she would want to remain Jewish after she grew up. She even chose to be converted orthodox when she was a teenager."

"She was adopted by a Jewish family who loved her and treated her like a queen. They were very wealthy and gave her a good life. But she has more love for herself than she has for them or for you, Eric; otherwise, she would try to protect you instead of disgracing you while trying to portray herself as the injured one."

Eric remembered Dawn's deliberate, inflammatory exaggerations to the neighbors, but he did not reply. "Thank you for being my friend, Rachel. For not cutting me off. I really love you."

"I love you too, Eric."

Eric looked at his watch. It was six o'clock. "Maybe they woke Paul for supper. Let's go back to his room and see if there is any difference after what happened today." Eric arose from his chair. "Come on."

"No, I'm dead tired. I want to go home. Call me when you can with a progress report on Paul, Okay?" Rachel said as she arose from her chair.

"Sure, bye, Rach." He planted a kiss on her forehead.

She kissed her fingers and pressed the kiss on the end of his nose. "So long, good luck." She turned and walked out of the cafeteria.

Eric watched her go with a lonely sadness. He did not tell Rachel that he wanted to go back to Paul because he did not want to go home to another confrontation with Dawn. He wanted very much to ask Rachel if he could come over to her home to relax a little, to have peace for just a little while, but he knew that after what happened the previous night, she would refuse him.

Fearing that Dawn would again call Rachel looking for him, Eric called Dawn to tell her where he was going. He felt nauseated. How he hated reporting his actions!

"How long will you be?" Dawn inquired.

"I don't know."

"What about dinner? I made dinner for you."

"I'll eat when I get home," insisted Eric.

"But everything will be cold and ruined."

"I don't care! So, I'll eat a cold and ruined dinner! I tell you what, Dawn. Come to the institution and sit with me while I talk with Paul. Maybe you can bring a dog collar and a leash, and afterwards, you can take me for a walk!" Sarcasm permeated his voice.

"Oaky, okay," Dawn backed off. "Go to your goy, but don't take too long."

"Thank you for your permission. I certainly appreciate it!" He put the phone away without waiting for a reply.

Eric went to Paul's room. Paul was still sleeping. Disappointed, he decided to go check the clergy list and see if there were any other Jewish patients. He would visit with them for a while and then come back. Maybe Paul would have awakened by then.

He found two Alzheimer patients and one schizophrenic. They all seemed happy to see a rabbi and repeated the special prayers with him. One of the Alzheimer patients thought he was a long-lost son

CHAPTER 28

and insisted on hugging and kissing him to which Eric complied with promises of returning "very soon."

With his spirits lifted, Eric returned to Paul's room, half-expecting to see him sitting up in bed and warmly greeting him as he came into the room. But the room was quiet as dusk descended. Only the dim light over the bed stood guard.

Paul lay on his right side, quietly sleeping. Eric pulled up a chair, sat down and studied Paul's face. His lips were slightly parted as he calmly breathed through his mouth. There was an ever so slight flush of color in his cheeks. There were no groans or mans or rapid movements under his eyelids.

Eric remembered sitting at Jacqueline's bedside the night she died, watching her the same way he was watching Paul. He covered his face with his hands and rock back and forth as the pain of memories lacerated his heart. "I lost Jacky, misjudged Sandra, and here I am now being suffocated by Dawn," he mumbled allowing self-pity to overwhelm his soul. "Will I ever find peace and happiness, or at least some sort of contentment?" he asked the ceiling as he looked up toward heaven.

A soft hand touched his shoulder from behind him. "Why don't you go home, Rabbi. There is nothing more you can do here." Eric turned and looked up into Dr. Siegelman's weary eyes.

Eric stood up. "I know, I was just witting here and thinking. The last time I sat at a bedside, I watched a noticeably young, extremely beautiful woman die." To his surprise, his eyes flooded with tears.

Doctor Siegelman walked over and sat down on the foot of the bed, spreading his hands on both sides of him for balance. "Did you know her?"

Eric sat back down in his chair facing the doctor and hesitated for a few seconds before he spoke. "Yes, I knew her. I had once hoped to marry her, but it didn't work out. She married someone else, a psychiatrist in fact." Eric hesitated.

"What happened?" Dr. Siegelman asked.

"He was killed in an automobile accident, and then she killed herself with an overdoes of drugs and alcohol. I didn't even know she was in town until I was called by the hospital to give her last rites. I didn't even know she had married. You can imagine my shock when I walked into that room and saw her lying on the bed, comatose." Eric's sorrowful eyes looked into the doctor's eyes.

Dr. Siegelman's dep sigh of compassion was more comforting to Eric than any words he could have spoken.

"Why are you here so late, Doc? Did you have an emergency?"

"No, sometimes my office here feels more like home to me than my home."

"I can relate with that. Are you married, Doc?"

"Yes, to a very fine lady."

"So, why do you choose to be here instead of home?" Eric asked softly.

"We seem to have grown apart. I guess a lot of it is my fault. She just got tired of me being out all hours and never having a set schedule... so she made a life of her own. Sometimes I feel I am going home to just a house, not a home. Big, beautiful and empty. She is rarely home, always busy with her charities, friends, clubs." his voice trailed off.

"Do you have any children?"

"No," the doctor answered with a sigh. "I wanted them, but Jenny said she didn't intend to raise children alone, and until I could buckle myself down to the responsibilities of being a father, she did not want to have children."

"When she married you, didn't she know that as a doctor, your schedule would be erratic?"

"Yes, but I guess she thought she could change me. But it didn't work. I get caught up in my work, and I just any sense of time."

Eric felt a close kinship to Dr. Siegelman. "How well I know what you are talking about!"

"I guess you experience it with a lot of your congregants?"

"With myself. I'm waiting here now because I don't want to go home to my wife!"

The doctor's sympathetic brown eyes waited for Eric to continue. Before he knew what happened, Eric had spilled out all his troubles with Dawn. "I love her, but I cannot tolerate the reporting every moment where I am, nor can I stand the abuse, physically and mentally." He looked at the doctor

For a comment.

CHAPTER 28

"Professionally, Rabbi, I am not supposed to comment or give advice. You know the procedure, you are not supposed to talk until you work out you own problems, but you are a professional with more wisdom than I have regarding the nature of people."

"Ho, hold it, my friend..."

"No, I graduated the Yeshiva. It was he wisdom of my rabbinical teachers that gave me the desire to go into the psychiatric field. I so admired the sagaciousness of the ancient Biblical world regarding human nature."

"What Yeshiva?

"Beit Yitzchok."

"I'm impressed. That is an exceedingly difficult Yeshiva. They specialize in Talmudic study. Some of the greatest rabbis teach there."

"Yes, that's true. Therefore, I always admired rabbis, especially the orthodox ones. They have an innate knowledge of life with a wonderful understanding how it should be lived."

Dr. Siegelman's words surprised Eric. His naivete was appealing and refreshing. Eric felt very old and weary.

"But back to the subject. You realize, Rabbi, your wife will never change. She will destroy you physically and emotionally."

"Why do you say that?" Eric was surprised. He had not expected to hear these words.

"I have had many cases like this before. You will always try to please her, and yet you never will."

"Don't you think we can maybe work things out?" Eric asked.

"Normally, I would say, possibly, but a woman like Dawn is unpredictable. One moment she is wonderful, the next moment she can be a holy terror. The tension of not knowing when there will be a flare-up will kill you. I have seen it happen more than once."

"Maybe I can learn to cope." Eric said hopefully.

"Some men thrive on tension. But not you, Rabbi, you are far too sensitive. You will never get used to the stress or the fits of violence."

"Why do they act like that, Doc?"

"It is the nature of some people to create tension around themselves. They enjoy it for they then become the center of attention, which gives them a kind of control. You would never believe cases that come before me sometimes."

"Yes, I would. I get them too! When they get too much for me to handle, I just send them to you!"

The ringing phone broke into the conversation. The doctor got up, walked around the bed and picked up the receiver.

"Hello."

"Yes, one moment please." He handed the phone to Eric and started to walk out of the room. Eric called out and motioned to him to wait.

"Hello, Dawn. I will be home in a little while. Goodbye." He placed the receiver back on the phone.

"Doctor, I guess I owe you for a session."

"True and I owe you for a session, so let's call it even."

"Not fair, I'm sure you get more money for a session than I do!"

"True, but maybe your advice is more valuable."

The phone rang again. Dawn's voice could be heard across the room. "You prefer to be with the goyim than with me. Is that despicable whore there too?"

"I am speaking with the doctor, Dawn. I'll be home in a little while. Now please don't call again." Eric gently hung up the receiver.

"Doc, is your wife ever abusive to you?"

"Oh no. She is very respectful. She is a lady in the full sense of the word."

"Did she ever speak of leaving you?"

"I suggested it once since I cannot live up to her expectations, but she only answered, 'I would rather be miserable with you than miserable without you.'"

"Honest, Doc. Do you love her?"

"Yes," the doctor answered without hesitation. "I love her, but I'm not good for her. I have made her life miserable."

"Listen to me, Dr. Samuel Siegelman. Learn a lesson from my experience. You could do a lot worse. Go home and take your wife in your arms, tell her you love her, and start your first son."

"But she already has a life of her own. We have drifted so far apart." He looked at his watch. "She probably is not even home now."

Eric pointed to the phone. "Call!" he demanded.

The doctor obediently picked up the phone and dialed. "Hi, Jenny. You're home? Oh, I just thought I would call you. Are you

CHAPTER 28

going out or will you be home tonight? Oh, I just wondered. I'm coming home now. Yes, I would like something to eat. A hamburger would be fine. Thanks. See you soon." He hung up the phone.

"Now, my friend. Stop off at a florist and pick up a bouquet of flowers, go home and start a new life!"

"Are you going to take flowers to your wife?" the doctor asked.

"No, my wife would probably make me eat them!"

"See, I told you, your advice is more valuable than mine." He put out his hand to shake hands with Eric. "Thanks, Rabbi, I don't know if it will work out but," he shrugged his shoulders, "What do I have to lose?"

"Only your loneliness." Eric answered. "And remember, I get to officiate at the briss!"

Again, the phone rang. Eric picked it up and when he heard Dawn's voice, he spoke between clenched teeth. "Damn it to hell! You call here one more time, I'll break off your finger, then you will really have something to show to the police!" Eric slammed the phone down with all his might. Paul stirred in his sleep. Eric reached over the bed and gently kissed Paul on the forehead.

"Good night, my friend, sleep well. I pray tomorrow will be a better day for you."

Eric thought he saw the wisp of a smile across Paul's lips. He watched him sleep for a few moments, then turned and walked out of the room.

CHAPTER 29

THE NEXT MORNING around ten o'clock, Rachel telephoned Paul's younger sister, Irene.

"Hello, my name is Jennifer Schmidt. I don't know if you remember me, but I was a friend of Christina's before she died. We went to school together."

"That's been a long time ago. I don't remember your name. Why are you calling?"

"I heard about your father and your brother. I always admired your father, and I want to express my sincere condolences to you and your family."

"That was quite a few months ago. How come you are only calling us now?" the sister's voice was suspicious.

"I have been away in the islands with my husband. I heard about the tragedy and wanted to contact you immediately, but my husband suffered a severe heart attack. I was involved with caring for him. I just got back to New York yesterday."

"I thank you very much for calling," Irene said, obviously ready to hang up the phone.

"Wait!" Rachel quickly responded. "I really was very upset when I heard your father had been killed. I guess as a young girl, I had a pretty big crush on him, and I never did get rid of it. In fact, I even married a man who resembled him."

"Yes, he was handsome. A lot of women had crushes on him." Irene's voice was shaky. "Listen, I thank you for calling, but… "

Rachel did not give her time to finish her sentence. "Irene," Rachel put a cry in her voice, "I know this is an imposition on you, and I am truly sorry to bother you, but I just lost my husband. I don't know how to explain it, but I feel like I have been dealt a double blow." Rachel hesitated and continued. I guess I am being

THE SECOND GENERATION

selfish and invading your privacy, but would you please meet with me and let's talk a little bit about old times?"

There was an audible sigh from Irene. "Well, I don't know. My husband wants it to be a closed subject."

Rachel picked up on the hesitation in her voice. "I don't think he would object to you meeting an old friend of the family. Please meet with me. Let's meet at uh, uh, the Mozart Café. It would be my pleasure for you to be my guest at lunch. I think I would feel much better if I could speak with you… just for a little while." Rachel did not let go. "I apologize for inconveniencing you, but it would mean an awful lot to me."

"Well, okay. When do you want to meet?"

"It's 10:10 now. Let's try to beat the lunch crowd. How about meeting around 11:30?"

"11:30 will be fine at the Mozart Café."

"Okay," Rachel responded, "I'll go ahead and get us a table. I'm wearing a light blue blazer, white shirt and dark blue skirt, in case you don't remember me."

"Fine, I'll see you in a little while." Irene answered without an enthusiasm. "Goodbye."

Rachel smiled as she picked up the small tape recorder from her desk and dropped it in her knitted shoulder bag. She called the synagogue secretary. "Is Rabbi Froman in?"

"No, he is not. Could I take a message, please?" Judy asked.

"This is Rachel, Judy. Could you please give the Rabbi a message for me?"

"Hi, Rachel. Sorry I didn't recognize your voice. He may still be home. Do you want to try him there?"

"No, just tell him the meeting is on for 11:30 today at the Mozart Café."

"Does he know what meeting you are talking about?

"Oh yes, he'll know. Thanks a million, Judy."

"You're welcome. Bye Rachel."

Rachel recognized Irene as she walked into the Café. She was exactly what Rachel had expected. She was a wispy sort of girl about five feet, six inches tall. Her blond hair was in a neat bun on the back of her neck with locks of curls in front of her ears. She

CHAPTER 29

was wearing a navy-blue suit with a crisp snow-white blouse. She held a small white leather clinch bag under her right arm. She walked with a purposeful stride to the three steps leading down to the dining area, hesitated and looked around, her eyes search for Jennifer Schmidt.

Rachel stood and waved until she caught Irene's attention, then motioned for her to come to the table for two she had reserved in the corner of the Café. With her left hand, she reached into her purse and activated the tape recorder she had placed at the mouth of the bag which was laying on the side of the table.

"I was planning on coming to town anyway." Irene smiled as she sat down. "Now refresh my memory about your relationship with Christina and my family."

Rachel's heartbeat faster. "She's smart." she thought. With a smile, she spoke fondly of the past. "Oh, in school, Christina and I were friends. She helped me a lot with work I did not understand. She was so intelligent! We both like the same boy. I pretended I liked him too, but I really was awed by your father. He was SO handsome, SO masculine. Oh my, such dreams I had of him. He was SO attractive!"

Irene smiled. "Yes, he was. We all admired him so much." Tears rose in her eyes.

The waitress handed menus to them. Rachel glanced through the menu. "All of the food here is really delicious. Please order something scrumptious."

"That's okay. You don't have to buy me lunch in return for information."

Rachel looked hurt. "No, Irene, I am not buying you a lunch in return for information. I just wanted to share a meal with you for old time's sake." Rachel bit her lips as she looked at Irene with pain in her eyes.

"Okay, I'll have the open-faced turkey sandwich with a chocolate ice cream soda."

Rachel ordered a large salad with hard-boiled eggs and a cup of coffee. "I would love to have what you ordered, Irene, but my buttons are popping, and I promise myself I would strictly adhere to my diet until I lose some of these love handles." Rachel pinched her

sides. It was the only time in her life that Rachel was happy to be slightly plum. "I admire people like you who are able to keep themselves so trim. I just look at food and inches appear on my hips!"

Irene laughed. It was obvious that she was beginning to like this person from her past. "I guess a lot of it has to do with genes, as well as with parents. Father was always insistent that we all remain in good shape. My, how he used to make us adhere to a rigorous routine of calisthenics and proper diet."

"And all the time, I was eating cream-puffs and admiring your family."

"I am trying awfully hard, but I just can't seem to recall any memory of you whatsoever. Did you continue to see our family after Christina died?"

"No, Christina was my friend, and it was through her I was able to visit you. After she died, there was no reason for me to come to your house. I don't think it would have been proper for a young girl to call on your father."

"Were your parents friendly with my parents? Did you live nearby?" Irene was probing.

"Only casually. Christina had many friends. She was popular in school. My parents rarely entertained in our home. My father always said he was too tired, and what little time he had at home, he wanted to rest and just be with his family."

"My father was the same way. Being a one-parent family was difficult for him, being both father and mother and running his book sales kept him quite busy. And then there was Paul. Whatever extra tie he had, he spent trying to rear Paul into manhood. I guess that was his biggest failure in life."

"Why? Don't you think being a priest is an honorable profession?"

"Of course, it is when there is more than one son in the family. Paul was father's only son. He was supposed to carry on the family name, to someday take my father's place as the patriarch of the family."

"I don't really remember Paul too well," Rachel said. "Wasn't he a bit of a weakling?" Rachel held her breath hoping that she had guessed correctly.

CHAPTER 29

"A little wimp, chubby little cry-baby, and the worst part of it was that he didn't want to even try to build himself up. Father tried everything, but nothing worked."

"That's surprising. Usually sons like to imitate their fathers." Rachel stated.

"I know. Father took him on overnight camping trips. He had his own backpack, the works. I remember the time when father even bought him real gun. Tell me, Jennifer, wouldn't every little boy just love to have a real gun!"

Rachel did not show her annoyance when the waitress arrived to inquire if they wanted dessert. Afraid the luncheon might come to an end; Rachel ordered another cup of coffee and a dish of vanilla ice cream. She insisted that Irene order a Sunday with all the works. When the waitress left, Rachel returned to the subject. "What happened with the gun? Did Paul refuse to touch it?"

"No, I think he was too frightened of father to reject his gift, but I think he wasn't too happy about it. H went out with father to practice shooting in the woods behind our home."

"What happened?"

"With beginner's luck, Paul killed a squirrel and then cried his eyes out. You should have seen the fit he threw. I distinctly remember it because the next day was when Christina got killed."

"That was a shocker. She was so young and beautiful." Rachel shook her head back and forth with sadness.

"Father personally shot the horse that threw her. It was hard on father; the two people he loved most in life dying. He never got over mother's death, and then to lose his favorite daughter as well, was just horrible. But he was so strong. Everyone admired the way he showed no emotion whatsoever but was a pillar of strength to us all." Irene spoke with great admiration.

"Christina never told me how your mother died. She always changed the subject when I asked her." Rachel said nonchalantly.

"Oh, she died giving birth to Paul. Her heart gave out. I know it wasn't right, but we all were angry with Paul for quite a while because we blamed him for killing other; that is, all except Christina, who took over the mothering." Irene looked down at her plat. "Maybe mother was lucky, not to have to see how her only son turned out." Irene was visibly holding back her tears.

Rachel reached over the small table and put her hand on Irene's. She spoke sympathetically. "I guess it was hard on all of you to lose a mother and a sister. But on Paul, it must have been twice as bad. He lost two mothers."

"Christina spoiled Paul. Especially when father would discipline or punish him, she would sneak into his room at night to comfort him or to bring him some food. We tried to tell her it wasn't good for him, that father was right; it was time that he grew up to be a an and stopped acting like a spoiled brat. But she wouldn't listen."

"I remember Christina as being a very kind person. I guess she felt sorry for a motherless little kid."

"To tell you the truth, later we all felt sorry for him, and I guess in a way, we all mothered hi when he was a little boy. Father warned us that we were spoiling him. Finally, he had to put down the law as to how we were to act with him. He wanted him to have discipline, self-reliance and independence."

"How old was Paul when Christina died?" Rachel asked.

"Seven years old. You would think that he would understand how much father was suffering, that he would try to be the kind of man that father wanted in order to comfort him. But, oh no, not Paul. He was a disappointment to father all of his life!"

"That's a shame. Do you think that is why he killed his father? Because he was a disappointment to him?" Unbelief was in Rachel's voice.

"No. Paul recently got mixed up with a group of Jews who were using him for their own aims. Father tried to warn him, but he wouldn't listen."

"No!" Rachel spoke with utter surprise.

Irene leaned forward and spoke in a low vice. "To tell you the truth, Jennifer, we all believe that the Jews are the ones who put Paul up to killing Father. He is their pawn." She leaned back with a smug look on her face.

"Really?" Rachel had a surprised look on her face. "Why would the Jews want to kill your father?"

CHAPTER 29

"For the same reason they wanted to destroy Germany. They are lower than vermin. Like a virus, they have conquered Paul's mind and made him an instrument of their plans." Irene was breathing hard with anger.

Revulsion permeated Rachel. With all her strength, she tried to keep a sweet smile on her face. "Have you tried to get Paul back again and find out if that is true? Have you gone to see him?"

Irene shook her head, "No, he is a diseased limb on the body of our family and our fatherland. He must be amputated to prevent the virus from spreading."

"How do you know? Maye he is just a weak person and was misled." Rachel pretended that she could not believe such a terrible thing and was groping for alternative reasons.

"No, he is far from weak. Father gave him a surprise 35th birthday party. He had gone to a lot of expense and trouble to make it perfect, and Paul had the nerve to stand up at the table and bad-mouth Germany when we all made a toast to the fall of the Berlin Wall and the unification of Germany. Can you imagine? The whole family sitting at the table and Paul accuses Germany of genocide and cruelty? Father almost slapped him to bring him back to his senses. Do you think that was a nice thing to do in front of his young nieces and nephews who are at a very impressionable age? See how a virus can infiltrate young minds and destroy them? God knows what thoughts our children may have after witnessing that fiasco!"

"Oh, I'm sure you have the ability to teach and guide your children with what you wish them to believe." Rachel struggled, trying to keep cynicism out of her voice.

Irene took it as a compliment. "You're damn right we shall. My children will know and appreciate their great heritage. They will know that Germany was stabbed in the back and betrayed by the Jews. They will to be always on guard not to let it happen again!" Irene was emphatic in her determination to rear the perfect Nazis.

Rachel was relieved when the waitress appeared with the check. As Rachel picked up the check, she looked at her watch. "Oh my, look at the time. It's almost one o'clock. I have to go." She extended a hand to Irene. "I was right. Seeing and talking with you has certainly enlightened my life!"

THE SECOND GENERATION

"Oh, must you go?" Irene said as she shook her hand. "You did not touch your ice cream."

"You were so interesting to speak with that I completely forgot. My hips don't need it anyway." Rachel joked.

"But I don't know anything about you." Irene was insistent.

"I'm sorry but I have a one o'clock appointment about my husband's estate and I'm late already. Please forgive me."

"Let's meet again. I really enjoyed talking with you." Irene stood up. "It was good seeing someone from the past." She gave Rachel a light hug. "Okay?"

Rachel returned the hug. "Sure, I'll call you." Rachel dropped $10.00 on the table for a tip and turned to go. "So long, Irene. Thanks again for meeting with me."

"My pleasure indeed. Bye Jennifer. Take care."

Raschel paid the bill and left without looking back to Irene. She stepped out of the Care and breathed deeply in the fresh air. She was surprised at how deeply Irene's words had disturbed her.

Rachel drove directly to Dr. Siegelman's office to give him the tape. "Eric will probably be angry I didn't let him hear it first, but I thought it was important for you to know this information as quickly as

Possible. You'll let the Rabbi hear it, won't you?

"No problem. Can you give me a hint as to what's on here?" He looked at the tape.

"Nope. I want you to form your own opinion. I'm curious what kind of reaction you will have to our conversation." Rachel turned to leave.

"Rachel?" Dr. Siegelman called her as she neared the door. Rachel turned around.

"Yes?"

"I just want you to know that I admire you. You must have really done a great job. I'm going to listen to the tape right now. Do you want to say and hear it again?"

"No thank you, Doctor. Once is enough for me. See Ya." She disappeared through the door.

CHAPTER 30

THE TAPE RACHEL had brought to Dr. Siegelman contained invaluable information for treating Paul.

Dr. Siegelman had permitted Eric to listen to the tape in the doctor's office. "Obviously, Paul has no one in this entire world. He has been exorcised from a family who considers him evil and a traitor to their cause." Eric remarked.

"That is not the real problem, Rabbi. He has gross stress reaction due to traumatic experiences in his childhood. From the tape, we see that his mother died when he was born which resulted in rejection by his family. Then his sister, who was a somewhat substitute mother, died when he was only seven years old, but most of all, think of the anguish he must have endured when his father tried to mold him into a 'macho man' even though he did not have the physical body or the mental desire to be a super Rambo."

"To me, it sounds like his father wanted Paul to be a super Nazi."

"Maye so," Dr. Siegelman shrugged his shoulders.

"What about the feelings of guilt he must have about killing his father?"

"I don't know how much guilt he feels, Rabbi, killing an abusive parent can be a catharsis for some people."

"But Paul is so sensitive; it must have some negative effect on him." Eric was insistent.

"You may be right, but right now, I'm concerned with getting Paul to release those repressed emotions and painful experiences he has buried in his unconscious."

"It looks like Rachel and I are the only family he has now. You know, Doc, as a rabbi, I am trained in working with troubled people. Could I please help in some way?"

"Yes, I know. My Talmudic learning has many times formed a basis of treating patients. I'm going to use the abreaction technique. First, we will try to drain off pent-up emotions and then we will try to open the way toward increased insight and desensitization. I'm going to try to reduce the emotional effects of disturbing experiences in his life through an understanding of their nature and origin."

"So, I should try to get him to talk about his past?"

"Yes, as his friend, he may talk with you. I surmise from what I heard on the tape; he is a very lonely person. Oh yes, by the way, I would appreciate it if you keep a tape recorder in your pocket and give it to me every time you speak with him."

"Suppose he won't talk about any of his past? What will happen to him? Will he remain like this the rest of his life?"

"Not necessarily. There are a number of special techniques which are employed today to recover repressed memories and emotions, that by the way, are effective in shortening the therapeutic process."

"Such as?" Eric inquired with interest.

"Hypnotic suggestion is sometime used, but more frequently the abreaction is induced by injection of narcotic drugs such as sodium pentothal and sodium amytal. In cases like Paul's, the success rate has been extremely high with drug therapy. I have had patients release intense emotions associated with painful memories."

"I feel so sorry for Paul, Doc. How he must have suffered in his life!" Eric rose to go.

"Rabbi, right now he doesn't need your pity, he needs your help." The doctor extended his hand. "And by the way, thanks for the advice you gave tome regarding my wife."

Eric had a pleased look on his face. "Everything worked out okay?"

"Well, we still have our problems, but we both think we can make a goal of it. At least, we have decided to try." There was an excited air about the doctor's shaggy appearance.

Eric placed his hand on Dr. Siegelman's shoulder. "Listen, Doc, we all have our specialties. I have been remarkably successful with family counseling, for everyone except myself, that is. If you and your wife have a sticky problem you are having difficulty in solving, promise me, you'll both come to me and we'll work it out together, okay?"

"Great idea. You have my word."

CHAPTER 30

Eric was out of the door when he turned around and came back to Doctor Siegelman. "I'm sorry to bother you, Doc, but would you have a small tape recorder? I'm going to see Paul now."

"Sure," the doctor reached into his middle desk drawer and handed a small Sony to Eric. "Good luck!"

"Thanks," Eric took the recorder and slipped it in his right jacket pocket. "So long, Doc."

"So long. If anything interesting happens, I'll be here for about another hour."

"Gotcha!" Eric disappeared down the hallway.

Eric's heart fell when he walked into Paul's room. Paul was lying on his back, with blank eyes staring at the ceiling. Eric sat down in the chair by the bed, took Paul's hand in his and began to rub it.

"Paul, I'm here. It's Eric. Paul, please look at me."

Nothing.

Eric took a deep breath and said softly but with a stern voice, "Paul, you have to fight it. YOU HAVE TO BE STRONG!"

Paul instantaneously covered his ears with his hands. "I killed those words! How can they keep tormenting me? Why?" His face was contorted.

"How can you kill words, Paul? How can you kill words? You have to be strong!"

"I don't know. I don't know!" He thrashed his head back and forth.

"Yes, you do, Paul. How did you kill the words, 'You have to be strong?'"

"I don't want to talk about it." He pulled the sheet over his head. "I can't talk about it!"

Eric pulled off the sheet with one swift jerk.

"Why did you do that, Eric? You are supposed to be my friend!" Paul sounded like a little hurt boy.

Eric sat down on the side of the bed. "Paul, I am your friend! I'm not only your friend, but I am your brother. Have you ever ha a brother, Paul?"

Paul slowly shook his head negatively as he investigated Eric's face with the wonder of a child.

THE SECOND GENERATION

Before Eric could speak the phone rang. Paul reached down to the sheet Eric had thrown on the bottom of the bed, grabbed it and covered his head with it as he lay back down on the pillow.

"Damn it to hell!" Eric said furiously as he picked up the receiver. "Hello!" anger radiated from his voice.

"Hi, honey. It is me. When are you coming home?"

"Dawn, will you please stop calling me all over the creation! I told you a thousand times I'll be home when I can. Now leave me alone!" He slammed the receiver down, hesitated a few moments and then took it off the phone and placed it on the nightstand. As Etic walked back around the bed, he automatically put his hands in his pockets and felt the tape recorder. "Oh hell!" he groaned as he realized his conversation with Dawn was also recorded. He went out into the hallway and played the tape recorder back to his last words with Paul.

Eric returned to Paul's bed, again sat down on the right side. He slowly lifted the side of the sheet covering Paul's face and with a wide smile said, "Peek-a-boo! Peel-a-boo, Paul, Peek-a-boo!" When he saw a smile on Paul's lips, he slowly pulled away the sheet without any objections from Paul.

"Now, where were we when the phone rang?"

The smile disappeared from Paul's face, replaced by fright. Eric took both of Paul's hands and held them. "Paul, please tell me how you killed the words, 'Y-O-U H-A-V-E T-0 B-E S-T-R-O-N-G."

Tears bubbled out of Paul's eyes, his mouth and chin shook as he tried to speak. His chest was heaving as he cried out. "I killed him, Eric. I killed my own father!"

"Oh, Paul," Eric hugged him in his arms and cradled him like a baby, rocking back and forth. "It's all right, Paul, it's all right!

Suddenly Paul pushed back from Eric's embrace. "You don't understand, Eric. I'm glad I killed him!" The tears were replaced by open defiance. "I'm not sorry! I do not feel any loss! I do not feel any regret! I know I am wicked, and I do not care! I killed my father and I am happy he is dead! I have sinned, and I don't care!" "No, Paul, you are not wicked. You saved my father's life! You may even have saved my life. Your father was going to kill us! You are a good person. I will be forever grateful to you."

CHAPTER 30

Paul looked straight into Eric's eyes. "I did not kill my father to save you or your father. I could have shoved him out of the way to keep him from killing your father. I saw myself in your father's place, and my father was shouting at me to be a man, to be strong, so I followed his orders. I was strong. I showed him I could be strong. I could be a man! I had courage. He killed my mother. He killed Christina. He killed the little squirrel!" The defiance disappeared, and the tears returned. "He took away my childhood from me. But he can't hurt me anymore. I showed him that I AM a man. I showed him that I am strong. I don't care if I burn in hellfire!"

"No, Paul. I believe there is no such thing as hellfire, and even if there were, you would not go there. You ae destined to go to the seventh heaven but not for many years to come. You are needed here on earth."

"Don't you hear me, Eric? I killed my father, and I do not even care! Shouldn't I feel some sort of remorse, some sort of pain, some sort of loss. I feel only peace, and that is wrong. It is against God's nature. A child should mourn the loss of a parent, not rejoice in it!" He wrapped his arms around his body and rocked back and forth.

A uniformed aide rapped twice in a perfunctory gesture and entered the room.

"Rabbi Froman?" she questioned the visitor. At Eric's nod, she went on, "your wife is on the phone." Her eyes caught the receiver off the hook. "Oh, no wonder she could not get through; the phone is off the hook!" She walked over and put the receiver back on its cradle, then she continued her sentence. "Your wife wants to know when you are coming home. We aren't supposed to allow visitors to receive calls at the nurses' station, but she insisted that she had to speak with you. She threatened to call the Director if we couldn't call you to the phone." Her small close-set eyes were indignant and her round cheeks very pink.

Eric stood up. "I am sincerely sorry and apologize for the inconvenience caused you. My wife is not well. Would you please be so kind as to tell her to hang up. I'll call her from here." The aide nodded approval and Eric thanked her. He arose and walked over to the phone. While he was waiting, he noticed that Paul had laid down in the bed, covered up, and gone to sleep

Damn, damn, damn! A golden opportunity lost!"

"Eric?" Dawn's reproving voice questioned after a half a ring.

"Did you call here to check up on me?" he demanded. "How dare you threaten the personnel here! What in the hell is the matter with you?"

"Honey, I just want to know when you'll be home." Her tone was close to a whine. "It's already after ten o'clock! Any normal husband would be home by now."

"Dawn, when you married me you knew that I do not have a nine to five job. I was at a critical point with Paul and you spoiled it!"

"So, you prefer to be with that goy than with me!" She stated with anger.

"When you act like this, maybe I do! Don't call here again. I mean it, Dawn. Goodbye!"

Weariness consumed Eric's body. He felt all his strength had been drained. He reached in his pocket for the recorder. "Shit, not again?!!" He went into the bathroom, closed the door and again rewound the tape back to his conversation with Paul. He went to Dr. Siegelman's office. It was locked. He went to the nurses' station and asked for an envelope. As he wrote "Dr. Siegelman" across the front, put in the tape and sealed it, he again apologized for Dawn's call.

"It's okay, Rabbi. We just don't like to keep the line tied up with personal calls in case there is an emergency."

"I know. Would you please see that Dr. Siegelman gets this the first thing in the morning? It is very important."

"Sure, Rabbi, no problem. You have a good night."

"You, too. May it be a peaceful night for all you 'angels of mercy!'"

Eric did not wait for an answer but walked back to Paul's room. Paul was deep in sleep, cuddled in the fetal position. Eric took the cotton blanket from the bottom of the bed and pulled it over the sheet. He stroked back the hair from Paul's face, leaned over and kissed his head. "Sleep well, my brother, sleep well," he whispered. He stood up, put both hands on the small of his back, stretched and then walked to his car. He prayed Dawn would not start a confrontation when he got home.

CHAPTER 31

AS THE DAYS turned into weeks, the weeks into months the relationship between Dr. Siegelman, Eric and Paul strengthened into a strong friendship. In the security of the warmth and affection of his friends, Paul found the courage to shakily climb out or the abyss of mental hell.

At times, Paul would be uplifted, full of hope and inspiration. Other time he would be withdrawn, depressed and sullen. His radical mood swings, however, never gave any hint of violence of uncontrollable behavior. With his improvement, however, Paul became afraid to leave the confines of his room.

In one of Paul's irascible moos, Eric strove to encourage him to talk about his feelings. Dr. Siegelman had told Eric that the more Paul spoke of his emotions and what caused them, the more successful would be his recovery. The idea was to bring the dark trauma of Paul's life into the light of day, thus exorcising them.

"Tell me about your mother, Paul. Do you remember your mother?" Eric asked, even though he knew she had died soon after he was born.

"No, I don't remember my mother. She died after giving birth to me. I know my father, my whole family, hated me because I killed my mother." Paul's eyes widened in panic. "My God, Eric, I killed both my father and my mother!" He began to wring his hands. "I killed BOTH of my parents!"

"Paul, you know the Bible well. Answer a question for me, please."

Paul looked at Eric disbelievingly. Here he was telling him that he committed the sin of parricide, and he talks about the Bible?

Eric continued, ignoring Paul's surprised look. "Did Benjamin kill Rachel in the Bible?" Eric asked softly.

THE SECOND GENERATION

"Why do you ask me that?" Paul was suspicious.

"Come on, tell me, Paul. How did Rachel die?"

"She died giving birth to Benjamin."

"Was its Benjamin's fault? In his mother's womb, did Benjamin say: 'Well, I am going to be born today so that I can kill my mother'?"

Paul just looked at Eric, his mouth open.

"Is that what you did, Paul? Did you say in your mother's womb, "Well, I am going to be born today so that I can kill my mother?"

"So why did my father hate me so much?"

"How do you know your father hated you?" Eric's voice was almost a whisper.

"Because he was never pleased with me as a human being. He wanted to mold me into what HE wanted me to be, with no appreciation of what and who I was. He constantly demanded perfection; he used fear and pain to punish me."

"Is that why you became a priest, Paul? To escape your father's insistence that you turn into a hard-core Nazi?"

"A hard-core Nazi?? What are you talking about?"

"Your father was an infamous Nazi, Paul. He was an escaped Nazi, who successfully assimilated himself and his family into the American community." Eric opened his briefcase, took out a large envelope and handed it to Paul. "Here are the records about your father."

Paul refused to take the envelope. He turned his head away from Eric.

Eric arose and threw the envelope on the bed. "I have to go, Paul; read what is in the envelope. God works in mysterious ways." Eric put out his hand. Paul ignored him but sat quietly in his chair, his face pale. Eric patted his shoulder. "So long, Paul, see you." He turned and walked out of the room.

Eric twisted and turned all night. His sleep was disturbed by the thought that the materials he had given Paul would cause a regression in his improvement. "Surely Paul had inner thoughts about his father being a Nazi. How could he live with him all his life and not see the signs? Paul was worldly and well-educated as well as well-read. Maybe he knew but refused to acknowledge it. Maybe it is suppressed in his subconscious. Maybe this is one

CHAPTER 31

of his problems." Thoughts were skaters in his brain, racing back and forth.

Eric went to the Institution the next day with a fast beating heart fearful of what he would find.

He was relieved to find Paul dressed and sitting in a chair by the window. He was clean-shaven and his hair was combed.

"My, my, look at you!" Eric exclaimed with pleased excitement.

"I read what was in the envelope, Eric."

"And?"

"I don't want to discuss it ever again. This whole thing is something I am going to have to work out for myself. The information you gave to me has helped considerably, but I am he son of this man. I carry his genes. This is something I have to resolve." Paul was halfway speaking to Eric and half to himself. A sorrowful sigh tore out of his throat. "Eric, you asked me last night whether I became a priest to escape my father?" Eric nodded. "Well, that question started me thinking. Maybe in the beginning I did, but later I knew that I wanted to be a priest because I truly feel a 'calling' to serve people."

"And you are truly a man of the people, Paul. I will never forget that stormy night we first met, how badly you felt when you lost someone. I'll lay odds that not every priest would come out on a fierce night like that one."

"Not too many rabbis would have come out that night either."

"You're right. Just you and me. I guess we were destined to meet that night."

"Well, I certainly was fortunate." Paul was sincere.

"Mutual feeling," smiled Eric. "Hey, come on Paul. It's a beautiful day today. Let's take a walk outside as we talk." He motioned for Paul to get up.

"NO!" Paul's exclamation surprised Eric. Seeing the look on Eric's face, Paul softened his tone. "I'm sorry, Eric, but I'm not ready to leave this room. Not yet."

"It's okay. I understand. I will bet there are flies and bees out there anyway. A bird would probably drop on us if we sat outside." Eric answered with half a laugh.

Paul nodded with a soft smile. "Eric are you ever frightened. Do you ever cry? Do you wish you could be stronger?" Paul hesitated and then continued. "I talk to people, Eric. I give them advice. I seem to help them. Why can't I help myself?"

"Why are you beating on yourself because you are human? Yes, I have been frightened in my life. In fact, I would say downright scared many times. Yes, I have also cried with pain from the depths of my soul. You are not the only one who wishes he could be strong like the macho men in the movies. But that is only in the movies, Paul. You, me, we're human, and we are the real stuff from which humans are made with all the frailties of human beings. We can give advice to other people because we see their problems from a different perspective, and we are not involved emotionally with their feelings of guilt or fear of inadequacy. But when it hits home, and we feel these emotions in ourselves… emotions that rip and tear at the fiber of our being, then it is more difficult to control, to comprehend, much less resolve."

"How can I help others anymore when I can't even help myself?" Paul rubbed his hand against his forehead.

Eric turned his eyes heavenward. "Did you hear that, God? Methinks Paul is feeling sorry for himself. What do you think, God?"

"How can I serve God when I don't have enough courage to even leave this room?!" Paul angrily declared.

Eric sat on the end of the bed and took Paul's hands into his own. "Paul, you are one of the most wonderful servants God has ever had. You have guided, comforted, given strength and helped people. And you will again."

Paul began to wring his hands. "But I feel so empty inside. I am just a piece of flesh wrapped around bone that walks this earth for a few years and then becomes part of the earth. What does my existence mean?"

"That part of you called 'the soul' makes you more than bone and flesh, Paul. That mysterious part of us called 'soul' lifts us up and lets us ascend to the greatest of heights. Communicate with your soul, Paul, and you will see that your life is more than a fleeting shadow. A bird casts a shadow as it flies overhead. The

CHAPTER 31

shadow may not represent anything of substance, but the bird that casts that shadow does. It is the same with human beings. Some people spend their whole life living only for themselves, satisfying the desires and wills of their bodies, but forgetting the spark of heavenliness that inhabits their bodies. They cry, they mourn, and they are depressed within themselves because they do not get what they want, yet around them is a most beautiful world full of meaning, full of beauty. In the time I have known you, Paul, you have been the kind of person who not only saw but appreciated life and the world around you.

"Appreciate life, Eric? I took a life."

"That took strength, Paul."

"Strength?! What is strength, Eric? Does one have to have strength to kill another person? Or to get up in the morning? Or to do what you do not want to do? What is strength?" Paul's voice was filling with hostility. "My father told me to have strength to kill an innocent squirrel. I didn't want to kill it. I hated the gun. I did not even want to touch it! Then he told me I had to have strength to let the straps of my backpack cut into my shoulders and not to cry out. Why must one suffer just to show he has strength?!" Tears began forming in Paul's eyes.

"No! No! No! What you are speaking of is not strength, it is sadism. Your father enjoyed torturing my father in the slave labor camp, yet my father had the strength to survive; and when it came to the point where my father could have killed your father, his tormentor, he didn't have the strength."

"My father had strength, Eric. Remarkable strength." Paul shook his head from side to side. "At times I wondered what he felt inside of himself. Did he have feelings? To this day, I never knew what his weaknesses were or if he had any. It was a half-statement, half-question.

"Oh, he had feelings, all right! Feelings of superiority, feelings of power which he acquired by trampling on and killing others. In his mind, he became God because he had the power of life and death. Whenever he saw fear, or terror in his victim's eyes, he felt superior. He felt strong."

"Why didn't he kill your father in the camp, Eric? Why did he let him live?"

"It is hard to say, Paul. But I think he did not kill my father because my father never showed fear of him, but always defied him. He wanted to see that fear in my father's eyes and had he once seen it, he would have killed him!"

"Your father must have been terrified. Living under the fear of instantaneous death would cause anyone to be afraid."

"I think my father's fear was transferred to anger. He was determined to live despite all that was done to him. He was determined to outlive his persecutors and that is what kept him alive and going on, to live and someday get even. When I was growing up, I heard my father's nightmares when he dreamed of choking your father to death. He would wake up shouting how at last he had his revenge!"

"And yet, Eric, when he had that chance, he didn't do it. Why?"

"I don't know, Paul. Maybe subconsciously he felt that if he did kill him, he would be no better than your father. Maybe he just froze and relived moments in the camp. To have struck out in the camp would have meant certain death. Maybe it was a moment of self-preservation. I don't know if we will ever know the reason."

"How is your father? Does he talk about what happened?" Paul asked.

"No. He never mentions it. The closest he come is when he asks how you are, which he does every time I see him or speak with him. He is different now. He sits quietly in his chair for long spans of time with his eyes closed. He refuses to discuss anything about what happened."

"And your mother, how is she?"

"Frightened," Eric answered. "She doesn't know what to expect from my father. She has suffered a lot with him. I think she was accustomed to his behavior before, even the abusive behavior, but this new quietness makes her very uneasy."

"Does your mother love your father, Eric? Is that why she put up with him all these years?"

"No. I don't think she really loves him. I think he loves her despite the things he did to her; but she stays by him because

CHAPTER 31

they have a common experience in life that welded them together. She knows he needs her, and I guess in her own way, she needs him also. Often, however, I think they feed off each other's misery. They both lost everything and everybody they loved during the war, and their sorrow and unhappiness calls out one to the other – maybe two negatives in this case make a positive. I don't know, but I can tell you this. Being a second-generation survivor is to relive emotionally what my parents experienced, repeatedly."

Paul was surprised. Eric had never spoken of his deep feelings before. "I think you and I have some things in common, Eric. We may have come from different backgrounds, different philosophies, but our feelings are parallel. Our experiences may have made us brothers."

Eric smiled. "Okay, and by the way, my mother wants you over for dinner one night as soon as you can break out of here."

Panic swept across Paul's face. "I can't leave here. I can't go out there!" His fingers grasped the arms of his chair until his knuckles were white from the pressure. "I can't face them out there, Eric. Please don't make me!"

Eric was taken by surprise. "I'm not making you do anything you don't want to, Paul. Take it easy. Nobody is forcing you to do anything. Relax… come on, relax!" Eric wiped the perspiration from Paul's brow with a towel. "It's okay, fellow. Do you want me to go get Dr. Siegelman?"

"No, please don't. I'm just tired, Eric. I want to go to bed."

"Okay, come on, I'll help you undress."

"No, I just want to lie down." Eric noticed Paul's hands were shaking as he arose from the chair, stood up straight and took a deep breath. "It's okay, Eric. I can manage." He walked shakily over to the bed and laid down with a thump. He closed his eyes and then immediately opened them. "Good night, Eric. I enjoyed our conversation very much."

"I'm sorry I upset you, Paul."

"No, it's okay. I'll be all right. Can we continue our conversation again?" Paul's eyes closed.

"Sure, any time you want… or feel like it."

"Tomorrow?"

"Fine, but maybe we should wait and see how you feel tomorrow."

"I'll be all right. Tomorrow's okay. I'll look forward to it." Paul's words ran together in a mumble as his body became limp on the bed.

Eric pulled the blanket over him, looked at him for a moment, and then left the room. He headed towards Dr. Siegelman's office to give him the tape and found the office closed. "Shesh!" Eric mumbled out loud. "I guess he and his wife are seriously involved."

CHAPTER 32

PAUL WAS WAITING for Eric by the door when Eric arrived the next day. "You're late!"

"I don't remember making any definite appointments for today. I said I would see you sometime today, and here I am."

"But you always come around three. It is now three forty-five." Paul pointed to his watch.

"So, call me the late Rabbi Eric Froman!" Eric laughed. "I had quite a few appointments today, but I saved you until last. Remember the old saying: 'the best s last'!"

"Bullshit!"

"My, my, such language! And for a priest!" Eric clicked his tongue and shook his head.

"I don't know if I am still a priest," Paul said softly.

"Of course, you are! Wait! I have an idea. Do you want to come with me?"

"No! Where are you going?"

"Just down the stairs to the office… come on!" Eric motioned for Paul to come.

"No, I'll wait here for you. Will you be long?"

"I'll be right back." Eric half walked and half ran to the elevator. In the office he checked the clergy's information book for names of patients who were Catholic. "Here's one on the floor below Paul. Room 203. Great!"

One of the girls in the office looked up. "Are you happy to find a patient HERE?" she asked with humor.

"This one I am!" Eric answered joyfully.

"Why, may I ask? Who is he or she?"

Eric shrugged his shoulders, "I don't know!" He quickly turned to leave. "See you," he waved to the girl.

She waved her hand to him and laughed, "You need a break, Rabbi, you've been working too hard."

Eric had been to the hospital so frequently to see Paul that he now knew most of the nurses, doctors and staff, and they in turn both welcomed his visits and treated him as though he were on the payroll. As a member of the clergy, he could come and go, without restriction, and if he so desired, he could speak with other patients. He would, on his way to see Paul, stop to acknowledge or talk with those who responded to his friendliness. But today, he did not stop to chat as he walked through the light blue halls, but only shook a hand or patted a shoulder as he continued to walk hurriedly to Dr. Siegelman's office. The door was closed. Eric knocked impatiently. A few seconds later the door opened.

"I am busy with a patient now, Rabbi."

"How long will you be? It is very important."

"What is it?" the doctor asked concerned.

"Oh, everything is all right. But I think I have a way of getting Paul out of his room. It must be right now, Doc, but I need your help. How long will you be?"

"I'm almost finished. Give me a few moments." He quickly closed the door.

Eric paced the hall outside of the office. "Come on, Doc. Come on, Doc," he softly repeated over and over.

Finally, the door opened and out came an elderly man and the doctor.

"Isn't it a shame about my children?" the elderly man kept saying as he shook his head.

"Everything will be okay, Mr. Kleinman. Your children have not forsaken you. We'll talk more tomorrow. Okay?"

"Okay, thanks, Doc. You are a nice guy! I wish you were my son."

"It would be my pleasure." The doctor shook hands with Mr. Kleinman and then turned to Eric as Mr. Kleinman started down the hall to his room.

"Listen, Doc, there is a Catholic girl on the second floor. If we can convince Paul that he is needed as a priest, it may be a first step to get him out of that room," Eric explained.

"Why do you think you can get him out today?"

CHAPTER 32

"Because he is waiting by the door for me. Please, Doc, let's give it a try. What have we got to lose?"

"How do you know the girl wants to see a priest?"

"She's Catholic, and you are her doctor?"

"Yes, that's Marybeth Miller. Tragic case."

"Come on, Doc, you're driving me nuts!"

"Well, okay, but let me call a nurse to go with us. I don't like to go into a female's room without a nurse present."

"Please, Doc, do what you have to do but just do it!" Eric said in exasperation.

"Take it easy, Rabbi, or you are going to wind up in a room here. Go on to Paul, we'll catch up with you."

Paul was still waiting by the door. He was surprised that Eric was not carrying anything, since he had surmised that he had gone to get something to show him. "Where did you go?"

Eric grabbed Paul's hand. "Come with e, someone needs a priest!"

Instinctively Paul took a few steps forward, then realized he was outside of the room; with a pale face he quickly stepped back into the security of his room.

"I can't go out!" He began to breathe heavily. "Don't make me. Please! I can't go out there!"

Dr. Siegelman and a nurse arrived on the scene. "Did you tell him, Rabbi, that we need a priest pronto?" Dr. Siegelman asked.

"Yes, I did. He is just getting ready to go." Eric answered.

Paul looked with pleading eyes at the doctor. "I can't go, Doc. Tell Eric I can't go!"

"There is a Catholic girl on the floor below you, Paul, and she needs you. She needs you badly. You are a priest, and when you are needed, you must go!" Eric completely ignored Paul's reaction.

"I can't!"

"You are a priest – you must! This person needs you. Can you turn your back on someone who needs you?"

"I am no longer fit to be a priest. I have blood on my hands. How can I be a priest when I have blood on my hands!" He held up his hands, looking at them and hen showed them to Eric. "See the blood, Eric. There is blood on my hands!"

Eric paid no attention to Paul's words. He took the trembling hands and held them between his own and then placed them together in a praying position, palm to palm with fingers pointing upward.

"I see two hands pointing towards God for direction, asking God to give you the knowledge to help a person close by who needs a priest desperately. Now come with me, Paul. You are a priest and you are needed." He pulled on Paul's hands and kept repeating over and over... "You are a priest and you are needed!" Paul never took his eyes off Eric's face as Eric walked backwards pulling Paul after him the 50 feet to the exit door. He led Paul down the stairway, then turned and walked beside him as they continued to Room 203, the doctor and nurse following. As luck would have it, this stairway was not used frequently. Therefore, Paul did not have to be confronted with anyone else as he walked slowly, hesitatingly. Eric continued to guide him forward as they walked side-by-side down the stairs.

"You are a priest, and you are needed," Eric repeated. Paul stopped at the doorway entering the second floor. Eric, without further comment, opened the door with one hand and gently pushed Paul through with his other hand. When they were both through the door, Paul looked at Eric. "You pushed me! You shouldn't do that!!"

Eric, smiling broadly said, "You mean like this?" as he pushed Paul forward to Room 203.

When they came into the room, there was a little girl who looked to be 5 or 6 years old, sitting on a chair holding a large rag doll. Her strawberry red hair was tied back with a blue ribbon. Eric was as surprised as Paul to see her. The name in the register had read Marybeth Miller. He had not expected to see a child.

"Hello, Marybeth!" Dr. Siegelman spoke.

The child looked up at the doctor and then at the two men. The later afternoon sun shining through the window touched her lovely face like a soft spotlight. Her bluish-green eyes were accented with long blond lashes. There was a sprinkling of little freckles on her nose.

Eric guided Paul to a nearby chair. "We must look like giants to her," he whispered.

CHAPTER 32

"How are you, Marybeth?" Dr. Siegelman asked.

"Hi, Dr. Siegelman. Hi Nurse Dorothy. Do you know that there are two men who came in with you?" She asked suspiciously.

"Yes, Marybeth. They are my friends… this is… "

Marybeth interrupted the doctor. "Are they real?"

"Of course, we are real. Do you want to touch us to see that we are real?" Eric responded.

"No. You may be playing a trick on me. You may be controlling my mind and making me think you are real. Who are you?" She was hugging the doll closer to her.

"This is Father Paul Steiger. Children call him Father Paul, and I am his friend, Eric. We came to see you today. Would you like to have visitors today?"

"You are a priest?" Marybeth leaned forward in her chair to peer more closely at Paul.

Paul looked at Eric. Beads of sweat were standing on his forehead and running into his eyes.

"Well, are you or aren't you a priest?" Marybeth asked again.

"The young lady is waiting for your reply, Father Paul. How are you going to answer her?" Eric asked with a movement of his hand towards Paul, palm up as if he were introducing him.

Paul wiped the sweat from his brow. "Yes, Marybeth, I am a priest."

"A Catholic priest?" Marybeth asked.

"Yes, I am a Catholic priest."

"Oh yeah, if you are a Catholic priest, then where is your white collar? You are trying to fool me, aren't you?"

"No, Marybeth, I'm not trying to fool you. I truly am a Catholic priest and I don't have my collar on right now because my friends here," he pointed to Eric, the doctor and the nurse, "just told me you were here, and I didn't have time to put it on. Does it bother you that I don't have my collar on?"

"I don't know. I don't think I have ever seen a priest before without a collar on. Why are you here? Who told you I was here? Weas it one of them?" she asked warily.

"Who is 'them'?" Paul asked.

"Those people that talk to me."

"What people?"

"Those who tell me to do things."

"What do they look like?"

"I don't know," she said simply. "They never show themselves to me. I only hear them talking. Sometimes I see them when I am sleeping; I see them in my dreams. Am I sleeping now? Are you part of my dreams?"

"No, I'm real. Eric, my friend, here, he is real, too. Paul got up and walked over to Marybeth with his hand outstretched. "Here, touch my hand."

Marybeth looked suspiciously at the outstretched hand for a moment. "Go ahead and touch it." Slowly, she extended her hand and placed it on Paul's. Then she smiled, and lifting her hand, slapped Paul's hand three times. "You are real, aren't you?" she asked with satisfaction.

Eric was noticing Marybeth's hand, long with graceful slim fingers. "I wonder if she likes music?" Eric thought to himself and made a mental note to bring a music box the next time he came to see Paul.

"Does your parish priest visit you, Marybeth?" Paul asked softly.

"Yes, there is one who comes to see me every so often. But I don't like him close to me."

"Why?" Paul asked apprehensively, fearing the answer.

"Because he smells like garlic all the time."

Eric turned away so Marybeth would not see him laugh.

"I don't smell like garlic, do I?" asked Paul.

"No, you smell nice, but you don't have a collar on."

"Would you like me to come see you again?" Paul asked.

"Oh yes, now since I know you are real, it would be 'real nice'." She began to laugh. "That's a joke."

"You're pretty smart, aren't you?!" Paul laughed too.

"Yep, but next time wear your collar."

"Okay, I'll do that."

"Will you please bless me, Father?"

His hands shaking, Paul placed them on Marybeth's head and blessed her, tears running down his cheeks.

CHAPTER 32

When Paul and Eric returned to Paul's room, Paul flung himself down on the bed, hands behind his head. Eric sat at the foot of the bed.

"How did you arrange for that child to be there?" Paul asked Eric.

"I didn't. It's God's mysterious way of showing you that it's time to come back to humanity. You have come a long way in just these last few weeks, and now it is time to begin work again."

"I'm not ready yet, Eric. To go down those stairs was hard for me. When I even think of getting on an elevator and walking out of her, I feel a panic."

"You took your first step today, Paul. Give it time. You'll do it."

"Will you help me?"

"I can't afford not to. I have taken a liking to you. What can I do?"

"Don't you think it's a pain coming here to see me all the time?"

"Coming here… to the hospital… yes, it is indeed hard… but to see you? No, that's a pleasure I look forward to."

"Good, then can you go by the rectory tomorrow and bring a few of my collars with you?"

"How am I to go through your stuff? Come on, Paul, I can't do that! I'll go buy you some. Tell me where to go. That will be a first – a rabbi buying priest collars! Can't you image the face of the salesperson?"

"All of my collars are ordered, Eric. Listen, I'll call Father McClellan and tell him to have my things packed and ready for you. He is a good man."

"Okay, just tell me when. I suppose this means you intend to visit Marybeth again?"

"I'm going to try. Maybe I'll be able to help her. But first, I need to find out what is wrong with her, why she is here, so young."

"How are you going to do that?"

"I'll ask Dr. Siegelman when he comes to see me tomorrow."

"Paul, I think that's wonderful. You are a priest and as a clergyman, should be able to obtain a release to read her medical records. She sure is a sweet girl, isn't she, and sharp too."

"That she is… a real beauty. Just looking at her, you would never think anything was wrong with her. She seems to be having trouble with reality," Eric said.

THE SECOND GENERATION

"Yes, she does, and she is suffering. I have never been reconciled to the fact that innocent children must suffer," Paul sighed. "Even as a priest, I question, why does God do this to innocent children?"

"Maybe God has a purpose for her life? Maybe we cannot pull out one little aspect of a giant picture and question that aspect without ever seeing the whole picture. I don't know why she is like that, Paul, but I do know that somewhere in time or in space, there must be a reason. Don't we have to believe that there is a purpose for everything and that maybe someday we will find out what that purpose is. Until that time, we just must believe, otherwise we will go crazy trying to figure out something for which there is no answer." Eric shook his head as he spoke.

"Yes, Eric, I question but still believe that everything is preordained, and everything has a reason for happening."

"In Judaism, there is a belief that everything is contingent upon heaven except the fear of heaven, which means that certain things are preordained to happen, but it is up to us how we conduct ourselves when those things happen. We are given 'free will' which means we must choose what we will do, and it is by the choices we make that we are judged on high. I sincerely believe that whatever one does, that action comes back upon him… maybe seven-fold. If I do good, then someday that good will be returned to me; and if I do wrong, then that wrong will be done back to me. You have a similar belief, Paul. Don't you say, 'Those who live by the sword shall die by the sword?'"

"Yes, and I believe God gave us a set of laws to follow as to what is good and what is bad, so when we choose, we can choose between the good and the bad. Doesn't it say in Deuteronomy, 'and Moses said in the name of God, I have placed before you tis day… life and death… the thou shalts and thou shalt nots… ' which sounds easy, Eric, but I have often wondered how in the world is the average common man to know all the laws. What about people who don't even know how to read? And if they know how to read, they will not understand what they were reading! The Bible is very confusing and hard to understand. You, yourself, showed me your Talmud, how great minds sat and studied the words and tried to find different meanings in them, and even they, minds I could never

CHAPTER 32

hope to come near in understanding, the differ and have conflicting opinions."

"Paul, we believe it is all based on one philosophy as portrayed by the great Sage, Hillel, which both Judaism and Christianity follow: 'Don't do anything to anyone else which you would not want done to you!' That, my friend, is within everyone's comprehension. It crosses all lines of religions, races or cultures."

"The Christians say, 'Do unto others as you would have them do unto you.' We take the positive rather than the negative connotation." "But the positive has a completely different meaning, Paul. Think about it! Do to people what you would like someone to do to you. Maybe a person is a masochist, enjoying his pain when he is hurt, or maybe he has a martyr complex. He could become a sadist because he would want others to hurt so they might enjoy pain. What a can of worms that would open! And it does! Christianity is supposed to be a religion of love, brotherly kindness, and so on, but look at its history. It is filled with violence, cruelty and murder. Why? Because each wants to turn everyone to their way of thinking. Every splinter sect wants to convert everybody and tries to force conversion where it is not accepted. The Inquisition is the most hideous example. The Crusaders themselves are a big blotch on history and fall under the category of 'man's inhumanity to man.' Look at the negative side of the 'Golden Rule'– don't do anything to anyone else which you certainly don't want done to you! No way can that be misinterpreted of subverted to cause suffering."

Paul did not respond, and for a few moments there was a strained silence between the two men. Then, Paul spoke. "My father was like that. He wanted to make me into what HE wanted me to be. He tried to make me do things that he called 'manly' because he always wanted to be tested to the limits of his strength, of both body and mind."

Unexpectedly, Paul burst into tears. "I AM a man. There isn't just one standard to dictate what a man is. A man can be a dancer, a soldier, a writer, or a wrestler, or he can even be a philosopher! And he can still be a real man! What do you think, Eric? Do muscles and cruelty make the man, or does manhood come from within one's soul?"

"You are right, Paul. I have seen a cripple in a wheelchair who was more of a man than some images of the 'macho man.' Some of our greatest men of accomplishment in history were gentle, short, crippled or malformed. I can't think of many who really contributed to the good of mankind who were the real so called 'macho' type except in the movies, can you?"

Paul wiped his eyes. "Forgive me, Eric, I don't know what the matter with me is. I cry at everything now. I look out the window and see a mother bird teaching her baby to fly, and I cry. I found a bug in the room this morning and I put him out on the windowsill, and I cried."

"So? Are you trying to apologize because you are a sensitive, kind human being who has concern for all God's creation, man and nature alike? Well, men do cry, Paul. Men cry a lot. Maybe not in public, because it is not acceptable in our society, but men are human, with the same emotions as anyone else. We hurt inside. Why should we have to swallow that hurt, and stifle our pain?"

"Do you ever cry, Eric?" Paul asked.

"Yes, I do. I have wet my pillow with tears many times, out of frustration, out of disappointment, out of pain. Even animals cry out, Paul. Are we any less than animals?"

"I love you, Eric. You bring a lot of comfort to me."

"I love you too, Paul. You bring a sincere friendship to me."

 # CHAPTER 33

November 1987

FEAR GNAWED AT Rachel as she drove along Route 95 to the Rochester Medical Center. Her mind raced with thoughts of long-ago conversations and events. Had she made right decisions? For herself? For her family? What did the future hold for her? Would time be her friend or her enemy? With apprehension about facing the future, her thoughts shifted to the past.

She thought of all that had happened to her since she came to the United States. She was especially proud of her professional achievements at Syracuse University. She had not only earned her Ph.D., but when Professor Solomon returned to Israel, she was appointed to his position as head of the Anthropology Department.

Personally, she was leading a fulfilling life. She had established rewarding friendships with many people; but none had more impact on her life than her relationship with Eric and Paul. They were special to her, each possessing the intellectual level and ethical character that enhanced her life. But most of all, she was comfortable enough to be herself in their presence. They gave her a sense of security, for she knew that the three of them had bonded into a family unit of affection and loyalty. They shared happiness and anguish together, each helping the other over the rough phases of life. However, she had kept from them the reasons for her periodic absences even when they gently prodded her for explanations. She did not want to create an atmosphere of dependency or sympathy. Now, she knew that she might have to leave not only her life in America, but her friends as well.

Rachel recalled how the doctors in Israel had been puzzled when they found an excess of normal lymphocytes in her blood.

"Lymphatic leukemia is most commonly found in individuals beginning in their late fifties," they had said. Due to her young age, they had recommended that she be treated by a hematologic specialist in Rochester, New York.

Rachel, even in the beginning, was adamant about keeping her illness a secret. "I don't want any pity!"

"No one has to know unless you want to tell them, Rachel. We will say that you are going to America to study for your doctorate," her father reassured her.

"My doctorate!? Great! Everyone knows I want a doctorate in anthropology. Come on, I am supposed to go to New York to study, when our whole country is a living example of anthropology with all the immigrants here from all over the world?"

"Oh, REALLY? Then why is Professor Uri Solomon, an ISRAELI, heading the Anthropology Department at Syracuse University? You can say you want to study under him. He IS one of the leading anthropologists of the world," her father suggested.

"I will go with you, dear," her mother said reassuringly. "Just until you are settled," she quickly added when she saw the look of disapproval on Rachel's face. Mrs. Winograd gave a deep sigh. Rachel had always been a difficult child, overly independent with a fierce determination to do everything by herself.

Dr. Winograd noticed the desperation on his wife's face. "Rachel," he said with a stern voice, "we are your parents. You have a serious illness. This is no time to lock us out of your life. We'll beat this but must beat it together. How would you feel if one of us were seriously ill and we refused to let you have anything to do with us... if we locked you out completely and said we would handle it ourselves? There is a time to be independent, but this is not that time. I am incredibly pleased that you feel you are strong enough t handle this... this trouble... by yourself, but maybe your mother and I are not that strong. Did you ever think that maybe, just maybe, we need you to let us be a part of your life, in bad as well as good times?"

Rachel and her parents left for America three days later. Her mother insisted that she find an apartment within walking distance

CHAPTER 33

of a synagogue. Rachel and her mother decorated the apartment while her father planned for her studies under Professor Solomon.

Though she refused to show any fear, Rachel was frightened at what was happening to her. When they reached the hospital, she placed herself between her parents, then with a smile, took their hands as they walked into the hospital together.

After a painful bout with shingles, Rachels chronic lymphatic leukemia was brought under control. For the first three years, she had taken the radioactive phosphorus once every month. Twelve years had now passed since the first treatment, and she was presently being given treatments only three times a year. The results had been successful, and she was living a useful, normal life, up until just recently when she began again to feel a tiredness she could not shake.

Rachel smiled as she drove, remembering how after three months in America, she had insisted that her parents return to Israel. Her mother's unwavering attention got on her nerves, as did her own efforts to show only a happy face to her parents to assure them that she was doing fine. She felt helpless and vulnerable, which aggravated her even more. At times she just wanted to crawl into the bed, cover up, and just lie there being miserable. But knowing that her parents were hovering outside the door, peeking in regularly to see if she was all right, kept her up and moving.

"Would you please stop it already!" she cried out in anger one day when she saw the worried look on their faces as they peered through the door. "I'm going to be fine!"

"But you look so pale, are you sure you are okay now? Maybe you need to go to the doctor. He could do something. Her mother worried, completely ignoring Rachel's outburst, as they both came into the bathroom.

"Do I have to get up, put on makeup, and comb m hair, just to prove I'm okay?" Rachel was almost shouting. "I know you are worried about me, and I know you want to see me well. I assure you; I will be just fine! Mom, why don't you and Papa go home already? I don't need you hanging over me all the time! If I am pale, maybe it's because of the strain of having you both worrying about me!" She turned her back on them, pulled the covers over her head. "Please, just get out of my room and leave me alone!" Muffled cries were heard from under the blankets.

As her mother and father left the room, she heard her mother whisper to her father. "It's your fault! That's the way you brought her up, a real Sabra, rough and tough on the outside and soft on the inside. Sometimes I even wonder if she is soft inside. Now how are we going to know how she really feels? Maybe she is just telling us she is okay now because she doesn't want to worry us."

"My fault?!! Really!" her father responded. "You aggravate her too much. Stop prodding her!" Leave her alone. She'll let us know if she needs help."

Feeling guilty, Rachel got out of bed, combed her hair, and put a little rouge on her cheeks, thoroughly rubbing it in to give her face a little color without it being obvious she had on makeup. She put on a pair of jeans and a heavy sweatshirt and went out to her parents who were sitting at the kitchen table drinking tea.

Her mother was delighted. "You ARE feeling better!" Her face lit up. She noticed her father looking at her with suspicious eyes.

"Yes, I am. I'm sorry I was impatient with you, but, Mom, you know that every time I get a treatment, it makes me very tired. I want to climb into bed and just sleep. I'm okay, but it bothers me when you keep peeking in at me with worried faces. You two are the dearest people I have in my life. I promised you that if I did not feel well, you would be the first ones I would come to for help. And you have helped me! You came with me to America; you helped me get settled in this beautiful apartment; you got the best doctors for me. Dr. Ohayon assured you that I'm doing great. You have done all you can. Now it is up to me, and I really can handle it now. In fact, I think it is time for you both to go home and leave me alone."

"No, it is too soon for us to go. Let us stay with you a little while longer," her mother objected with a worried look on her face.

"Mom! We are getting on each other's nerves, and that I the best sign that it is time for you to go home. I will call you every week. I'll write everything going on. I promise!"

Her mother looked helplessly at her father for support.

"Rachel, suppose we stay just a little longer... say, another month. Two weeks even?" Her father tried to mediate.

CHAPTER 33

"Papa, please, this tension is killing Mama, and it is not doing me any good either. There is simply no need for it. You see that between treatment, I'm just fine… just like nothing is wrong with me. You know me. I like to be alone. I have all my studies to do. If I am studying and I get tired, which is normal, and I put my head down for two minutes, Mom thinks I'm dying already! Please, Papa, I love you both very much, but if you really want to help me… go home. Go home now."

Her father and mother looked at each other. From the time Rachel was a small child, she had marveled at how her parents could communicate by merely looking at each other without any words.

Her father was the first to speak. "Okay, Rachel, we will leave on one condition."

"What's that?" Rachel was suspicious.

"The Rabbi in the synagogue is a very compassionate, caring individual. He and his wife are good people. Let me speak with him… see that he just keeps an eye on you."

Rachel was horrified. "I'm not a little child that I need someone to look out for me!"

Breezily her father answered. "Then we don't go!"

Rachel drew in a large breath of air and slowly blew it out. "Okay, but don't you date tell them about my treatments!"

"No, I won't. I promise. I'll just tell them that your mother and I are returning to Israel. We feel insecure about leaving our daughter alone; an ask if you could please call them in case of an emergency."

Her mother jumped in. "It will sound like any parent who is leaving a child alone, dear. I'll feel better if I know there is someone looking out for you rather than just leaving you here all by yourself."

"Mama, you know I can take care of myself."

"I know that, dear, I know you can take care of yourself. But just in case of an emergency, any kind of emergency, I will feel better if I know there is someone you can call." Mrs. Winograd set her lips tightly. "Otherwise, I AM NOT going, and you will just have to put up with one or both of us here!"

"Okay, okay," Rachel answered in frustration. "But you are only going to tell him that you would feel better if you thought I had someone reliable to call in case of an emergency. You promise?"

"I promise," her father replied, but this means you will have to go to services every Saturday."

"What?"

"It won't kill you to go to Synagogue once a week! You need a home base, Rachel, and if you are doing as well as you claim, then you should thank God that you are recovering. Don't take your recovery for granted. Be thankful for every day of life. Who you tell what, and what you tell whom, is your business, but God knows everything, and you are not to neglect him! Now, do YOU promise you will go to services?"

Rachel knew that her father's strength was in his religious convictions, a strength that he had tried to impart to her since she was a small child. She realized also that this strength was now seeing her through the present crisis as it had all the crises in their lives, like the terrible days following the death of her older brother who was killed in the Yom Kippur War. "I'm being selfish," thought Rachel. "I'm all they have left. They don't want to lose me too."

"You are right, as usual, Papa, I promise." She went over to them, hugged and kissed both. "I think I'll keep you both until your warranties run out; then maybe I can get spare parts," she laughed to cover the sudden sadness she felt. "I love you both very much!"

Rachel's thoughts came back to her as she was driving. She concentrated on the trees whizzing by, and then returned to her memories.

That had been twelve years ago, and she had certainly come a long way. Rabbi Marcus and his wife had kept their word to her father. The had taken her into their lives as if she were their own child. She was a frequent guest for the Sabbath meals and celebrations.

Three years later, Rabbi Marcus was killed by a mugger as he walked to services one Saturday afternoon. The mugger had become enraged when he discovered the Rabbi did not carry money on the Sabbath and had shot him without mercy. Soon after, Mrs. Marcus had moved back to Brooklyn to be with her family and the synagogue began its search for a new Rabbi.

Rachel, bereft of her surrogate "parents," stopped going to services because she could not bear to see Rabbi Marcus' empty seat

CHAPTER 33

on the pulpit or a new rabbi taking his place. It was only when she was present when the new Rabbi, Eric Froman, spoke on Columbus Day from the City Hall steps, and again at the Holocaust Commemoration, that she decided to return to the synagogue.

Now as she drove the route to the hospital which she had taken so many times in the past, she felt a deep sadness. She was worried that something was terribly wrong. What if the leukemia is no longer in remission and is active again? Will the radioactive phosphorus still work? Her mind was racing. "If I get sicker what will I do? Maybe I'll go back to Israel... but I love my work. I hate to leave it. Maybe I'll just take a leave of absence. That way, if things improve, and I am not happy in Israel, I can always come back." The entrance to the hospital was in view. She glanced at the car clock. "I have only 15 minutes! I must find out what is happening. Suppose it is not meant for me to live. Is it best not to tell anyone?

Should I stay in America and pretend everything is all right?"

"Oh God, please..." She began repeating the Shema – the prayer of declaration of God's justice, "*Shma' Yisroel, Adoni, Eoheynu, Adoni Echad* – Hear O' Israel, the Lord is Our God, The Lord is One!" And then the 24th Psalm, "The Lord is my Shepherd..."

 # CHAPTER 34

FOR THE FIRST time in weeks, Eric felt good when he awakened Saturday morning. Relishing a few moments in bed, he mulled over his thoughts.

His parents were well. His father was returning to his old self again but with a calmer attitude. His mother had not complained about anything in quite a while. Paul was improving with each day. Their conversations and discussions were intellectually stimulating and exciting, that contributed a great deal of pleasure to Eric's life.

Eric's marriage to Dawn was still far from ideal, but at least there had been no recent uncontrollable fights or arguments. They had tremendous difficulty living together in everyday mundane life. Whenever they were in the house together, Eric was always tense not knowing when Dawn's temper would erupt. They had been able to work out ways to lessen some of the stress. Whenever Dawn was preparing meals, Eric stayed out of the kitchen because if he tried to help or make suggestions, she would become defensive, and an argument would ensue. There was an unspoken agreement in the house that the kitchen, living room and bedroom were Dawn's domain, and the study belonged to Eric. They tried to share the family room, but usually a feeling of tension arose between them.

Eric would constantly try to appease Dawn by buying special gifts and foods for her and by saying the words he knew she wanted to hear. The only part of their marriage that was satisfying was their sex life. Their lovemaking was passionate, fulfilling and gratifying. After each episode, they would agree, "Things have to improve, we must give it a chance!"

When they were out together, away from the house, in neutral territory, the pressure disappeared. Only then could they relax and enjoy each other's company.

THE SECOND GENERATION

Eric turned over on his back. He placed his hands behind his head and looked up at the ceiling.

When the atmosphere was tense, Eric would find himself thinking of Rachel. He missed being with her, talking with her, and discussing issues without fear of things degenerating into a quarrel. He realized he was looking forward to seeing Rachel at services this morning. He wished Dawn would not come to synagogue so he could spend a few minutes speaking with Rachel during Kiddish, the reception after services. At the same time, he hated and wondered why he felt he had to be constantly answerable to Dawn. "Why do I feel that I must always strive to please Dawn?!" he asked himself over and over. He felt as he had when he was a small child, trying to please his father and yet fearful of his father's temper.

"I had better get moving," he mumbled out loud, as he rolled over and sat up on the side of the bed. Dawn rolled over and grabbed him around the waist. "Come on, honey, I'm in a good mood for love," she cooed as she nibbled the back of his neck, running her fingers down his backbone.

He reached behind him, caught her arms and pulled them around him. He turned his head sideways and gave her a kiss on the mouth. "I would love it, too, but it's late. I have to be in the synagogue in 20 minutes."

You'll be a little late, so what?" She pulled him back onto the bed.

Eric gently pulled her arms away. "Come on, Dawn, I have to be at services. We'll continue when I get home!"

"You are anxious to go see that slut in Schule, aren't you?" her eyes flashed hated.

Eric did not answer her. He got up and began pulling clean underwear from drawers, quickly choosing clothing from the closet.

"Why don't you answer me?" Dawn demanded as she got out of bed.

Eric quickly dressed as he said, "Your remarks don't deserve an answer."

He was straightening his tie, when her hands grabbed his shirt by the collar and ripped it, spitting buttons as she torn the front open, her long nails cutting into his chest as they tore down the shirt.

300

CHAPTER 34

"Go ahead, hit me!" she yelled. "You know you want to!" Her hands were on her hips and her jaw jutted forward daring him to do it.

Eric went to the closet and stripping off yet another ruined shirt, put on the fresh one, then his jacket, coat and hat. "Good Shabbos, Dawn." He said as he walked out of the room softly closing the door behind him. He did not allow her to see his shaking hands. As he left the house, his whole body was trembling, his heart pounding and he felt light-headed. Walking to the synagogue, he kept repeating repeatedly. "Got to get hold of myself. Maybe I'll go to Rachel's house after services. No, I can't go there, Dawn will come after me for sure, and there will be another scene. I'll just stay in my office until evening services. I don't want to go home. I don't want another confrontation."

"Good Shabbos, Rabbi," he heard a voice sing out. He turned and faced Rachel.

"My God, are you okay? You are pale as a ghost!" Her smile turned to alarm, her hands instinctively reaching toward him.

"I'm okay. I'm okay. I am happy to see you, Rachel." He reached out his hands to grasp hers. He wanted desperately to hug her.

She released his hands quickly. "Not in the street," she said. "You don't know who is watching. You really look awful, Eric. What happened? ANOTHER fight with Dawn?" Her eyes searched his face.

"I don't want to talk about it. Come on, let's walk, talk to me, tell me anything new in your life, anything exciting?" He tried for composure.

"Yes! Yes! A room filled with artifacts has just been unearthed near the Western Wall... " her face with joyous.

"How big a room? What did they find?" Eric excitedly inquired. "Can I tell the congregation today? It is wonderful news!"

"I really don't know that much about it yet. Well, here we are. You're late. You had better move fast."

"Let's talk after services, okay?" Rachel nodded in agreement. "I've missed you," Eric whispered. "Don't leave, stay, okay?"

"Yeah, okay, Eric, we'll talk after services."

Rachel went to the women's side in the sanctuary and sat in the back pews. She did not look up when Dawn came in, walking past her without acknowledgement on her way to the front of the

THE SECOND GENERATION

women's section to sit. Dawn was elegantly dressed in a black leather suit and white silk blouse. She wore a matching black leather hat with a white feather attached to it. Her hair was pulled back into a French twist. Large golden rings hung from her ears. "She looks like she stepped out of a fashion magazine," Rachel thought.

Eric disappeared into his office on the side of the bimah, the stage, for several minutes before joining the services. He sat in his chair behind his desk, leaning backward with his hands rubbing his forehead. "How can I go out there and face my people? I am their rabbi, their leader, teacher, their comfort in time of trouble. But I am… but I am… I can't even handle my own life… my own marriage…" Trembling, he went to the lavatory, where only the mirror watched him splash cold, bracing water on his face again and again. He looked up and his eyes met his mirrored eyes, penetrated, assessing, measuring, asking, "Ready, now, Rabbi? You can go out there and do it. You will do it. You must do it." He picked up a folded paper towel and wiped his face and hands. The man in him diminished and the religious leader took over. Squaring his shoulders and holding his head erect he walked out to again lead his people in the Sabbath prayers of peace.

Each Saturday, Rabbi Froman interpreted and discussed the portion of the Torah after it was read in Hebrew, answering the congregants' questions. This week the segment was about the giving of the Torah on Mount Sinai.

"It is a tree of life to all those who grasp it." Eric explained. "The roots of a tree, which grow deep and strong, will prevent the tree from being blown over, even by the fiercest storm. So, it is with life. If we are steeped in knowledge of the Torah, the Bible, there is no adversity which can overthrow us. In the Torah, God's gift to the world, we find ethics, morals, justice for all. The laws of life are all in the Torah."

A man raised his hand from the congregation. Eric acknowledged him.

"Rabbi, I was reading in a book about the Jewish Community in Europe, when they lived in ghettos. Was it true that if anyone had a grievance about anyone else, he could rise at the reading of

CHAPTER 34

the Torah and present his case and ask for justice? Does that still hold today, Rabbi? What I mean is, do they still do it?"

"What you read is true. The reasoning behind it was that with the Torah before us, which represents God, one would not dare to lie; therefore, one would receive justice for his grievance."

"I want justice for my grievance?" Dawn stood up. A dead quiet fell over the congregation. Eric turned white. Before he could speak, Dawn continued. "My husband... my husband, THE RABBI, claims he loves me, yet he spends time in another woman's company. He runs to her when we have difficulties in our marriage, to consult with her. He even spent the night with her! Now he is sneaking around to be with her. I ask this congregation before the open Torah, that I be given justice for my plight!" Her face was frightening, ugly with rage, as she publicly accused him.

No one spoke, but all eyes turned towards their rabbi.

Eric vet his heart pounding in his ears. Like another voice speaking, he heard himself quietly say, "You did not take your medicine this morning, did you, Dawn? I knew I should have made you take it before I left the house. Excuse me, my friends, I'll be right back. Please continue with the services." Eric coolly came off the bimah platform, took Dawn by the arm and led her into the synagogue office. He closed the door behind them. Very calmly he informed her with a commanding, stern voice, "I'm leaving you, Dawn. I cannot take your outbursts any longer. Now sit here until services are over."

Dawn began to cry, "I'm sorry, please, let's talk. I'll be different from now on, I promise. I swear I'll never do that again. I'll promise anything, just don't leave me. I love you. I love you. I love you."

"You stay here in this room. Don't leave it. When services are over, I will take you home."

"Please don't leave me in anger. Take me in your arms and tell me everything will be all right. I said I'm sorry." She was sobbing loudly.

From the side of his eye, Eric saw a few members of his congregation peering at them through the glass in the office door. Eric knew that Judy, his secretary, kept a bottle of aspirins in the desk which was at a right angle to the door. Leading Dawn to a chair beside the desk, the reached into the desk drawer, keeping his body between the desk and his viewers outside the office door. Fumbling the bottle open, he shook two aspirins into his hand, closing the drawer and sliding his hand into his pocket. He turned, walked toward the office door and opened it, calling out, "Please, Mr. Goldman, would you get a cup of water for me?"

"Sure, Rabbi." Within minutes Mr. Goldman returned with a plastic cup of water.

Eric's hand dipped into his pocket, flourishing the two aspirins he hoped the men would believe were Dawn's desperately needed medication, the lack of which had supposedly caused her wildly hysterical behavior.

"Here, Dawn," Eric said, "Take our pills and you will feel better." She dutifully took the two aspirins and swallowed them. "Thank you." She smiled demurely and sweetly at Mr. Goldman, "And thank you for being such a good and patient husband." She smiled in turn to Eric.

"Now, I must get back to services. Put your head down on the desk and rest, Dawn. You'll be okay now." He turned to the door.

"Should I get the janitor to turn on the lights, Rabbi?" Mr. Goldman asked.

"No, leave them out. Dawn must rest now!"

When Eric returned to the sanctuary, services stopped, and voices pressed him anxiously. "How is she, Rabbi? Is she okay? Can we do anything for you? For her?"

"I gave Dawn her medication. She is resting now. I apologize for the interruption."

Eric stole a glance at Rachel. She was sitting quietly looking at him, her face without expression. Eric was relieved that she had not left. All the members knew the two were friends, and if she had gone, it would have raised the possibility she was the woman of whom Dawn spoke.

Eric continued with services as if nothing had happened, with iron control over his inner turmoil, hands clenched on the podium to hide their trembling.

As the Torah was being carried among the congregants before being replaced in the Ark, Eric whispered in Hebrew to Rachel.

CHAPTER 34

"Do not leave immediately after services. Go to Kiddish as always." Eric nodded as he said it, as if he were only greeting her as he did the other members. Rachel responded with a confirming nod as if it were just a hello, but her heart was racing so fast, she felt like fainting.

During the Kiddish, Eric and Rachel acted as if nothing had happened. Rachel circulated among the people who were, of course, talking about Dawn. Finally, as usual, Eric came to talk with Rachel.

"I have to go, Eric, I am in a panic. If she sees me, I know there will be a terrible confrontation." Wide eyes begged him as she softly spoke.

"I know, I know, but you have to act as if you are not involved. Have you heard any comments from the people?" He kept his voice very low.

"Yes, I think most of the people have compassion for you. I didn't hear anything negative about you. They are talking about all kinds of illnesses Dawn probably has. Remember also, Eric, many of them knew her long before she knew you. Her reputation precedes her."

Eric just shook his head. "I guess you could leave now. Not immediately, but in a few minutes. Okay?"

"I haven't done anything, Eric. I hate having to act a part, to provide a cover for something I'm not guilty of."

"I know. I'm sorry. Please don't let this get you down. Everything will be all right." He tried to sound sure.

"I have heard that line before and too often," Rachel muttered in a very low voice, as she began to circle the room unobtrusively, speaking to first one and then another of the people she knew among the congregants, before she left the building.

After everyone else had left, Mrs. Bronstein lingered. "Rabbi, I would like to talk with you, please," she said as she followed Eric out of the social hall.

"Yes? Mrs. Bronstein." Eric impatiently waited for her to reply.

"I feel sorry for your wife, Rabbi," her face was cool, accusing.

"She'll be all right. Thank you for your concern."

"I don't mean that, Rabbi. When she was over at my house last week, she told me what a rough life she has."

The hair rose on the back of Eric's neck and his heart quickened again.

"Oh, in what way?" he tried a casual tone.

"Well, being a rabbi's wife is not easy. She suffers a lot!"

"Being a rabbi's wife is an honor. In what way do you think she is suffering?" He was firm and a little indignant.

"Well, she is alone a lot and rarely has your attention." Eric must have had a surprised look on his face because Mrs. Bronstein quickly added, "Oh, Rabbi, I know you are a very busy man and as a rabbi, you must always be on call. It's your job, but your wife… "

"But what, Mrs. Bronstein?" Eric could not keep the annoyance out of his words.

"Well, all the time you spend with that priest… you know, the one who killed his own father… and time with Rachel, too! Oh, I know she is a very interesting person, but unless she has a special problem you can help her with, don't you think it would be better for your marriage if you spent that time with your wife? I know this is none of my business, Rabbi, but I really feel sorry for your poor wife. She is intelligent and beautiful. It is a shame she suffers so much. A real shame!"

"Mrs. Bronstein, I thank you again for your concern. However, this is Shabbos. It is supposed to be a peaceful day of rest. Now go home and have a good Shabbos." As he spoke, he guided her toward the front door.

Eric sat down in the lobby and put his head back against the cool metal of the Tree of Life. He tried to dissipate his anger before he confronted Dawn. After five minutes he arose and went into the office. Dawn was asleep in the chair with her head on her arms, folded on the desk.

"That's a break! Thank God." Eric whispered to himself. He knew many of the members had probably passed by the office and looked in to see how she was and to wish her a good Shabbos. When they found her asleep, he also knew they would not wake her to speak with her.

When Eric looked at her, with her swollen eyes and white face, he viewed her not as he had in the past with feelings of sorrow for her, but with contempt.

CHAPTER 34

"Come on, Dawn," he roughly shook her shoulder. "Wake up. It's time to go home."

Dawn blinked, picked up her head, yawned and stretched. "Hi, honey, I love you."

"If you loved me, why do you try to destroy me?" his voice was hard and cold.

"Me? I would never try to hurt you. I love you!"

"Then why did you say that in front of everybody? How could you? That isn't love and trust."

"It is not my fault. Did you not say that grievances should be brought before the Torah? I was following Jewish law!" Unbelievably, her tone was all injured innocence.

"Dawn, there is a difference between the letter of the law and the spirit of the law! Our problems are ours to solve. They are not for public display before the world."

"And what did you do? You lied before the whole congregation. I don't take any medicine. Now they will think I'm a nut case."

"I had to save myself from what you said." Eric was defensive.

"I have to think of myself, too!"

"And what about pouring your guts out to Mrs. Bronstein?"

"I'm so lonely," Dawn began to cry again. "You are always surrounded by people who love you. You have Paul and Rachel. I have no one! Now you are even trying to take away the one person I have to talk to!"

"You could have been a part of the circle of Paul, Rachel, and me, but you are jealous of them. You want to own me a hundred percent. You have never learned that one person cannot own another. Each one is an individual entitled to his own life. Marriage means sharing a life together, not having ownership of another human being!" Eric knew his words fell on deaf ears. She didn't even want to understand.

"Do you blame me for wanting to be with you? I relish every moment we are together."

"Come off it, Dawn! It is a matter of control to you. I told you, you cannot control my life!" He was almost shouting.

"No! It is your fault. You caused everything. You know I am insecure. I need to feel safe with you. You are the one whose cheap affair with that whore has wrecked our marriage!"

"She is not a whore, Dawn. Stop calling her that!"

"She is taking away another woman's husband! What else would she be called? Slut! Hussy! Whore! Whore! Whore!" She taunted him, eyes flashing.

"Being your husband does not mean I have to give up all my friends. I knew Rachel eight years ago. Do you expect me to take eight years of loyal friendship and throw it away… just like that!" Eric snapped his fingers in her face.

"Yes, I am your friend as well as your wife. I'm all you need! You don't need other friends."

"No, you are not my friend. No friend would hurt me the way you hurt me. You have no loyalty. You are a selfish, cruel, controlling manipulator. You don't know how to be a friend!"

"I am not your friend, huh? Just look what I gave up to marry you! And I only ask one thing of you to prove your love for me. If it means making me happy and securing our marriage, why won't you get rid of her?"

"Dawn, if Rachel were the only issue standing in our way of a happy marriage, I would sacrifice my friendship with her. But Rachel has nothing to do with our problems, because if is not Rachel, it will be someone else. Why are you also insisting that I drop Paul as a friend? He is a male. There is no love interest there. No, Dawn, you look at marriage as a swap-off, you give me this if I give you that." Eric gestured with his hands.

"No, Eric, you don't understand."

"Yes, I do understand. Marriage is mutual cooperation, and most of all, mutual respect. A couple should work with each other for the benefit of both, not against each other to get what each one wants!"

"But look at you," Dawn sneered. "You are the rabbi of the community. Everyone admires you and looks up to you. What am I? A nobody? What do I have in life?"

"So, you are even jealous of me. You are supposed to be my wife, to stand beside me, not behind me or in front of me. You are supposed

CHAPTER 34

to be my inspiration, my security, my helpmate, not my antagonist!" Eric felt a lump in his throat. Tears were burning his eyes.

"I don't want to ride on your coat-tails. All anybody sees is YOU! All I am to them is your wife! I am not even a person!"

Eric sighed from the depths of his soul. He felt drained. He knew within himself that Dawn would never understand what he was trying to tell her.

"I'm going home, Dawn, I'm exhausted." His voice was flat.

"But I want answers!"

"Dawn, I have given you answers over and over again. You want control and ownership, not answers. This is the Sabbath. A time of peace and relaxation. I have to be back here in two hours for evening services. I have to get some rest, or I am going to fall on my face. If you want to come, I don't care. Do what you want." He turned and walked out.

Dawn got up and ran after him. She hugged his arm as they walked. "When we get home, we'll make love," she cooed.

"I told you I'm dead tired, Dawn." He pulled his arm away. "Just leave me alone!" This was incredible. Was she insane? Was he insane?

"Oh, come on, sweetheart, remember all the great times we have had together. Let's not let this foolishness come between us now." Her words purred, and she leaned close against him.

Eric stopped walking and faced Dawn. "Foolishness? You may have ruined my life today, Dawn. You planted the seeds of destruction into fertile ground. I don't know what will happen because of your actions today and your false tales told to Mrs. Bronstein. Don't you even realize what you have done?"

Dawn began to cry. "I'm sorry. I'm sorry. I don't understand what I did that's so terrible, but if I did do something that bad, then I am sorry." She tried to snuggle up to him, like a repentant child.

Eric pushed her away.

"Come on, Eric, don't be angry. I can make everything all right. If we only get into each other's arms, I know everything will be all right!"

Eric took Dawn by the shoulders and shook her, demanding, "Who is a whore now? You are trying to sell yourself, to get me to

THE SECOND GENERATION

say that everything you did to destroy me is okay, forgotten, as if nothing happened!"

A brisk slap twisted Eric's head.

"Go home, Dawn. I'm going back to the synagogue. I'll rest in my office." Her handprint immediately began to redden on his cheek.

"Let me come with you, we'll talk."

Tears of frustration ran out of Eric's eyes. "I have told you a thousand times. There is nothing more to talk about. Please, Dawn, please. I'll drop dead of a heart attack right here in the street in front of you. Go! Go home!"

"When will you be home?"

"When you see me!" Eric turned and almost ran back toward the synagogue.

After the services and the Sabbath had ended, Eric did not go home but went directly to see Paul. When he came into Paul's room, he walked past Paul reading in his chair and threw himself face-down on the bed.

"Rough day?" Paul questioned, amused.

Eric replied with a deep groan.

Paul put down the book he was reading, arose from his chair and sat down on the side of the bed. Eric flipped over on his back, his hands across his eyes.

Paul put his hand on Eric's chest over his heart and held it there for a few moments.

"I feel a broken heart," he said softly.

Eric grabbed Paul's hand and held it. "It's all over, Paul. I can't take it anymore! My marriage is a disaster."

Paul said nothing but put his other hand over Eric's and looked into his face with sympathetic eyes.

Eric poured out all that occurred that day. Paul did not interrupt or comment until Eric had finished.

"What do you plan to do?" Paul asked.

"I have to leave her, Paul. I can't take it anymore. I will have a heart attack or a stroke, or something!"

Paul nodded his head in agreement.

CHAPTER 34

"When we are in bed together, everything is beautiful. I love her then and have been able to forget the bad things. It is something I have never felt in my life... so wonderfully intense. But after today... "

"Is there any way you think you could settle this between you?" Paul inquired.

"I have tried. We talk it out and agree that it is silly to argue. We both say it won't happen again, but it always does." Eric shook his head.

"So, what goes wrong?" Paul asked.

"When she gets those jealous fits, there is no telling what she will say or do. Today, she went public. She has no control over herself!"

"Have you explained to her about public outbursts. Does she realize what the means to you and even to her? The damage she is doing to you both?"

"Oh yes, we have talked until I am totally exhausted. She always apologizes and promises never again; but then she does it again, and when I confront her, she says it is my fault. Paul, I can't take it anymore. Sometimes I do love her, and at times like today, I only have contempt for her. I don't know what will happen after today. I love my profession, my work. I love being a rabbi. I don't know what to do about the Bronsteins now or the members of my congregation."

"She doesn't realize that when she brings you down, she is also ruining herself?" Paul asked again in disbelief.

"She doesn't care what anyone says or thinks. At that moment when she becomes crazy, nothing matters for her except revenge. A month or two later, out of a clear blue sky, she will get back at me for some instance I don't even remember." Eric said in frustration.

"See, this is what I mean!" Dawn came stomping into the room. "You run to strangers and complain about me. You talk about our troubles. It is none of his business what goes on between us!"

Her eyes were flashing fire as she stood with her hands on her hips, legs spread apart.

"This is my friend, Dawn, a colleague. I need his advice. I need someone to talk to about our situation. I have a right to talk to my friend."

"And yet, you complained when I talked with the Bronsteins. Did you ever consider that I need a friend too? How is it different?" she accused.

"The Bronsteins are members of my congregation. They have lots of friends in the synagogue. How do you know they won't talk to other members about us? Dawn, it is not the same and you know it!"

"So, what if they do? Let people know the truth of how you treat me!"

"Are you aware, Dawn, that in the Bible, Miriam was cursed with leprosy when she spoke of Moses, even though she spoke what she thought was the truth?" Paul asked gently.

"You are on his side, I see that."

"All I know is that Eric is a rabbi and apparently he is a rabbi because God chose him to be one. Have you any right to speak against one chosen by God?" Paul reasoned.

"It does not matter anymore, Paul." Eric said with resignation. "I cannot live with you, Dawn. I just cannot take it. Whether it is my fault or your fault, it doesn't matter. I am going to divorce you." Tears were streaming down Eric's face.

"No, Eric, please don't leave me!" Dawn was frantic. "I'll control myself. I won't do it again. I'll suffer to myself. Give us another chance. We have too much going for us. You can be friends with whomever you want, I won't care. I can't live without you! Please, Eric?"

Eric looked hopelessly at Paul and said to Dawn. "Please, go home, Dawn, go home. Just go on home and leave me alone!"

Dawn tuned and slowly walked to the door, then she turned around and sweetly said: "I'm so glad you're feeling better, Paul. See you later, Eric." She threw a kiss and left.

CHAPTER 35

"MY, MY, MY!" exclaimed Eric as he walked into Paul's room a few weeks later. "What do we have here?"

Paul was dressed, with his priest's collar, black shirt and pants. He was sitting in a chair at the side of his bed. On the bed, spread in neat stacks, were papers, and what appeared to be blueprint plans.

Paul's face lit up when he saw Eric. "Hey, Eric, come over here! I have something to show you!" He beckoned with his hand for Eric to join him. "Don't pay any attention to the formal dress, I just came back from visiting my children."

Dr. Siegelman appeared at the door. "Hi, fellows. How were the children today, Paul?"

"Oh, just great, Doc. There's a lot of excitement generated down there. Come on in, have a seat. You may enjoy Eric's reactions when I tell him the news."

"What news?" Eric looked at the two men who were grinning like the Cheshire cat.

"Come on, what have you two cooked up behind my back?"

"Eric, you know where my church is?"

"Of course, I do. So, what?" Eric asked impatiently.

"Well, do you remember seeing that old, dilapidated, fantastically large house next door to the rectory?"

"The one with the big porch that wraps around the front and side?" Eric asked.

"Yes, yes, that's the one!" Paul was animated with excitement. Dr. Siegelman was grinning as he chewed on his pipe.

"Come on, Paul, would you please get to the point? You are killing me with suspense."

"Well-l-l-l, that's where I am going to live when the good doctor lets me out of here!" Paul said with a big smile.

"They won't let you live in the rectory anymore?" Eric asked.

"I don't want to live in the rectory. I want to live in my own big house with all my children." Paul nonchalantly declared.

"All your children?" Eric looked at Dr. Siegelman. "Has he flipped out, or what?"

"If you don't tell him, Paul, I'm afraid I am going to have another patient here!" Dr. Siegelman laughed.

"Eric, I'm going to convert that old house into a 'home' for children who are well enough to leave this Institution but have nowhere else to go."

"That is just fantastic!" Eric was amazed. "How did you do it?"

"Well," Paul leaned back in his chair. "With the help of the Doc here, this Institution has agreed to let some of the children come live with me, under the supervision of Dr. Siegelman, who has agreed to volunteer his time."

"How long have you been working on this? Why didn't you tell me?" Eric felt left out.

"I advised him not to tell anyone," the doctor interjected. "This is something he needed to do on his own. It's a very important endeavor, and Paul had to prove to himself he could do it."

"Apparently, he passed the test with flying colors!" Eric declared proudly.

"Oh yeah, we have been monitoring Paul's effect on Marybeth and the other children. Paul has found people to love, to take care of, to guide and to nurture. In return, these children, cut off by tragedy, from family life, feel a kinship toward this kind, loving man who has an aura of trust about him."

"Oh, Paul, that's wonderful!" Eric reached over and touched Paul's arm. "What have you planned?"

"I've already hired a housekeeper, Mrs. Hannah Cadwell, a lovely, early-middle-age widow. She is the motherly type of lady. I remember before her husband died, she used to come into the Church regularly to pray for children. Now her prayers have been answered. She will have plenty of children to take care of."

"Where is all the support money to come from? Do you think I could help you with fund raising?" Eric asked eagerly.

"Oh, the Church is supplying support."

CHAPTER 35

"The Church?!!" Eric's mouth fell open in surprise. "How in heaven's name did you swing that deal?"

"It WAS accomplished in heaven's name," laughed Paul.

"Hold it. I remember your Bishop was reluctant to even allow you to return to your priestly duties. What did you do? Go over his head to the Pope?"

"I went to an even higher authority than the Pope. I prayed a lot, but I also reminded my Bishop that I was sure the media had not forgotten the sensationalism of a Nazi war criminal being killed at a Holocaust Commemoration. I also reminded him of the Church's protection of Nazi criminals after the war as well as its failure to fight Nazism during the war. Wouldn't it be a shame if one of the investigating programs or tabloid shows on television picked up the information that a well-known priest, who had killed his own father, a Nazi war criminal, was denied the right to save children – ironic sine his father had sent thousands of children to their death?"

"Why Father Paul, would that be under the category of blackmail?" Eric teased.

"Don't you think it could be more like a command from heaven, that the son try to counterbalance the evil deeds of the father?"

"Absolutely!" Eric agreed. "How many children are you going to begin with?"

"Five now, but we'll probably have more later. I was just studying the blueprint here to see what rooms I would put the children in. I want to put a library in here, I asked Rachel to help with that, a playroom here, and here, in this little room in the attic, I'm going to put in a 'growlry.'"

"A growlry? What's that?" Eric asked.

"From Mark Twain. He said he had a 'growlry' – a special room that he had so when he was in a bad mood, he would go in there, close the door, and think out his bad mood. I want to have that room also for my kids. When one gets in a bad mood, then he or she will go to the growlry and think about their bad mood until they solve it. I intend to put in a punching bag figure, you know the kind with the sand in the bottom, to let the kids punch out their anger on it."

"You are a born psychiatrist, Paul!" Dr. Siegelman said as he chewed on his pipe.

THE SECOND GENERATION

Eric turned to the doctor. "Can Paul tell me about the children? Maybe I could come and help out sometimes."

Dr. Siegelman nodded his head to Paul as he puffed on his pipe.

"Well, Marybeth – she is eight years old. When she was five, her parents and little brother were killed when a drunk driver, going over 90 miles an hour smashed head-on into their station wagon on the New York Freeway. The car burst into flames with everyone trapped in the car except Marybeth, who miraculously escaped when she was thrown out of the rear gate onto the roadway. She had apparently been playing with her seatbelt and it had come loose. Hearing the cries of her family as they burned to death forced her mind to cut off from reality and escape into its own fantasy world where she created a genealogy of demons and saints, with whom she constantly communicates."

"She has greatly improved with Paul's friendship," Dr. Siegelman interjected. "She is slowly letting go of her imaginary companions. Bright children often create different imaginary characters. They are also likely to construct more elaborate fantasies such as those Marybeth has created. We believe when she is in the family atmosphere Paul creates, she will let them all go as she heals."

"I don't believe you will ever be able to blot out those cries of her family dying," Eric remarked. "I know my father still hears the cries of his first wife and children, and he was an adult when it happened."

"That's true, Eric, but since she was so young, maybe they will dim with time and love," answered the doctor.

Paul continued. "Then there is Steven, a ten year old, small for his age, who was chained in the closet by his parents to 'keep him out of the way' when they did not want to bother taking care of him and when they went to work. He literally turned into an animal which made them chain him permanently. The police found him after a neighbor reported hearing moans and groans from the house when everyone was away. They have done an unbelievable job of rehabilitation on Steven here, but he still has his problems."

"You may have a little trouble with him, Paul. He still regresses sometimes," Dr. Siegelman commented.

"What child is not trouble?" asked Paul. "He'll be okay! I'm sure. And then, there is Karen, also a ten-year-old going on forty. Her

CHAPTER 35

father, brother and uncles have sexually abused her since she was five. They kept her in the house for their use and passed her from one to the other."

"My God!" Eric exclaimed. I have heard of abuse cases, but this sounds like fiction."

"Oh, it is true enough. The poor girl thinks she is property to be used. Yet, she has an unbelievably strong spirit of survival," Dr. Siegelman added.

Before Paul could continue, the phone rang. Paul reached over and picked it up. "Hello. Hi Rach, what's doing? Yes, Eric is here. Dr. Siegelman is here also. How about bringing some coffee and donuts and joining us? It is a time for celebration! Oh, okay. Here, Eric," he held out the phone, "Rachel wants to speak with you."

Eric took the phone. "Hi, Rach. Who? Is she there right now? Please don't cry. I'll be right over." He hung up the phone, his face pale. "Dawn is at Rachel's house. I'm sorry, Paul, I really want to hear about your plans and your children, but I must go. Please excuse me, Doc."

"It's okay. Go. I understand." Paul arose from his chair and walked Eric to the door. He patted his back, "Good luck, my friend."

"Thanks, I'll need it." Eric almost ran down the hall.

When Eric arrived at Rachel's, he found Dawn sitting on a chair, her legs crossed, swinging the upper leg. Her arms were folded defensively in front of her. How well he knew that look!

Rachel was sitting on the couch; her right eyes was beginning to discolor and swell. Dawn's fingerprints were visibly showing against her upper right cheek.

Dawn uncrossed her legs. "Well, it is about time you got here!" she said angrily.

"What are you doing here, Dawn?" Eric demanded.

"I want to settle this once and for all!" Dawn answered.

"Settle what?" Eric was raising his voice.

"Settle this despicable whore breaking up our marriage!" she pointed to Rachel with an accusing finger.

"Why did you hit Rachel?" Eric's face was red with anger.

"Because she deserved it!" Dawn arose and started towards Rachel. "And I'll hit her again if you dare take up for her!"

THE SECOND GENERATION

Eric stepped in front of Dawn and took her by the arm. "Come on, you're getting out of here."

"Where are we going, sweetheart?" Dawn asked sweetly with a smile.

"You are going to MY house to pack your stuff. I have had enough of our wild craziness!" Eric spoke calmly and softly.

"You will let this slut break our marriage?" Tears filled her yes.

"Come on, Dawn. And you had better not say one word from this door to the door of the car, or I will personally give you more than a black eye. You have my word!" Eric's voice was stern and uncompromising.

As they walked out of Rachel's door, a man commented with a smile. "Tough taking care of two women, isn't it, Rabbi?"

"I should have such problems," Eric smiled back but he felt his face turn fire-red.

Eric's fingers cut into Dawn's arm as they walked but she did not protest or say anything. Eric opened the passenger's side of the car and helped Dawn into the car. If women had not been sitting on benches watching them, Eric knew he would have thrown her into her seat.

He went to the driver's side and got in.

"Darling, my car is here. Are we going to leave it?"

Eric did not answer but started the car and pulled out into the road. Dawn reached over and touched his crotch. "Come on, lover boy, give your sweetie a kiss," she puckered up her lips.

Eric took her hand and threw it back in anger. He did not answer her but looked straight ahead. The rode the rest of the way home in silence.

When they arrived at the house, Eric reached over Dawn and opened the door. "Get out, Dawn. Go into the house and pack your things. When I get back with your car, you are to be ready to put your bags into it and leave. Do you understand me?" His voice was cold and grim.

Dawn began crying hysterically. "Please, Eric. Don't do this to me. Come into the house and let's talk. We can work things out. You know we can."

CHAPTER 35

Eric saw the curtains move in his neighbor's window. He knew they were being watched. "Okay, I'll go in with you." As he expected, Dawn's tears immediately ceased, and she got out of the car with a smile.

When they got into the house, Dawn threw her arms around Eric and rubbed her body against his. "You are such a good man. I wish I could be as good as you are. Please teach me to be good like you are. It is true you don't deserve a bitch like me. I'm no good. I was lucky to get such a wonderful man and I've spoiled it. Please, my wonderful, sweet man, please help me. I need your help. I want so much to be good, to be the perfect wife for you. I know I can, if you will only help me." She began to cry again.

Paul took Dawn's arms from around him and gently pushed her back. "I am very, very angry now, Dawn. I don't feel like talking. I am going to get your car." He turned and strode out of the house and began walking the mile to Rachel's house.

The exercise calmed Eric. He no longer felt the blood beating in his temples.

Rachel opened the door to him. Her eye was swollen completely closed, turning black and blue colors. She was holding an ice pack against it.

"Why didn't you call the police and have her arrested?" he asked Rachel when he saw the swollen eye.

"Great! I can just see the headlines: 'Rabbi's wife arrested from home of Rabbi's girlfriend!'

It would be the end of my career and reputation as well as yours. You know all police actions are reported in the paper."

"I'm terribly sorry, Rachel. I really am!"

"I know you are, Eric, but it doesn't help the situation."

"I'm going to leave Dawn, Rachel. I can't take it anymore."

"You are not going to get rid of her so easily, emotionally or physically."

"I just can't take it anymore. She is killing me."

"Well, what you do is our business, Eric. But I have made up my mind. I'm going home for a while."

"You mean to Israel?" Eric's heart fell.

"Yes, I have done a lot of thinking and I have decided to go home."

THE SECOND GENERATION

"Is it because of Dawn and me?" Apprehension was on Eric's face.

"I just feel that I need some time away, to be by myself. I need to go home for a while." Her reply was tentative.

"I really don't know. It depends." She shrugged her shoulders.

"Depends on what?" Eric pressed.

"Depends on my mood, I guess."

"What about your work at the university?" Eric was grabbing at straws.

"Well, I have the total summer in front of me. I have at least a month before I have to notify the University." Rachel turned her face away from her friend. "I have to go, Eric. I just have to go."

◦ ◦ ◦

Two weeks later, Eric, Paul and Dr. Siegelman stood outside of the El Al Air Lines gate and waved goodbye to Rachel as she departed toward the waiting plane. She turned, threw them a kiss, and quickly disappeared through the security doors.

Paul turned to Eric. "She'll be back soon, won't she?"

"Oh, I'm sure she will," Eric replied, "How can she get along without us?"

"Very well, I'm afraid," Paul remarked.

"If not, then why not just go and get her?" Dr. Siegelman inquired.

"Spoken like a true psychiatrist!" commented Eric. "We could use a psychiatrist. Would you go with us to get her?"

"Sure, I have always wanted to visit Israel."

"Me, too," chimed in Paul.

Paul took one last look at the door through which Rachel had disappeared. He half-hoped he might see her one more time.

As they walked out of the El Al building, Eric looked up at the clear blue sky. A brisk breeze blew through his clothing. His body shivered. He was struggling to hold back his tears. He softly repeated Dr. Siegelman's words.

Paul turned around and placed his hand on Eric's shoulder. "Yep, that's what we'll do. We'll just go and get her!"

THE END

Lightning Source UK Ltd.
Milton Keynes UK
UKHW020832111120
373203UK00009B/186